# How to Complete a Risk Assessment in 5 Days or Less

# How to Complete a

# Risk Assessment in

# 5 Days or Less

## THOMAS R. PELTIER

CRC Press
Taylor & Francis Group
Boca Raton   London   New York

CRC Press is an imprint of the
Taylor & Francis Group, an **informa** business
AN AUERBACH BOOK

Auerbach Publications
Taylor & Francis Group
6000 Broken Sound Parkway NW, Suite 300
Boca Raton, FL 33487-2742

© 2009 by Taylor & Francis Group, LLC
Auerbach is an imprint of Taylor & Francis Group, an Informa business

No claim to original U.S. Government works
Printed in the United States of America on acid-free paper
10 9 8 7 6 5 4 3 2 1

International Standard Book Number-13: 978-1-4200-6275-5 (Hardcover)

---

**Library of Congress Cataloging-in-Publication Data**

---

Peltier, Thomas R.
  How to complete a risk assessment in 5 days or less / Thomas R. Peltier.
     p. cm.
  Includes bibliographical references and index.
  ISBN 978-1-4200-6275-5 (alk. paper)
  1. Risk assessment. 2. Risk management. 3. Crisis management. 4. Emergency management. I. Title.

HD61.P45 2008
658.15'5--dc22                                                              2008019340

---

**Visit the Taylor & Francis Web site at**
**http://www.taylorandfrancis.com**

**and the Auerbach Web site at**
**http://www.auerbach-publications.com**

To Lisa and Winston, my two best buddies.

# Contents

# Acknowledgments

No one ever writes a book by himself and this book is no exception. As I worked on a third version of the risk assessment process I found myself going back to the people on whom I relied when I was creating the initial Facilitated Risk Assessment Process (FRAP). Good friends and associates such as John Blackley and David Lynas have been and continue to be sources to information. Additionally, they are excellent at providing feedback when new ideas and concepts are being formulated.

This process has come a long way since Lisa Bryson, Sherry Giardano, Ken Jaworski, Mike Kadar, and I put it together nearly fifteen years ago as a way to implement risk assessment quickly and efficiently within our company. It was founded on solid concepts and ideas, some of which we got from Gareth Davis and Dan Erwin.

When undertaking a book such as this, it helps to have a publisher/editor who understands what the process is and why the deadline seems to keep moving. Rich O'Hanley has been an excellent editor and friend.

A number of years ago the FRAP was introduced to a company called Netigy. This company, under the direction of Mike Corby, put together the best security team ever: Alec Bass, John Blackley, Genny Burns, Terri Curran, Stan Dormer, Beck Herold, Pat Howard, Cheryl Jackson, David Lynas, Justin Peltier, Nan Poulios, John Sherwood, Peter Stephenson, and Fred Trickey.

Establishment of a good foundation of learning and experience began at Chevrolet Engineering with my boss Larry Degg, who encouraged and supported me as I moved the security program further down the road. My best friend, Mike Cannon, was part of this team which included John Riske and Gene Traylor.

The Computer Security Institute, founded by John O'Mara, was where I got my start presenting risk assessment concepts. When I contacted John circa 1988 and told him I needed a class on risk analysis, he told me the best way to get a good class was for me to develop one. I did research and created a risk analysis class, and for the first two years prayed that no one would ask any questions. Over the past twenty years I think I have finally begun to understand a little bit about risk assessment. Working alongside John O'Leary, Richard Power, Patrice Rapalus, and Pam Salaway, I was able to improve the risk assessment classes.

I have enjoyed the challenges presented by the risk assessment process and I hope you find the concepts easy to use.

# About the Author

**Thomas R. Peltier** is the president of Thomas R. Peltier Associates, LCC, an information security training and consulting firm that conducts training on topics such as risk analysis, policies, standards, procedures, network vulnerability assessments, fundamentals of information security, and Certified Information Systems Security Professional (CISSP®) prep courses in North America as well as on four other continents. He is also the founder of the Southeast Michigan Computer Security Special Interest Group, one of the largest information security professional organizations in the United States, and has taught the information security curriculum for a master's certificate at Eastern Michigan University. Currently he is an adjunct professor at Norwich University in the Information Assurance master's program.

Prior to this, Peltier was director of policies and administration for Netigy Corporation's Global Security Practice, where he helped integrate security services and solutions into the Netigy Corporation suite of offerings. He also refined the techniques for policy and procedure development and the Facilitated Risk Analysis and Assessment Process (FRAAP) based on the ISO 17799, managed the Total Information Protection Strategies (TIPS) team, consisting of seven senior subject matter experts, and helped establish a consultant training program to prepare personnel to sit for the CISSP exam.

For CyberSafe Corporation, Peltier was the national director for consulting services, which included conducting network security assessments using a top-down, bottom-up approach and the development and implementation of the Facilitated Risk Analysis Process (FRAP).

At Detroit Edison, Peltier implemented the development of a corporate information protection program that was recognized for excellence in the field of computer and information security by winning the CSI's Information Security Program of the Year for 1996.

Peltier has also served as president at Blaier & Associates, as an information security specialist for General Motors Corporation, as an information security officer for the Chevrolet-Pontiac-Canada Group, and in various positions at the Chevrolet Engineering Center (CEC).

In 1993, Peltier was awarded the Computer Security Institute (CSI) Lifetime Achievement Award, and in 1999 the Information Systems Security Association (ISSA) Individual Contribution to the Profession Award. In 2001, Mr. Peltier was inducted into the ISSA Hall of Fame. He was also awarded the CSI Lifetime Emeritus Membership Award.

Peltier is the former chairman of the Computer Security Institute's Advisory Council, and chairman of the 18th Annual CSI Conference. He has also served as technical advisor to Commonwealth Films, Boston, in the production of nationally distributed films including *Locking the Door; Virus: Prevention, Detection, Recovery; Back in Business*; and other security awareness and training films. Peltier's published works include *The Complete Manual of Policies and Procedures for Data Security; Information Security Policies and Procedures: A Professional Reference; Information Security Risk Analysis; Information Security Policies, Standards, and Procedures; How to Manage a Network Vulnerability Assessment*; and *Information Security Fundamentals*. Peltier also coauthored the *2007 Complete Guide to CISM Certification,* and has been both a contributing author and editor of *The Total CISSP Exam Prep Book (2002),* as well as a contributing author to the *Computer Security Handbook* and *Data Security Management.*

# Introduction

The goal of *How to Complete a Risk Assessment in 5 Days or Less* is to give you the tools and skill set needed to do exactly that. Over the course of this book we will examine many different ways to improve the risk assessment process to work best for you and your organization.

The book is designed in such a manner that the initial discussions will relate to the actual risk assessment process. We will examine each of the steps necessary to complete a successful risk assessment. We will discuss the basic concepts and then we will entertain variations of the theme.

The process that we will use is called the Facilitated Risk Analysis and Assessment Process (FRAAP). This is a qualitative risk assessment process that has been used throughout the world for the past fifteen years. The guiding factor in the development of the FRAAP was that we had neither a budget to purchase a risk assessment product nor the time to implement a product. My team and I began to discuss what the outer limits of time were that we could expect the infrastructure and business people to be able to complete one risk assessment. It was this time factor that drove the development of the FRAAP and over the years added to its refinements. Throughout the book you will be given examples of checklists, forms, questionnaires, and other tools needed to complete a risk assessment.

Once we have covered the basics on how to complete a risk assessment, we will then examine other important concepts and how to implement them. We will examine the concept of risk analysis and how it relates to the risk assessment process. We will discuss where risk analysis fits into the system development life cycle (SDLC) and how it is used in project management processes.

We will discuss the SDLC and how risk analysis, risk assessment, risk mitigation, and vulnerability assessment fit into this structure. We will also review the gap analysis process and see how this can be used to support the quality control objectives of the risk assessment process. We will examine the difference between a gap analysis and a security or controls assessment.

It will be necessary to discuss the cost–benefit analysis process because it is found in a number of other concepts we will discuss.

We will discuss also how to use the concepts developed throughout the book to implement a business impact analysis (BIA) process and an information classification methodology.

The final concept we will explore is the pre-screening methodology. Over the years we have come to the conclusion that not every application, system, or business process needs to have a full-blown risk assessment or BIA run against it. To reach that conclusion, it will be important to create a methodology that will enable the organization to determine what needs analysis and what can benefit best by implementation of a baseline set of controls. Through understanding gap analysis, controls assessment, and information classification requirements, we will be able to generate a baseline set of controls and a methodology to determine whether a risk assessment or BIA is required.

The book is meant to be a reference guide to help you create the components you will need to implement a successful risk assessment process. I have included sample documents that include a management summary and a completed risk assessment action plan. Copies of many of the checklists presented in the book, as well as a chart comparing the old and revised ISO 17799 Standard and CIP-002 to CIP-009, ✓ are available at http://www.infosectoday.com/Risk_Assessment.

During the discussions additional material is given that can allow you to present a more quantified view of risk assessment. The key element of risk assessment in our business environment is time. If you have more time, you can do more things. During my days in the business world, time was always at a premium.

## Chapter 1

# The Facilitated Risk Analysis and Assessment Process (FRAAP)

## 1.1 Introduction

After being in the information security profession for over thirty years and information technology for over forty, I have found that most organizations have the ability to identify threats that can impact the business objectives or mission of the organization. What they cannot do in a systematic manner is to determine the level of risk those threats pose to the organization.

Years ago I worked with a delightful gentleman named Irving Ball. Irv was six feet seven inches, and I am five feet two. One morning Irv came in with a fresh abrasion on his forehead. I inquired about what happened, and Irv said, "Didn't you see that scaffolding in the parking lot?" I said that I thought that I had. As we headed to my car at lunchtime, we passed the scaffolding and noted that it posed a threat to both of us; however, the probability of my hitting the portion of the scaffolding that Irv had hit was much lower. So the scaffolding was a threat for both of us but the risk to me was lower because the probability and impact were lower.

Just because a threat exists does not mean that the organization is at risk. This is what risk assessment is all about: identifying the threats that are out there and then determining if those threats pose a real risk to the organization.

With the changing business culture, successful security professionals have had to modify the process of responding to new threats in the high-profile, ultra-connected business environment. With outside regulatory agencies and external auditors gaining more oversight strength over recent years, organizations are met with an increased motivation to implement an effective, inexpensive risk assessment process.

Even with the change of focus, today's organizations must still protect the integrity, confidentiality, and availability of information resources they rely on. Although senior management is becoming increasingly interested in security, the fact remains that the business of the enterprise is business. An effective security program must assist the business units by providing high-quality, reliable service in helping them protect the assets of the enterprise.

## 1.2 FRAAP Overview

The Facilitated Risk Analysis and Assessment Process (FRAAP) was developed as an efficient and disciplined methodology for ensuring that threats to business operations are identified, examined, and documented. The process involves analyzing one system, application, platform, business process, or segment of business operation at a time. By convening a team of internal subject matter experts, the FRAAP will rely on the organization's own people to complete the risk assessment process. These experts must include the business managers and system users who are familiar with the mission needs of the asset under review, and the infrastructure staff who have a detailed understanding of potential system vulnerabilities and related controls. The FRAAP sessions follow a standard agenda and are facilitated by a member of the project office or information security staff. The facilitator is responsible for ensuring that the team members communicate effectively and adhere to the project scope statement.

The team's conclusions about what threats exist, what their risk level is, and what controls are needed are documented for the business owner to use in developing an effective action plan. The FRAAP is divided into three phases:

1. The pre-FRAAP
2. The FRAAP session
3. Post-FRAAP

During the FRAAP session, the team will brainstorm to identify potential threats that could impact the task mission of the asset under review. The team will then establish a risk level of each threat based on the probability that the threat might occur and relative impact in the event that it actually does occur. We will go into more detail on this process later in the book.

The team does not usually attempt to obtain or develop specific numbers for the threat likelihood or annual loss estimates unless the data for determining such factors is readily available. Instead, the team will rely on their general knowledge of threats and probabilities obtained from national incident response centers, professional associations and literature, and their own experience.

When assembling the team, experience causes them to believe that additional efforts to develop precisely quantified risks are not cost effective because:

- Such estimates take an inordinate amount of time and effort to identify and verify or develop.
- The risk documentation becomes too voluminous to be of practical value.
- Specific loss estimates are generally not needed to determine if a control is needed.

After identifying the threats and establishing the relative risk level for each threat, the team identifies controls that could be implemented to reduce the risk, focusing on the most cost-effective controls. The team will use a common set of controls designed to address various types of threats. We will discuss the controls selection process later in this chapter. Ultimately, the decision as to what controls are to be identified in the action plan rests with the business owner.

Once the FRAAP session is complete, the security professional can assist the business owner in determining which controls are cost effective and meet the business needs. Once each threat has been assigned a control measure or has been accepted as a risk of doing business, the senior business manager and participating technical expert sign the completed document. The document and all associated papers are owned by the business unit sponsor and are retained for a period to be determined by the organization's records-management procedures (usually seven years).

Each risk assessment process is divided into three distinct sessions:

1. The pre-FRAAP meeting, which normally takes about an hour, is attended by the business owner, project lead, scribe, and facilitator, and has seven deliverables.
2. The FRAAP session takes approximately four hours, and includes fifteen to thirty people though sessions with as many as fifty and as few as four people have occurred.
3. Post-FRAAP is where the results are analyzed and the management summary report is completed. This process can take up to five work days to complete.

Over the course of this chapter we will examine why the FRAAP was developed, what each one of the three phases entails, and what the deliverables from each phase are.

## 1.3 FRAAP History

Prior to the development of the FRAAP, risk assessment was often perceived as a major task that required the enterprise to hire an outside consultant, and could take weeks, if not months to complete. Often the risk assessment process was shrouded in mystery and it seemed that elements of voodoo were being used. The final report sometimes looked as if the name of an organization was simply edited into a standard report template.

By hiring outside consultants, the expertise of the in-house staff was often overlooked and the results produced were not acceptable to the business unit manager. Additionally, business managers who were not part of the risk assessment process found that they did not understand the recommended controls, did not want the recommended controls, and often worked to undermine the controls implementation process.

What was needed was a risk assessment process that:

- Was driven by the business owners
- Took days instead of weeks or months to complete
- Was cost effective
- Used the in-house experts

The FRAAP meets all of these requirements and adds another: it can be conducted by someone who has limited knowledge of a particular system or business process but good facilitation skills.

The FRAAP is a formal methodology developed through understanding the previously developed qualitative risk assessment processes and modifying them to meet current requirements. It is driven by the business side of the enterprise and ensures that the controls selected enable the business owners to meet their mission objectives. With the FRAAP, controls are never implemented to meet audit or security requirements. The only controls selected focus on the business need.

The FRAAP was created with an understanding that the internal resources had limited time to spend on such tasks. By limiting the information-gathering session to four hours, the subject matter experts (SMEs) are more likely to participate in the process. Using time as a critical factor, the FRAAP addresses as many risk assessment issues as possible. If there is more time, then there are more tasks that can be performed.

By involving the business units, the FRAAP uses them to identify threats. Once resource owners are involved in identifying threats and determining the risk level, they generally see the business reason why implementing cost-effective controls is necessary to help limit the exposure. The FRAAP allows the business units to take control of their resources. It allows them to determine what safeguards are needed and who will be responsible for implementing those safeguards.

The results of the FRAAP are a comprehensive set of documents that will identify threats, prioritize those threats into risk levels, and identify possible controls that will help mitigate those high-level risks.

The FRAAP provides the enterprise with a cost-effective action plan that meets the business needs to protect enterprise resources while ensuring that business objectives and mission charters are met. Most importantly, with the involvement of the business managers, the FRAAP provides a supportive client or owner who believes in the action plan.

## 1.4   Introducing the FRAAP

As with any new process, it is always best to conduct user awareness sessions to acquaint employees before the process is rolled out. It will be necessary to explain what the FRAAP is, how it works, and how it will help the business meet its specific objectives.

To be successful, the awareness program should take into account the needs and current levels of training and understanding of the employees and management. There are five keys to establishing an effective awareness program:

1. Assess current level of risk assessment understanding.
2. Determine what the managers and employees want to learn.
3. Examine the level of receptiveness to the security program.
4. Map out how to gain acceptance.
5. Identify possible allies.

To assess the current level of risk assessment understanding, it will be necessary to ask questions of the audience. Although some employees may have been part of a risk assessment in the past, most employees have little firsthand knowledge of risk assessment. Ask questions such as why they believe there is a need for risk assessment. Listen to what the employees are saying and scale the training sessions to meet their specific needs. In the awareness field, one size or plan does not fit for everyone.

Work with the managers and supervisors to understand what their needs are and how the risk assessment process can help them. It will become necessary to understand the language of the business units and to interpret their needs. Once you have an understanding, then you will be able to modify the presentation to meet these special needs. No single awareness program will work for every business unit. There must be alterations and a willingness to accept suggestions from non-security personnel.

Identify the level of receptiveness to the risk assessment process. Find out what is accepted and what is meeting with resistance. Examine the areas of non-compliance and try to find ways to alter the program, if at all possible. Do not change fundamental risk assessment precepts just to gain unanimous acceptance; this is an unattainable goal. Make the process meet the greater good of the enterprise and then work with pockets of resistance to lessen the impact.

The best way to gain acceptance is to make employees and managers partners in this process. Never decree a new control or policy to the employee population without involving them in the decision-making process. This will require you to do your homework and to understand the business process in each department. It will be important to know the peak periods of activity in the department and what the manager's concerns are. When meeting with the managers, be sure to listen to their concerns and be prepared to ask for their suggestions about how to improve the program. Remember: the key here is to partner with your audience.

Finally, look for possible allies. Find out which managers support the objectives of the risk assessment process and those that have the respect of their peers. This means that it will be necessary to expand the area of support beyond risk management and the audit staff. Seek out business managers that have a vested interest in seeing this program succeed. Use their support to springboard the program to acceptance.

A key point in this entire process is never to refer to the risk assessment process or the awareness campaign as "my" program. The enterprise has identified the need for risk assessment and you and your group are acting as the catalysts to moving the process forward. When discussing the process with employees and managers, it will be beneficial to refer to it as "your" risk assessment process or "our" process. Make them feel that they are key stakeholders in this process.

Involve the user community and accept their comments whenever possible. Make the risk assessment process their process. Use what they identify as important in the awareness program. By having them involved, the risk assessment process truly becomes theirs and they are more willing to accept and internalize the results.

### 1.4.1 Key Concepts

The FRAAP is a formal methodology for risk assessment that is driven by the owner. Each FRAAP session is called by the owner, and the team members are invited by the owner. The concept of what constitutes an owner is normally established in the organization's information security policy. The policy generally addresses the concepts of information asset owner, custodian, and user. A typical company policy may resemble the following:

Information created while employed by the company is a company asset and is the property of the company. All employees are responsible for protecting company information from unauthorized access, modification, destruction, or disclosure, whether accidental or intentional. To facilitate the protection of company information, employee responsibilities have been established at three levels: owner, custodian, and user.

*Owner:* The highest level of company management of the organizational unit where the information resource is created, or management of the organizational unit that is the primary user of the information resource. Owners have the responsibility to:

- Establish the classification level of all corporate information within their organizational unit.

- Identify reasonable and prudent safeguards to ensure the confidentiality, integrity, and availability of the information resource.
- Monitor safeguards to ensure they are properly implemented.
- Authorize access for those who have a business need for the information.
- Delete access for those who no longer have a business need for the information.

*Custodian:* Employees designated by the owner to be responsible for maintaining the safeguards established by the owner.

*User:* Employees authorized by the owner to access information and use the safeguards established by the owner.

Senior management must ensure that the enterprise has the capabilities needed to accomplish its mission or business objectives. As we will see, senior management of a department, business unit, group, or other such entity is considered to be the functional owner of the enterprise's assets, and in their fiduciary duty, act in the best interest of the enterprise to implement reasonable and prudent safeguards and controls. Risk management is the tool that will assist them in the task (Table 1.1).

As you can see in Table 1.1, the risk assessment process assists management in meeting its obligations to protect the assets of the organization. By being an active partner in the risk assessment process and acting in the owner capacity, management gets the opportunity to see what threats are lurking around the business process. The FRAAP allows the owner to identify where control weaknesses are and to develop an action plan to remedy the risks in a cost-effective manner.

The results of the FRAAP are a comprehensive risk assessment document that has identified the threats, risk levels, and controls as well as an owner-created action plan, which includes action items, identifies responsible entities, and establishes a time frame for completion. The FRAAP assists management in meeting its obligation to perform due diligence.

The FRAAP is conducted by a trained facilitator. This individual will lead the team through the identification of threats, the establishment of a risk level by determining probability and impact, and the selection of possible safeguards or controls. Because of the subjective nature of qualitative risk assessment, it will be

**Table 1.1  Management Owner Definition**

| Typical Role | Risk Management Responsibility |
|---|---|
| Management owner | Under the standard of due care, senior management is charged with the ultimate responsibility for meeting business objectives or mission requirements. Senior management must ensure that necessary resources are effectively applied to develop the capabilities to meet the mission requirements. They must incorporate the results of the risk assessment process into the decision-making process. |

**Table 1.2  FRAAP Facilitator Definition**

| Typical Role | Risk Management Responsibility |
|---|---|
| FRAAP facilitator | A facilitator is someone who skillfully helps a group of people understand their common objectives and assists them to plan to achieve them without taking a particular position in the discussion. The facilitator will try to assist the group in achieving a consensus on any disagreements that pre-exist or emerge in the FRAAP so that an action plan can be created. |

**Table 1.3  Fraap Scribe Definition**

| Typical Role | Risk Management Responsibility |
|---|---|
| FRAAP scribe | The scribe is the individual responsible for recording the oral discussions in a written format. The scribe ensures that the threats are properly recorded and all actions of the risk assessment team are captured accurately. |

the responsibility of the facilitator to lead the team into different areas of concern to ensure that as many threats as possible are identified (Table 1.2).

Instead of concentrating on establishing audit or security requirements, the facilitator ensures that the risk assessment process examines threats that might impact the business process or the mission of the enterprise. This ensures that only those controls and countermeasures that are truly needed and cost effective are selected and implemented.

Helping the trained facilitator is an individual acting as a recording secretary that will transcribe the meeting and help create the risk assessment documentation. As a scribe, this individual will accurately record the identifications of threats and all other relevant information. Unlike an editor, the scribe does not alter the written word once the team has agreed that the meaning of the statement has been properly captured (Table 1.3).

## 1.5  The Pre-FRAAP Meeting

The pre-FRAAP meeting is the key to the success of the project. The meeting is normally scheduled for an hour and a half and is usually conducted at the business owner's office. The meeting should be attended by the business owner (or representative), the project development lead, facilitator, and the scribe. The session will result in seven deliverables.

1. *Pre-screening results*: The pre-screening process is conducted earlier in the system development life cycle. Because the risk assessment is a historical record of the decision-making process, a copy of the pre-screening results should be

entered into the official record and stored in the risk assessment action plan. The pre-screening process is discussed in chapter 3.

2. *Scope statement:* The project lead and business owner will have to create a statement of opportunity for the risk assessment. They are to develop in words what exactly is going to be reviewed. The scope statement process is discussed in detail in Appendix C and an example of a risk assessment scope statement can be found in Appendix C. During the pre-FRAAP meeting, the risk assessment scope statement should be reviewed and edited into final language.

   It is during the development of the scope statement that threat categories need to be determined. In a typical information security risk assessment, we would include the C-I-A triad of confidentiality, integrity, and availability. For a more-detailed discussion on threat category issues, refer to Appendix E.

3. *Visual diagram (visual model):* This is a one-page or foil diagram depicting the process to be reviewed. The visual model will be used during the FRAAP session to acquaint the team with where the process begins and ends.

   There is a good reason to require the inclusion of a visual diagram or an information flow model as part of the FRAAP. Neural-linguistic programming is the study of how people learn. This process has identified three basic learning types:

   i. *Auditory:* These people have to hear something in order to grasp it. During the FRAAP, the owner will present the project scope statement to the team and those that learn in this manner will be fulfilled.

   ii. *Mechanical:* These people must write down the element to be learned. Those taking notes during meetings are typically mechanical learners.

   iii. *Visual:* Most of us fall into this category. Visual learners need to see a picture or diagram to understand what is being discussed. People that learn via this method normally have a whiteboard in their office and use it often. So the visual diagram or model will help these people understand what is being reviewed.

4. *The FRAAP team established:* A typical FRAAP has between fifteen to thirty members. The team is made up of representatives from a number of business infrastructure and business support areas. FRAAP team makeup is discussed in Appendix B.

5. *Meeting mechanics:* This is the business unit manager's meeting. The business unit manager is responsible for scheduling the room, setting the risk assessment time, and having the appropriate materials (overhead, flipcharts, coffee, and doughnuts) on hand.

   This risk assessment meeting is the responsibility of the owner. As the facilitator, you are assisting the owner in completing this task. It is not an information security, project management office, audit, or risk management meeting. It is the owner's meeting and that person is responsible for scheduling the place and inviting the team.

**Table 1.4  Risk Assessment Definitions**

| Term | Definition |
| --- | --- |
| Asset | A resource of value. An asset may be a person, physical object, process, or technology. |
| Threat | The potential for an event, malicious or otherwise, that would damage or compromise an asset. |
| Probability | A measure of how likely it is that a threat may occur. |
| Impact | The effect of a threat being carried out on an asset, expressed in tangible or intangible terms. |
| Vulnerability | Any flaw or weakness in the asset's defenses that could be exploited by a threat to create an impact on the asset. |
| Risk | The combination of threat, probability, and impact expressed as a value in a pre-defined range. |

6. *Agreement on definitions:* The pre-FRAAP session is where agreement on FRAAP definitions is completed. These definitions will eventually become a standard used in the risk assessment process. However, it is always a good idea to review the concepts that will be used in the risk assessment (Table 1.4).

7. *Mini-brainstorming session:* Once agreement has been reached on the other 6 items in the pre-FRAAP session, I have found it helpful to conduct a mini-threat identification session. Here the assembled members would identify four of five threats for each business attribute. Table 1.10 is an example of the results of this process. These threat examples will be used in the FRAAP session.

You will want to agree on the definitions of the business attributes be used as the will review elements. For many of risk assessments we have examined the (integrity, confidentiality, availability). Recently a group of my fellow information security professionals and I examined the idea of what attributes should be examined. For years we have concentrated on examining the threats associated with the C-I-A security triad.

Although C-I-A is a traditional form for a risk assessment, it is important to understand that there are other business attributes that can be used in the process. When I was in Psychology 101 class, we discussed functional fixedness, which is a cognitive bias that limits a person to using an object only in the way it is traditionally used. When you give a child a present, the child will oftentimes have more fun playing with the wrapping or the box. That is because the wrapping can be anything. I use this example in my training classes to remind audit, information security, and risk management that there are a vast number of business attributes that can be used to determine risk. Even if your primary use of risk assessment is to determine threats to assets based on examining confidentiality, integrity, and availability, try to remain open to other possibilities.

I posed the following to my colleagues:

When we are conducting risk assessments, we often examine threats based on C-I-A. We also discussed earlier this week that instead of C-I-A, we could consider reliability -performance -cost (for capital) or portability -scalability -market penetration (for software) as examples. Does the use of these categories confuse our way of thinking — instead of risk categories could these be titled Threat Categories? Also, do we do it this way because it is required or because it helps us think better within set boundaries?

C-I-A, reliability -performance -cost, and portability -scalability -market penetration are just 9 of the hundreds of such things defined in the SABSA method since 1996. We call them "business attributes" and the business attributes profile is used as the basis for all risk management.

The default prompt list/modeling tool kit has the 80 attributes that are most often re-used internationally (see http://www.sabsa.org) although each organization has a different context and thus a different set.

We have a whole section dedicated to users' definitions of these things and demonstrating case studies on the Institute's web site. Sadly that part of the site (it is in the member discussion area) isn't publicly accessible yet but we've about 200 people impatiently waiting on it out of the hundreds that are now certified in the method. We have 60 courses already on the schedule for 2008 so it will be well over a thousand by end of year and that's not counting what happens with it as an MOD standard or as a built-in part of the CISM exams.

*Could this be titled Threat Categories?*

I don't believe so. They are not threats but the areas/things of value we want to protect from the threats, i.e., ultimately the business issues that are at risk. Thus the use of the term "business attributes" seems to fit best.

However, they can easily be used to create a threat modeling taxonomy ... and they often are used that way in daily practice. Also, while you have correctly seen potential demarcation lines between different types (you used capital and software) a whole enterprise-wide taxonomy can be constructed that defines the things of value both unique to a division/stakeholder/department/team/project and to the enterprise as a whole. That in turn provides the basis for risk aggregation ... see my article in your year-in-review thingy.

*Also, do we do it this way because it is required or because it helps us think better within set boundaries?*

I believe that it is the latter. It isn't actually required but it helps. Boundaries and structure of many kinds help to remove the horrendous subjectivity and variable response we would get from a blank unbounded or unstructured risk management canvas.

**Table 1.5 Business Attribute Definitions (C-I-A)**

| Term | Definition |
| --- | --- |
| Confidentiality | The assurance that information is not disclosed to inappropriate entities or processes. |
| Integrity | Assuring information will not be accidentally or maliciously altered or destroyed. |
| Availability | Assuring information and communications services will be ready for use when expected. |

**Table 1.6 Business Attribute Definitions (Capital Expenditure)**

| Term | Definition |
| --- | --- |
| Reliability | The extent to which the same result is achieved when a measure is repeatedly applied to the same asset. |
| Performance | A quantitative measure characterizing a physical or functional attribute relating to the execution of a mission/operation or function. |
| Cost | The total spent for goods or services including money, time, and labor. |

**Table 1.7 Business Attribute Definitions (Software Procurement)**

| Term | Definition |
| --- | --- |
| Portability | A measure of system independence; portable programs can be moved to a new system by recompiling without having to make any other changes. |
| Scalability | The ability to expand a computing solution to support large numbers of users without impacting performance. |
| Market penetration | The share of a given market that is provided by a particular good or service at a given time. |

The business attributes that are going to be used in the risk assessment process must be discussed and agreed upon during the pre-FRAAP session. A formal set of definitions must also be established. Table 1.5 through Table 1.7 are examples of some of the many business attributes that can be used to examine threats and establish risk levels.

During the pre-FRAAP session, it will be important to discuss the process for prioritizing the threats. When examining the probability and impact of threats, it will be necessary to determine before the meeting if the threats are to be examined as if no controls are in place. This is typically the case when doing a risk assessment on an infrastructure resource. These resources include the information processing network, the operating system platform, and even the information security program.

For other applications, systems, and business processes, the examination of threats takes into account existing controls. When we discuss the FRAAP session, we will examine each of these methods and how they work. This decision should be made during the pre-FRAAP meeting. Once the risk assessment process has been established, this discussion will not be necessary as the organization will standardize the risk-level protocol.

## 1.5.1 Pre-FRAAP Meeting Checklist

When I attend a pre-FRAAP meeting, I like to take with me a checklist (Table 1.8) that will ensure that I receive all of the items I need to complete the pre-FRAAP process. (Table 1.9 lists the directions to fill out the pre-FRAAP meeting checklist.) By completing this checklist the elements for the project scope statement will be nearly complete. The categories of assumptions and constraints are two of the key elements contained in the checklist and must be part of the project scope statement. It is important that we understand what these are and how they impact the risk assessment process.

I have a client who brings me in from time to time to conduct FRAAP refresher training for employees; those who have taken the training before have an opportunity to be exposed to new ideas and concepts, other employees have the opportunity to be exposed to the process for the first time. Typically this process is done over three or four days. It consists of a day and a half of training, and the pre-FRAAP meeting is conducted during the afternoon of day two. The following day the FRAAP session is conducted, and then that afternoon and the following day I work with the project lead and the facilitator to complete the risk assessment documentation. On the afternoon of day one, the project lead and project lead backup informed me that they had a meeting to attend and would be back the following day. Not only did they miss the afternoon training of day one, they also did not return for any of the day-two training. On the afternoon of day two, the attendees decided to try to put together a project scope statement. The audience was almost exclusively information security and audit professionals. The scope statement lacked the business side, but at least we were able to be ready for the following day. Because of the team makeup, we did not address assumptions or constraints.

On the day of the FRAAP session, the project leads returned with the owner. This was the first time the owner had ever been exposed to a risk assessment process. We presented them with the scope statement that we had created and the owner said that it looked OK to her. So after a brief introduction and an overview of the methodology, we began the process of identifying threats. After about two hours the team had identified nearly one hundred fifty threats. As we were working through the FRAAP session, I noticed that the owner seemed very concerned and I approached her during the break to see if there was a problem. She informed me that the system was going into production on the following Monday and there was no way she could tell her bosses that one hundred fifty threats were uncovered. I sat down with her to review the scope statement and to fill in the assumptions area. A number of the identified threats were directly related to elements within the information security program:

**Table 1.8   Pre-FRAAP Meeting Checklist**

| Issue | Remarks |
|---|---|
| **Prior to the meeting** | |
| 1. *Date of pre-FRAAP meeting:* Record when and where the meeting is scheduled. | |
| 2. *Project executive sponsor or owner:* Identify the owner or sponsor who has executive responsibility for the project. | |
| 3. *Project leader:* Identify the individual who is the primary point of contact for the project or asset under review. | |
| 4. *Pre-FRAAP meeting objective:* Identify what you hope to gain from the meeting — typically, the seven deliverables will be discussed. | |
| 5. *Project overview:* Prepare a project overview for presentation to the pre-FRAAP members during the meeting. | |
| Your understanding of the project scope | |
| The FRAAP methodology | |
| Milestones | |
| Pre-screening methodology | |
| 6. *Assumptions:* Identify assumptions used in developing the approach to performing the FRAAP project. | |
| 7. *Pre-screening results:* Record the results of the pre-screening process. | |
| **During the meeting** | |
| 8. *Business strategy, goals, and objectives:* Identify what the owner's objectives are and how they relate to larger company objectives. | |
| 9. *Project scope:* Define specifically the scope of the project and document it during the meeting so that all participating will know and agree. | |
| Applications/systems | |
| Business processes | |
| Business functions | |
| People and organizations | |
| Locations/facilities | |

**Table 1.8 (continued)  Pre-FRAAP Meeting Checklist**

| Issue | Remarks |
|---|---|
| 10. *Time dependencies:* Identify time limitations and considerations the client may have. | |
| 11. *Risks/constraints:* Identify risks and constraints that could affect the successful conclusion of the project. | |
| 12. *Budget:* Identify any open budget/funding issues. | |
| 13. *FRAAP participants:* Identify by name and position the individuals whose participation in the FRAAP session is required. | |
| 14. *Administrative requirements:* Identify facility and equipment needs to perform the FRAAP session. | |
| 15. *Documentation:* Identify what documentation is required to prepare for the FRAAP session (provide the client the FRAAP document checklist). | |

- Passwords being posted on workstations
- Employees leaving workstations logged on and unattended
- Employees leaving work materials out after hours
- Shoulder surfing for passwords or other access codes
- Unauthorized access to restricted areas

Although these were important threats, they were already addressed in the risk assessment conducted on the information security infrastructure and were not unique to the specific application under review. We modified the assumptions section of the scope statement to include a reference to the fact that it was assumed that a risk assessment had been conducted on the information security infrastructure and that compensating controls were in place or were being implemented. We also addressed the processing infrastructure and applications development methodology in the same manner. By making sure the assumptions were properly identified, we reduced the number of threats from approximately one hundred fifty to about thirty.

The FRAAP was not diminished in any way. The one hundred twenty or so threats that were excised from the risk assessment report had already been identified in the infrastructure risk assessments and were being acted upon.

If other risk assessments have been conducted, enter that information into the assumptions area. If the infrastructure risk assessments have not been conducted, enter that information into the constraints area. This allows the risk assessment to

**Table 1.9  Pre-FRAAP Meeting Checklist Directions**

| Issue | Activity |
|---|---|
| **Prior to the meeting** | |
| 1. Date of pre-FRAAP meeting | Record the date the actual pre-FRAAP meeting is scheduled to occur. |
| 2. Project executive sponsor or owner | Record the full name and proper title of the owner of the asset that is to be reviewed. |
| 3. Project leader | Record the full name and proper title of the project lead for this specific asset or task. |
| 4. Pre-FRAAP meeting objective | There are seven deliverables for the pre-FRAAP meeting:<br>■ Scope statement<br>■ Visual model<br>■ Assessment team<br>■ Definitions<br>■ Meeting mechanics<br>■ Pre-screening results<br>■ Mini brainstorming results |
| 5. Project overview | If the FRAAP is a new concept to the owner or project lead, provide an overview of the process. |
| Your understanding of the project scope | |
| The FRAAP methodology | |
| Milestones | |
| Pre-screening methodology | |
| 6. Assumptions | Record any issues that are needed to support the project scope statement. |
| 7. Pre-screening results | Record the pre-screening results. |
| **During the meeting** | |
| 8. Business strategy, goals, and objectives | Record the mission of the asset under review and how it supports the overall business objectives or mission of the enterprise. |
| 9. Project scope | Draft the FRAAP scope statement. |
| ■ Applications/systems | |
| ■ Business processes | |

**Table 1.9 (continued)   Pre-FRAAP Meeting Checklist Directions**

| Issue | Activity |
|---|---|
| ■ Business functions | |
| ■ People and organizations | |
| ■ Locations/facilities | |
| 10. Time dependencies | Identify any time issues and enter them into the constraints section of the scope statement. |
| 11. Risks/constraints | Record any issues that may impact the results of the FRAAP. |
| 12. Budget | Where appropriate, establish a work order number or project identification number that FRAAP team members can use in time reporting. |
| 13. FRAAP participants | Record who the stakeholders and other team members are, as requested by the owner. |
| 14. Administrative requirements | Record any special requirements needed for the FRAAP session. |
| 15. Documentation | Record all laws, regulations, standards, directives, policies, and procedures that are part of the infrastructure supporting the asset under review. |

concentrate on the specific asset at hand, but puts the organization on notice that other risk assessments must be scheduled.

Other constraints might include the concerns about the use of obsolete operating systems, those that are no longer supported by the manufacturer. The back level of patch applications might also be a constraint to identify.

Assumptions and constraints allow the risk assessment team to focus on the asset at hand. The organization must conduct the other risk assessments to make certain that the infrastructure is as secure as possible.

In recent years an extra process has been added to the pre-FRAAP portion of the risk assessment process. That extra element is a brief mini-brainstorming process (Table 1.10). At the end of the pre-FRAAP session, those in attendance should conduct a quick threat identification process. Using each of the business attributes that are to be examined, the pre-FRAAP team will identify threats to the asset just as the entire team will during the FRAAP session. It will be important to get four or five threats for each business attribute. This information will be used by the FRAAP facilitator during the FRAAP session.

**Table 1.10  Mini-Brainstorming Results**

| Integrity | Confidentiality | Availability |
|---|---|---|
| Data stream could be intercepted. | Insecure e-mail could contain confidential information. | Files stored in personal directories may not be available to other employees when needed. |
| Faulty programming could (inadvertently) modify data. | Internal theft of information. | Hardware failures could impact the availability of company resources. |
| Written or electronic copies of reports could be diverted to unauthorized or unintended persons. | Employee is not able to verify the identity of a client, e.g., phone masquerading. | A failure in the data circuit could prohibit system access. |
| Data could be entered incorrectly. | Confidential information is left in plain view on a desk. | "Acts of God": tornado, tsunami, hurricane. |
| Intentional incorrect data entry. | Social discussions outside the office could result in disclosure of sensitive information. | Upgrades in the software may prohibit access. |

### 1.5.2   Pre-FRAAP Meeting Summary

The pre-FRAAP meeting sets the stage for the FRAAP session and all of the work that is to follow. It is very important that each of the seven deliverables is as complete as possible. If they are not complete, then this could be a major constraint to the risk assessment process.

## 1.6   The FRAAP Session

### 1.6.1   Overview

The FRAAP session is typically scheduled for four hours. This is a very tight time frame that can be expanded if you have the time and resources available. In recent years I have been out in the field conducting FRAAPs for various clients and I have found that the four-hour window is sufficient to capture threats associated with the business attributes of a specific asset. Then identify existing controls and conduct a risk-level analysis of the threats to identify those that require risk remediation.

As we discussed earlier, the key component in the development of the FRAAP was the time commitment that was available from the team members. Think about the typical employee's weekly work schedule. How much free or available time

**Table 1.11 FRAAP Session Agenda**

| Agenda | Responsibility |
|---|---|
| ■ Explain the FRAAP process | Facilitator |
| ■ Review scope statement | Owner |
| ■ Review visual diagram | Technical support |
| ■ Discuss definitions | Facilitator |
| ■ Review objectives<br>  – Identify threats<br>  – Establish risk levels<br>  – Identify possible safeguards | Facilitator |
| ■ Identify roles and introduction | Team |
| ■ Review session agreements | Facilitator |

does an employee have each week? Many of us spend at least twelve hours of our workweek in meetings. For the people that will be asked to participate in the risk assessment process, there will be an impact to their available time. The FRAAP is designed to meet the needs of an effective risk assessment while impacting the team members as little as possible.

## 1.6.2   FRAAP Session Introduction

Once the FRAAP session is called together, the executive responsible for the asset under review will address the team with opening remarks. This overview will help the team members understand why they were asked to be part of the FRAAP and how important senior management considers the risk assessment process to be. When the overview is complete, the facilitator will present the agenda to the team. A typical agenda might resemble Table 1.11.

The facilitator will explain the FRAAP to the team. This will include a discussion of the deliverables expected from each stage of the process. With the assistance of the facilitator, the team will identify threats to the asset under review. Using a formula of probability and impact, the team will then affix a risk level to each threat and will finally select possible controls to reduce the risk intensity to an acceptable level.

The business manager owner will then present the project scope statement. It will be important to discuss the assumptions and constraints identified in the statement. The team should have a copy of the scope statement to refer to as needed during the FRAAP session. The assumptions and constraints will be helpful in ensuring that the deliverables are as accurate as possible.

Technical support will then give a five-minute overview of the process using an information flow model or diagram. This will allow the team to visualize the process under review.

**Table 1.12    FRAAP Session Agreements**

| |
|---|
| ■ Everyone participates. |
| ■ Stay within identified roles. |
| ■ Stick to the agenda/current focus. |
| ■ All ideas have equal value. |
| ■ Listen to other points of view. |
| ■ No "plops"; all issues are recorded. |
| ■ Deferred issues will be recorded. |
| ■ Post the idea before discussing it. |
| ■ Help scribe ensure all issues are recorded. |
| ■ One conversation at a time. |
| ■ One angry person at a time. |

The facilitator will then review the term definitions to be used for this FRAAP session. Once the risk assessment process becomes part of the organization's culture, these definitions will become standard and the need for review will diminish. To expedite the process, the FRAAP session definitions should be included in the meeting notice.

The facilitator will then reiterate the objectives and deliverables of this initial stage. At this point, stage two of this process should be briefly discussed. The meeting notice should mention that those individuals needed for stage two will be staying for an additional hour.

At this point, the FRAAP team members should introduce themselves, and the following information should be recorded by the scribe:

■ Team member name (first and last)
■ Department
■ Location
■ Phone number

After the introductions, the facilitator will review the session agreements with the team members (Table 1.12).

## 1.6.3    FRAAP Session Talking Points

■ *Everyone participates.* It is important to get input from everyone in attendance. Some will want to sit back for the first few minutes to get comfortable with the lay of the process. Some of this apprehension can be alleviated by having a FRAAP awareness session throughout the organization. Many times, it is the fear of the unknown that causes team members to hold back. Brief awareness sessions that explain the reasons for and the process done by the risk assessment process will afford the team members a greater feeling of participation.

- *Stay within identified roles.* Introduce the facilitator and scribe. Explain that your job is to get the FRAAP completed within the limited time frame. The scribe will record all of the agreed-upon findings of the risk assessment. All others present are team members. As they enter the room, they step out of their regular roles and assume their roles as team members
- *Stick to the agenda/current focus.* The reason that the scope statement and visual model are discussed early in the process is so that everyone is reminded of the focus of the FRAAP meeting. We all have attended meetings where the intended purpose seems to get thrown out and anything else is discussed. It will be your job to keep the team focused.
- *All ideas have equal value.* This one is very difficult. As discussed earlier, some people are a bit intimidated by other team members. Sometimes the users are apprehensive about discussing threats to applications or systems while IT infrastructure personnel are present. It will be necessary for everyone to feel that their ideas are just as important as anyone else's.
- *Listen to other points of view.* Many times in meetings, some attendees break out of the group and carry on private conversations. At the beginning of the session we try to remind the team that the best way we can gain the respect we want is by showing respect to others.
- *No "plops"; all issues are recorded.* At least once in every session someone will comment that "this may seem stupid, but…" and then present a unique twist to the issues being discussed. The question of what was considered is one of many that arise when a risk assessment decision is being questioned. This very question ("what did you consider?") is why it is important to record all issues.
- *Deferred issues will be recorded.* In the FRAAP documentation, there is a spot to record any issue that is outside the scope of the current meeting. This will allow the team to record the concern and assign someone to follow up on it.
- *Post the idea before discussing it.* There will be a period of discussion on a particular threat, followed by some editing, and finally the scribe will post the agreed-upon item.
- *Help the scribe ensure that all issues are recorded.* Although there are time constraints on completing the session, it is vitally important to capture the issues and comments correctly.
- *One conversation at a time.* As we discussed earlier, it is important for the team to keep focused on the task at hand. If a number of separate conversations break out, then the objectives of the FRAAP session may not be completed during the allotted time.
- *Apply the three- to five-minute rule.* When discussing the risk level-setting factors, it is important that, after the first three or four discussions, a time limit be more or less adhered to.

When all of the preliminary activities have been concluded, it is time to begin the risk assessment process.

## 1.6.4 FRAAP Threats Identification

When I conduct a FRAAP, I like to have the room set up in a "U" shape. This allows me to work closer to the team members and it allows the process to flow around a conference room table. Having the room set up in this manner means everyone is in the front row; if the room is set up classroom style, it is harder to get the people in the back to feel that they are part of the team.

In the room setup it is important to include pads of paper and pens or pencils for the team to use. The team will be writing down ideas, and it is always best to have the implements readily available rather than taking up valuable time trying to find them.

During the FRAAP session, I normally discourage the use of laptops or PDAs. The team has been called by the owner to assist in meeting a due diligence obligation. If the team members are busy answering e-mail or distracted by other activities, the risk assessment will suffer. I also request that all cell phones and pagers be placed on "stun" or vibrate so as not to disturb the other team members.

To begin the brainstorming process, the facilitator will put up the first business attribute to be reviewed (Table 1.13). This will include the definition of the review element and some examples of threats that the team can use as thought-starters. I normally use a PowerPoint slideshow for this process so that the entire team can see what it is that the FRAAP is trying to identify.

The team is given three to five minutes to write down threats that are of concern to them. The facilitator will then go around the room getting one threat from each team member. Many will have more than one threat, but the process is to get one threat and then move to the next person. This way everyone gets a turn at participating. The process continues until everyone passes (that is, there are no more threats that the team can think of).

During the first two rounds, most of the team members will participate. As the rounds progress, the number of team members with new threats will diminish. When it gets down to just a few still responding, you can ask for a new threat from anyone rather than going around the table and calling on each person again.

**Table 1.13  FRAAP Brainstorming Attribute 1: Integrity**

| Definition | Threats |
|---|---|
| Assuring information will not be accidentally or maliciously altered or destroyed. | Data stream could be intercepted. |
| | Faulty programming could (inadvertently) modify data. |
| | Written or electronic copies of reports could be diverted to unauthorized or unintended persons. |
| | Data could be entered incorrectly. |
| | Intentional incorrect data entry. |

If a person passes, it does not mean that person is then locked out of the round. If something new comes into their mind, then they can join back in when it is their turn to do so again. They may hear a threat from someone else that will jog their thought process. This is why I recommend that there be paper and pens available for the team members to write down these quick-hitting ideas. Most of us suffer from terminal CRS (can't remember stuff). By providing paper and pens, the team members can capture these fleeting thoughts.

I am sad to point out that to some people everything is a contest. Too often the brainstorming round will dwindle down to two team members. When this occurs, the battle to be "King of the Threats" begins. They will continue to throw out ever-more-absurd threats until one combatant will finally yield. I share this with you only so that you can be on the alert for such behavior.

Once all of the integrity threats have been recorded, it is time for the facilitator to display the second review element with threat examples and give the team three to five minutes to write down their ideas (Table 1.14).

During this phase, I like to start the threats identification on the opposite side of the room from where I started last time. This allows those who were last to be first and get the best threats. The collecting of threats will continue until everyone has passed and there are no more confidentiality threats. After the scribe has indicated that everything has been captured, it will be time to go to the third element (Table 1.15).

Once the threats have been recorded, the FRAAP documentation will look like Table 1.16.

When I am conducting a FRAAP session, I use different colored pens for each element. Integrity might be recorded in blue, confidentiality in green, and availability in black. This will allow me to keep track of the threats by color coding them. As a flipchart page is filled up, I post it around the conference room. I record each threat sequentially within an element. For example, I will record all integrity threats in blue and number each threat in the order it was received, starting with

**Table 1.14   FRAAP Brainstorming Attribute 2: Confidentiality**

| Definition | Threats |
|---|---|
| The assurance that information is not disclosed to inappropriate entities or processes. | Insecure e-mail could contain confidential information. |
| | Internal theft of information. |
| | Employee is not able to verify the identity of a client, e.g., phone masquerading. |
| | Confidential information is left in plain view. |
| | Social discussions outside the office could result in disclosure of sensitive information. |

**Table 1.15    FRAAP Brainstorming Attribute 3: Availability**

| Definition | Threats |
|---|---|
| Assuring information and communications services will be ready for use when expected. | Files stored in personal directories may not be available to other employees when needed. |
| | Hardware failures could impact the availability of company resources. |
| | A failure in the data circuit could prohibit system access. |
| | "Acts of God": tornado, tsunami, hurricane. |
| | Upgrades in the software may prohibit access. |

**Table 1.16    FRAAP Worksheet 1 after Threats Have Been Identified**

| Business Attribute | Threat |
|---|---|
| Integrity | Data stream could be intercepted. |
| | Faulty programming could (inadvertently) modify data. |
| | Written or electronic copies of reports could be diverted to unauthorized or unintended persons. |
| | Data could be entered incorrectly. |
| | Intentional incorrect data entry. |
| Confidentiality | Insecure e-mail could contain confidential information. |
| | Internal theft of information. |
| | Employee is not able to verify the identity of a client, e.g., phone masquerading. |
| | Confidential information is left in plain view. |
| | Social discussions outside the office could result in disclosure of sensitive information. |
| Availability | Files stored in personal directories may not be available to other employees when needed. |
| | Hardware failures could impact the availability of company resources. |
| | A failure in the data circuit could prohibit system access. |
| | "Acts of God": tsunami, tornado, hurricane. |
| | Upgrades in the software may prohibit access. |

threat #1. When I move to confidentiality threats, I will switch to a green marker and start the numbering over again with #1. I will do the same when I get to the availability threats.

When all the threats have been posted, I recommend that the team take a fifteen-minute coffee break to do three important activities:

1. Check messages.
2. Get rid of old coffee and get new.
3. Clean up the raw threats.

During the break, have the team review the threats, and delete duplicate threats and combine like threats within a specific element. If a threat is repeated in the integrity and confidentiality elements, it is not considered to be a duplicate. It is only a duplicate if it appears more than once within a specific element. Only allow the break period, fifteen minutes, for the cleanup process.

## 1.6.5 *Identifying Threats Using a Checklist*

In recent years, some organizations have faced the task of doing a large number of risk assessments to become compliant with new laws and regulations. The Health Insurance Portability and Accountability Act of 1996 (HIPAA) is a specific example. A number of healthcare organizations contacted me to help them put together their risk assessment program. When we began to examine their specific needs, we found out that they did not have four hours for the risk assessment process, but they could get people to commit to a two-hour window. So from there we worked to find ways to streamline the process. We were able to meet the two-hour window by creating a checklist of threats to work from. The results of this work are available in Appendix G; also see Table 1.17.

To keep the risk assessment as clear as possible, we will concentrate on the activities that take place using the brainstorming techniques. When we have completed that discussion, we will turn our attention to the checklist style of risk assessment.

**Table 1.17 Sample Threats Checklist**

| Threat | Applicable (Yes/No) |
|---|---|
| Environmental | |
| Power flux | |
| Power outage — internal | |
| Power outage — external | |
| Water leak/plumbing failure | |
| HVAC failure | |

## 1.6.6  Identifying Existing Controls

Once the threats list has been completed, the team should quickly review each threat to determine whether there are any existing controls in place that address the threat issue. By identifying those threats that have existing controls in place, the team will be better able to determine the real level of current risk. This is one of the many reasons that the FRAAP needs representation from the various infrastructure groups. Typically, they will know best what controls and safeguards are already implemented (Table 1.18).

## 1.6.7  Establishing Risk Levels

This is probably the most important portion of the FRAAP and often the most confusing and most fun. You will want to ensure that the team has had an opportunity to examine the definitions used to establish probability and impact threshold levels. I like to include this information in the meeting notice attachments. This process will also be discussed during your FRAAP awareness program and briefly reviewed in the FRAAP session opening remarks.

For our initial review of the risk level-setting process, we will use a very simple example of the probability and impact thresholds. Appendix N has additional examples of more-intricate processes to establish the threat risk level. Recently, I have become aware that management likes "heat maps." The color coding of issues helps management and the team quickly identify where those issues fall in the severity levels.

At this point in the FRAAP, we have identified threats to the asset under review using the agreed-upon business attributes. We then examined each threat and identified those that had existing controls or safeguards in place. Our next task will be to determine the likelihood of the occurrence of a threat over a specific period of time and the impact to the organization in the event that it did occur (Table 1.19).

The team will discuss how likely the threat is to occur during the specified time frame. You will want to apply a good dose of common sense to the discussion. One of the examples that I like to use is the threat that an unattended workstation could be used by some other person to access the system. A good reality check is what you want to instill in this process. In the thirty years I have been in information security, this threat has always made every discussion list. I am not certain that I can cite one example of this threat actually occurring. So when you discuss probability, you will want them to address whether this threat has actually occurred. If so, when was the last time? This will provide the team with an ongoing reality check. You will want to keep them focused on the fact that the threats are being examined with existing controls in place.

Once the probability has been established, you will want to identify the impact presented by that threat to the asset under review (Table 1.20). Here, again, it will

**Table 1.18   FRAAP Worksheet 2 after Existing Controls Have Been Identified**

| Business Attribute | Threat | Existing Controls |
|---|---|---|
| Integrity | Data stream could be intercepted. | Vacant ports are disconnected. |
| | Faulty programming could (inadvertently) modify data. | Programs are tested before going into production, and change management procedures are in place. GLBA's Information Technology Policies & Procedures Manual No. 5-11, ISD Documentation; Test Plan and Test Analysis Report Standard. |
| | Written or electronic copies of reports could be diverted to unauthorized or unintended persons. | |
| | Data could be entered incorrectly. | Transaction journals are used. Contracts with third parties include language that addresses data integrity and service level agreements are designed to protect against this risk. |
| | Intentional incorrect data entry. | Transaction logs are maintained and reviewed to detect incorrect data entry. |
| Confidentiality | Insecure e-mail could contain confidential information. | |
| | Internal theft of information. | GLBA's Code of Conduct Policy. |
| | Employee is not able to verify the identity of a client, e.g., phone masquerading. | Customer must provide the date of last deposit or other confidential personal information within their file before information is released. |
| | Confidential information is left in plain view. | |
| | Social discussions outside the office could result in disclosure of sensitive information. | Code of Conduct/Conflict of Interest Policy; Annual Awareness item. |

*continued*

**Table 1.18 (continued)  FRAAP Worksheet 2 after Existing Controls Have Been Identified**

| Business Attribute | Threat | Existing Controls |
|---|---|---|
| Availability | Files stored in personal directories may not be available to other employees when needed. | GLBA 's management has established written policies and procedures to ensure information resources are available. See GLBA's Information Technology Policies & Procedures Manual No. 8-1 and Information Technology Policies & Procedures Manual No. 7-4. |
| | Hardware failures could impact the availability of company resources. | GLBA 's management has established written policies and procedures to ensure information resources are available. See GLBA's Information Technology Policies & Procedures Manual No. 8-1 and Information Technology Policies & Procedures Manual No. 7-4. Vendor maintenance agreements are established to support timely resolution of hardware failures. Files are imaged and stored to support recovery of information (ghost files). |
| | A failure in the data circuit could prohibit system access. | Vendor maintenance agreements are established to support timely resolution of hardware failures. See GLBA's Information Technology Policies & Procedures Manual No. 2-2. |
| | "Acts of God": tornado, tsunami, hurricane. | |
| | Upgrades in the software may prohibit access. | GLBA 's management has established written policies and procedures to ensure that software is tested prior to use in a production environment. See GLBA's Information Technology Policies & Procedures Manual No. 3-1 and Information Technology Policies & Procedures Manual No. 4-18. |

**Table 1.19   FRAAP Probability Thresholds**

| Term | Definition |
| --- | --- |
| Probability | A measure of how likely a threat may occur. |
| **Threshold level** | |
| High | Very likely that the threat will occur within the next year. |
| Medium | Possible that the threat will occur within the next year. |
| Low | Highly unlikely that the threat will occur within the next year. |

**Table 1.20   FRAAP Impact Thresholds**

| Term | Definition |
| --- | --- |
| Impact | The effect of a threat being carried out on an asset, expressed in tangible or intangible terms. |
| **Threshold level** | |
| High | Entire mission or business is impacted. |
| Medium | Loss limited to single business unit or business objective. |
| Low | Business as usual. |

be necessary to work with the team to ensure that the impact level is actually understood. Many times in the FRAAP, the business owner or users will get the impression that if their business unit is impacted, then the impact level is rated "High." Typically, that is not the case. The impact level of "High" is used to identify those threats that would affect the entire organization. One way to help the team see the issue in the proper light is to ask whether the threat has ever occurred. If it has, then you want to discuss what the impact really was.

I recently conducted a risk assessment where the threat identified was that contractors could enter data incorrectly into the system. Initially, the discussion was that the probability of occurrence was high and that it had the possibility to impact the entire mission of the agency severely. I asked the question about the high probability and found out that this issue happened almost daily. With that information we turned our attention to the impact. Although it was true that there was a chance that the entire agency could be impacted, the fact that existing controls had prevented it from reaching that level seemed to mean that something less than a "High" impact was the correct answer.

It helps to work with the team for the first few threats to make certain that everyone sees how the process works. Once the probability and impact have been selected, it will be easy to identify the risk level (Table 1.21).

The team can examine where the probability and impact levels fall and then can assign a risk level (Table 1.22).

So the results will resemble Table 1.23.

**Table 1.21   FRAAP Probability: Impact Matrix**

|  | Impact | | |
|---|---|---|---|
| *Probability* | *Low* | *Medium* | *High* |
| High | Yellow | Red | Red |
| Medium | Green | Yellow | Red |
| Low | Green | Green | Yellow |

**Table 1.22   Risk Level Color Key**

| Color | Risk Level | Action |
|---|---|---|
| Red | High | Requires immediate action. |
| Yellow | Medium | May require action, must continue to monitor. |
| Green | Low | No action required at this time. |

## 1.6.8   Residual Risk

When examining a threat, two types of risk typically will be identified. In Table 1.24, three total risks are identified. The first two have existing controls in place and the third threat does not. After performing the probability/impact process, the risk level that will be established for the first two threats is termed the "residual risk." The risk remaining after the implementation of new or enhanced controls is the residual risk. Practically no system is risk free, and not all implemented controls can eliminate the risk they are intended to address or reduce the risk level to zero.

For the third threat, because there are no existing controls in place, the risk level established is termed the "baseline" risk level. The reason that a control from the organization's standard control list was not selected (discussed later in this chapter) is that the baseline risk may be within the acceptable range even without any specific controls selected.

After the risk levels have been established, it will be necessary to assess whether the risk level is acceptable. A number of factors will ultimately determine the acceptability of risk level. For the purposes of this exercise, we will state that any risk level of "Medium" (Yellow) or "High" (Red) must be re-examined to determine whether additional controls could lower the risk level (Table 1.25).

The final process in the FRAAP session is to identify controls for those threats identified as having a high risk level. In our example, those would be anything identified as having a risk level of "High" or "Medium." A sample controls list should be sent out to all team members with the meeting notice, and copies should be available for the team during the FRAAP session.

During this step, the risk assessment team will determine which security controls generally could best reduce threat risk level to a more-acceptable level. A number of

**Table 1.23 FRAAP Worksheet 3 with Risk Levels Assigned**

| Business Attribute | Threat | Existing Controls | Probability/ Impact | Risk Level |
|---|---|---|---|---|
| Integrity | Data stream could be intercepted. | Vacant ports are disconnected. | L/M | Low |
| | Faulty programming could (inadvertently) modify data. | Programs are tested before going into production, and change management procedures are in place. GLBA's Information Technology Policies & Procedures Manual No. 5-11, ISD Documentation; Test Plan and Test Analysis Report Standard. | L/L | Low |
| | Written or electronic copies of reports could be diverted to unauthorized or unintended persons. | | M/M | Moderate |
| | Data could be entered incorrectly. | Transaction journals are used. Contracts with third parties include language that addresses data integrity and service level agreements are designed to protect against this risk. | M/L | Low |
| | Intentional incorrect data entry. | Transaction logs are maintained and reviewed to detect incorrect data entry. | L/M | Low |
| Confidentiality | Insecure e-mail could contain confidential information. | | L/H | Moderate |
| | Internal theft of information. | GLBA's Code of Conduct Policy. | L/L | Low |
| | Employee is not able to verify the identity of a client, e.g., phone masquerading. | Customer must provide the date of last deposit or other confidential personal information within their file before information is released. | L/H | Moderate |

*continued*

**Table 1.23 (continued)   FRAAP Worksheet 3 with Risk Levels Assigned**

| Business Attribute | Threat | Existing Controls | Probability/ Impact | Risk Level |
|---|---|---|---|---|
| Confidentiality (continued) | Confidential information is left in plain view. | | M/M | Moderate |
| | Social discussions outside the office could result in disclosure of sensitive information. | Code of Conduct/Conflict of Interest Policy; Annual Awareness item. | M/M | Moderate |
| Availability | Files stored in personal directories may not be available to other employees when needed. | GLBA 's management has established written policies and procedures to ensure information resources are available. See GLBA's Information Technology Policies & Procedures Manual No. 8-1 and Information Technology Policies & Procedures Manual No. 7-4. | L/H | Moderate |
| | Hardware failures could impact the availability of company resources. | GLBA 's management has established written policies and procedures to ensure information resources are available. See GLBA's Information Technology Policies & Procedures Manual No. 8-1 and Information Technology Policies & Procedures Manual No. 7-4. Vendor maintenance agreements are established to support timely resolution of hardware failures. Files are imaged and stored to support recovery of information (ghost files). | L/L | Low |

| Availability | A failure in the data circuit could prohibit system access. | Vendor maintenance agreements are established to support timely resolution of hardware failures. See GLBA's ITP&P Manual No. 2-2. | L/L | Low |
| | "Acts of God": tornado, tsunami, hurricane. | | M/H | High |
| | Upgrades in the software may prohibit access. | GLBA 's management has established written policies and procedures to ensure that software is tested prior to use in a production environment. See GLBA's ITP&P Manual No. 3-1 and Information Technology Policies & Procedures Manual No. 4-18. | L/L | Low |

**Table 1.24  FRAAP Residual Risk: Baseline Risk Level**

| Business Attribute | Threat | Existing Controls | Probability/ Impact | Risk Level |
|---|---|---|---|---|
| Integrity | Data stream could be intercepted. | Vacant ports are disconnected. | L/M | Low |
| | Faulty programming could (inadvertently) modify data. | Programs are tested before going into production, and change management procedures are in place. GLBA' s Information Technology Policies & Procedures Manual No. 5-11, ISD Documentation; Test Plan and Test Analysis Report Standard. | L/L | Low |
| | Written or electronic copies of reports could be diverted to unauthorized or unintended persons. | | M/M | Moderate |

sources for standards can assist the risk assessment team in establishing an effective set of controls. These sources might include some of the following:

- Information Technology — Code of Practice for Information Security Management (ISO/IEC 27002)
- Security Technologies for Manufacturing and Control Systems (ISA-TR99.00. 01-2004)
- Integrating Electronic Security into Manufacturing and Control Systems Environment (ISA-TR99.00.02-2004)
- Federal Information Processing Standards Publications (FIPS Pubs)
- National Institute of Standards and Technology
- CobiT® Security Baseline
- Health Insurance Portability and Accountability Act (HIPAA)
- The Basel Accords
- Privacy Act of 1974
- Gramm–Leach–Bliley Act (GLBA)
- Sarbanes–Oxley Act (SOX)
- Information Security for Banking and Finance (ISO/TR 13569)
- FFEIC Examination Guidelines

**Table 1.25  FRAAP Worksheet 4: Acceptable Risk Level Determined**

| Business Attribute | Threat | Existing Controls | Probability/ Impact | Risk Level | Acceptable Level (Yes/No) |
|---|---|---|---|---|---|
| Integrity | Data stream could be intercepted. | Vacant ports are disconnected. | L/M | Low | Yes |
| | Faulty programming could (inadvertently) modify data. | Programs are tested before going into production, and change management procedures are in place. GLBA's Information Technology Policies & Procedures Manual No. 5-11, ISD Documentation; Test Plan and Test Analysis Report Standard. | L/L | Low | Yes |
| | Written or electronic copies of reports could be diverted to unauthorized or unintended persons. | | M/M | Moderate | No |
| | Data could be entered incorrectly. | Transaction journals are used. Contracts with third parties include language that addresses data integrity and service level agreements are designed to protect against this risk. | M/L | Low | Yes |
| | Intentional incorrect data entry. | Transaction logs are maintained and reviewed to detect incorrect data entry. | L/M | Low | Yes |

*continued*

**Table 1.25 (continued)   FRAAP Worksheet 4: Acceptable Risk Level Determined**

| Business Attribute | Threat | Existing Controls | Probability/ Impact | Risk Level | Acceptable Level (Yes/No) |
|---|---|---|---|---|---|
| Confidentiality | Insecure e-mail could contain confidential information. | | L/H | Moderate | No |
| | Internal theft of information. | GLBA's Code of Conduct Policy. | L/L | Low | Yes |
| | Employee is not able to verify the identity of a client, e.g., phone masquerading. | Customer must provide the date of last deposit or other confidential personal information within their file before information is released. | L/H | Moderate | No |
| | Confidential information is left in plain view. | | M/M | Moderate | No |
| | Social discussions outside the office could result in disclosure of sensitive information. | Code of Conduct/Conflict of Interest Policy; Annual Awareness item. | M/M | Moderate | No |
| Availability | Files stored in personal directories may not be available to other employees when needed. | GLBA 's management has established written policies and procedures to ensure information resources are available. See GLBA 's Information Technology Policies & Procedures Manual No. 8-1 and Information Technology Policies & Procedures Manual No. 7-4. | L/H | Moderate | No |

| Availability | | L/L | Low | Yes |
|---|---|---|---|---|
| Hardware failures could impact the availability of company resources. | GLBA's management has established written policies and procedures to ensure information resources are available.<br>See GLBA's Information Technology Policies & Procedures Manual No. 8-1 and Information Technology Policies & Procedures No. 7-4.<br>Vendor maintenance agreements are established to support timely resolution of hardware failures.<br>Files are imaged and stored to support recovery of information (ghost files). | L/L | Low | Yes |
| A failure in the data circuit could prohibit system access. | Vendor maintenance agreements are established to support timely resolution of hardware failures.<br>See GLBA's Information Technology Policies & Procedures Manual No. 2-2. | L/L | Low | Yes |
| "Acts of God": tornado, tsunami, hurricane. | | M/H | High | No |
| Upgrades in the software may prohibit access. | GLBA's management has established written policies and procedures to ensure that software is tested prior to use in a production environment.<br>See GLBA's Information Technology Policies & Procedures Manual No. 3-1 and Information Technology Policies & Procedures Manual 4-18. | L/L | Low | Yes |

For this example we will be using a set of controls based on the IT organizations and groups that support the business processes. There are thirty-four controls that the team can select from. It is not necessary to try to select the one perfect control at this time. Remember one of the goals of risk assessment is to record all of the alternatives that were considered (Table 1.26).

The team will be selecting controls for only those threats that registered as high risks (those with "High" or "Medium" levels). Those threats with a risk level of "Low" will be monitored for change. All possible controls should be entered into the FRAAP worksheet (Table 1.27).

The FRAAP team must understand that trade-off must be made between business objectives and controls. Every control or safeguard will impact the business process in some manner as resources are expended to implement the control. Accidents, errors, and omissions generally account for more losses than deliberate acts. No control can or should be one hundred percent effective. The ultimate goal is to achieve an acceptable level of security.

The FRAAP will not eliminate every threat. Management has the duty to determine which threats to implement controls on and which ones to accept. The FRAAP team is to assist management in making that informed business decision.

## 1.7   Using a Threats Identification Checklist

As we briefly examined earlier in this chapter, it is possible to use a checklist to help the team through the threats identification process. In Appendix G, there are two sample threats checklists. The first is a checklist of threats based on the business attributes of confidentiality, integrity, and availability. This list contains nearly one hundred twenty threats. The second list is based on the business attributes of natural-human accidental-human deliberate-environmental. The second checklist contains sixty threat possibilities.

When using the checklist approach to any activity, there is a concern about the likelihood that when the team completes the checklist, there will be a feeling that all issues have been covered. What we want to make certain is that the risk team understands that the checklist contains only examples of threats. It usually contains some that do not apply, but more importantly, it may lack specific threats that do apply. You will want to provide the team with time to brainstorm additional ideas and add them to the threats list.

The first question to be answered is whether the identified threat is applicable to the asset currently being reviewed. This is usually quickly identified by a simple "Yes" or "No" on the worksheet (Table 1.28).

Once the threats have been identified, the process is much the same as the brainstorming process for the FRAAP. The next step is to identify any existing controls. That process would look something like Table 1.29.

**Table 1.26   FRAAP Controls List by IT Organization**

| Control Number | IT Group | Control Category | Definition |
|---|---|---|---|
| 1 | Operations controls | Backup | Backup requirements will be determined and communicated to Operations including a request that an electronic notification that backups were completed be sent to the application system administrator. Operations will be requested to test the backup procedures. |
| 2 | Operations controls | Recovery plan | Develop, document, and test recovery procedures designed to ensure that the application and information can be recovered, using the backups created, in the event of loss. |
| 3 | Operations controls | Risk assessment | Conduct a risk assessment to determine the level of exposure to identified threats and identify possible safeguards or controls. |
| 4 | Operations controls | Anti-virus | (1) Ensure LAN administrator installs the corporate standard anti-virus software on all computers. (2) Training and awareness of virus prevention techniques will be incorporated in the organization IP program. |
| 5 | Operations controls | Interface dependencies | Systems that feed information will be identified and communicated to Operations to stress the impact to the functionality if these feeder applications are unavailable. |
| 6 | Operations controls | Maintenance | Time requirements for technical maintenance will be tracked and a request for adjustment will be communicated to management if experience warrants. |
| 7 | Operations controls | Service level agreement | Acquire service level agreements to establish level of customer expectations and assurances from supporting operations. |

*continued*

**Table 1.26 (continued)    FRAAP Controls List by IT Organization**

| Control Number | IT Group | Control Category | Definition |
|---|---|---|---|
| 8 | Operations controls | Maintenance | Acquire maintenance and/or supplier agreements to facilitate the continued operational status of the application. |
| 9 | Operations controls | Change management | Production migration controls such as search and remove processes to ensure data stores are clean. |
| 10 | Operations controls | Business impact analysis | A formal business impact analysis will be conducted to determine the asset's relative criticality with other enterprise assets. |
| 11 | Operations controls | Backup | Training for a backup to the system administrator will be provided and duties rotated between them to ensure the adequacy of the training program. |
| 12 | Operations controls | Backup | A formal employee security awareness program has been implemented and is updated and presented to the employees at least on an annual basis. |
| 13 | Operations controls | Recovery plan | Access sources: Implement a mechanism to limit access to confidential information to specific network paths or physical locations. |
| 14 | Operations controls | Risk assessment | Implement user authentication mechanisms (such as firewalls, dial-in controls, secure ID) to limit access to authorized personnel. |
| 15 | Application controls | Application control | Design and implement application controls (data entry edit checking, fields requiring validation, alarm indicators, password expiration capabilities, checksums) to ensure the integrity, confidentiality, and/or availability of application information. |

**Table 1.26 (continued)   FRAAP Controls List by IT Organization**

| Control Number | IT Group | Control Category | Definition |
|---|---|---|---|
| 16 | Application controls | Acceptance testing | Develop testing procedures to be followed during applications development and/or during modifications to the existing application that include user participation and acceptance. |
| 17 | Application controls | Training | Implement user programs (user performance evaluations) designed to encourage compliance with policies and procedures in place to ensure the appropriate utilization of the application. |
| 18 | Application controls | Training | Application developers will provide documentation, guidance, and support to the operations staff (Operations) in implementing mechanisms to ensure that the transfer of information between applications is secure. |
| 19 | Application controls | Corrective strategies | The development team will develop corrective strategies such as reworked processes, revised application logic, etc. |
| 20 | Security controls | Policy | Develop policies and procedures to limit access and operating privileges to those with business need. |
| 21 | Security controls | Training | User training will include instruction and documentation on the proper use of the application. The importance of maintaining the confidentiality of user accounts, passwords, and the confidential and competitive nature of information will be stressed. |
| 22 | Security controls | Review | Implement mechanisms to monitor, report, and audit activities identified as requiring independent reviews, including periodic reviews of user-IDs to ascertain and verify business need. |

*continued*

**Table 1.26 (continued)   FRAAP Controls List by IT Organization**

| Control Number | IT Group | Control Category | Definition |
|---|---|---|---|
| 23 | Security controls | Asset classification | The asset under review will be classified using enterprise policies, standards, and procedures on asset classification. |
| 24 | Security controls | Access control | Mechanisms to protect the database against unauthorized access, and modifications made from outside the application, will be determined and implemented. |
| 25 | Security controls | Management support | Request management support to ensure the cooperation and coordination of various business units. |
| 26 | Security controls | Proprietary | Processes are in place to ensure that company proprietary assets are protected and that the company is in compliance with all third-party license agreements. |
| 27 | Security controls | Security awareness | Implement an access control mechanism to prevent unauthorized access to information. This mechanism will include the capability of detecting, logging, and reporting attempts to breach the security of this information. |
| 28 | Security controls | Access control | Implement encryption mechanisms (data, end-to-end) to prevent unauthorized access to protect the integrity and confidentiality of information. |
| 29 | Security controls | Access control | Adhere to a change management process designed to facilitate a structured approach to modifications of the application, to ensure appropriate steps and precautions are followed. "Emergency" modifications should be included in this process. |
| 30 | Security controls | Access control | Control procedures are in place to ensure that appropriate system logs are reviewed by independent third parties to review system update activities. |

**Table 1.26 (continued)  FRAAP Controls List by IT Organization**

| Control Number | IT Group | Control Category | Definition |
|---|---|---|---|
| 31 | Security controls | Access control | In consultation with Facilities Management, facilitate the implementation of physical security controls designed to protect the information, software, and hardware required of the system. |
| 32 | Systems controls | Change management | Backup requirements will be determined and communicated to Operations including a request that an electronic notification that backups were completed be sent to the application system administrator. Operations will be requested to test the backup procedures. |
| 33 | Systems controls | Monitor system logs | Develop, document, and test recovery procedures designed to ensure that the application and information can be recovered, using the backups created, in the event of loss. |
| 34 | Physical security | Physical security | Conduct a risk assessment to determine the level of exposure to identified threats and identify possible safeguards or controls. |

Once the existing controls have been identified, the team examines each threat to establish the probability of occurrence and relative impact, which will lead to an assigned risk level (Table 1.30).

We have found that the use of a checklist can speed up the process, but it comes with a price of perhaps missing some of the threats and some team interaction.

## 1.7.1  FRAAP Session Summary

At this point, the FRAAP session is complete. The team was given an overview of the risk assessment process and what will be expected of them. The owner then discussed the scope of the risk assessment and a technical support person reviewed the information flow model. The facilitator then walked the team through the review business attributes (integrity, confidentiality, and availability). Once all threats were identified and recorded, the team took a few minutes to edit and consolidate the threats. Once the consolidation was complete, the team examined each threat

**Table 1.27  FRAAP Worksheet 5: Additional Controls and New Risk Levels**

| Threat | Existing Controls | Select New or Enhanced Control(s) | New Probability/ Impact | New Risk Level | Acceptable Level (Yes/No) |
|---|---|---|---|---|---|
| Written or electronic copies of reports could be diverted to unauthorized or unintended persons. | Information classification policy in place. Information handling standards are being developed. | Information classification policy in place. Information handling standards are being developed. | L/M | Low | Yes |
| Insecure e-mail could contain confidential information. | Information handling standards are being developed. Concern to be addressed in GLBA 's employee awareness program and new employee orientation. | Information handling standards are being developed. Concern to be addressed in GLBA 's employee awareness program and new employee orientation. | L/M | Low | Yes |
| Employee is not able to verify the identity of a client, e.g., phone masquerading. | In addition to existing controls. Concern to be addressed in GLBA 's employee awareness program and new employee orientation. Continue to monitor. | In addition to existing controls. Concern to be addressed in GLBA 's employee awareness program and new employee orientation. Continue to monitor. | L/M | Low | Yes |
| Confidential information is left in plain view. | Information handling standards are being developed. Concern to be addressed in GLBA 's employee awareness program and new employee orientation. | Information handling standards are being developed. Concern to be addressed in GLBA 's employee awareness program and new employee orientation. | L/M | Low | Yes |

| Risk | Control | Control | | | |
|---|---|---|---|---|---|
| Social discussions outside the office could result in disclosure of sensitive information. | Code of Conduct/Conflict of Interest Policy. Information handling standards are being developed. Concern to be addressed in GLBA 's employee awareness program and new employee orientation. | Code of Conduct/Conflict of Interest Policy. Information handling standards are being developed. Concern to be addressed in GLBA 's employee awareness program and new employee orientation. | L/M | Low | Yes |
| Files stored in personal directories may not be available to other employees when needed. | GLBA 's management has established written policies and procedures to ensure information resources are available. Employee awareness program will reinforce the requirements. | GLBA 's management has established written policies and procedures to ensure information resources are available. Employee awareness program will reinforce the requirements. Verify compliance. | L/M | Low | Yes |
| "Acts of God": tornado, tsunami, hurricane. | Senior management to champion business continuity planning program. The BCP will also drive emergency response procedures and an IT disaster recovery plan. | Senior management to champion business continuity planning program. The BCP will also drive emergency response procedures and an IT disaster recovery plan. | M/M | Moderate | Yes |

**Table 1.28   FRAAP Checklist Worksheet**

| Threat | Applicable (Yes/No) |
|---|---|
| **Environmental** | |
| Power surge — a prolonged high voltage condition | Yes |
| Blackout (minor) — loss of power for less than four hours | Yes |
| Blackout (moderate) — four to eight hours | Yes |
| Blackout (severe) — more than eight hours | Yes |
| Sag — brief period of low voltage | Yes |

**Table 1.29   FRAAP Checklist Worksheet with Existing Controls**

| Threat | Applicable (Yes/No) | Existing Controls |
|---|---|---|
| **Environmental** | | |
| Power surge — a prolonged high-voltage condition | Yes | Surge suppressors installed on all computer systems. |
| Blackout (minor) — loss of power for less than four hours | Yes | Surge suppressors, UPS |
| Blackout (moderate) — four to eight hours | Yes | Surge suppressors, UPS, diesel generator |
| Blackout (severe) — more than eight hours | Yes | Surge suppressors, UPS, diesel generator |
| Sag — brief period of low voltage | Yes | |

and identified any existing controls or safeguards in place. When that process was completed, the team examined each threat for probability of occurrence and the impact to the business process. The team examined each threat using the existing controls as a guide. The result of this activity was to assign a relative risk level to each threat.

Once the risk levels were established, the team identified possible controls that could reduce the threat risk level to an acceptable range. The team then reviewed the probability and impact of those specific threats to see whether the new or additional control would be effective. For each new control, the team identified either a person or group that would be responsible for the implementation of the control.

When this process is complete, the FRAAP session is complete and the meeting is adjourned. A total of four deliverables come out of the FRAAP sessions:

1. Threats were identified.
2. Risk levels were established.
3. Compensating controls were selected.
4. Control "owner" was identified.

**Table 1.30   FRAAP Checklist Worksheet Complete**

| Threat | Applicable (Yes/No) | Existing Controls | Probability/ Impact | Risk Level | Acceptable (Yes/No) |
|---|---|---|---|---|---|
| **Environmental** | | | | | |
| Power surge — a prolonged high-voltage condition | Yes | Surge suppressors installed on all computer systems. | L/L | Low | Yes |
| Blackout (minor) — loss of power for less than four hours | Yes | Surge suppressors, UPS | M/L | Low | Yes |
| Blackout (moderate) — four to eight hours | Yes | Surge suppressors, UPS, diesel generator | M/L | Low | Yes |
| Blackout (severe) — more than eight hours | Yes | Surge suppressors, UPS, diesel generator | L/L | Low | Yes |
| Sag — brief period of low voltage | Yes | | L/M | Low | Yes |

# 1.8   Post-FRAAP Process

The FRAAP session will typically take the entire four hours scheduled for it. I like to take a break for lunch and then begin the process of creating the reports that afternoon. One important element that needs to be stressed is the presence of the scribe. This person (oftentimes it is me doing both roles) will record the activities of the FRAAP as the four-hour session is unfolding. Typically, I use my computer and a projector to show the risk action plan on a screen or wall in the FRAAP workroom. Using this, all of the threats and subsequent decisions are recorded in real time. This allows the facilitator and scribe to begin the process of preparing the final documents.

The first document I begin to prepare is the management summary report. A sample copy of this report can be found in Appendix I. We will now review each section of the management summary report.

This document is very important to the entire FRAAP. It is here that you will quickly present the findings of the FRAAP and identify the actions that are to be taken. All of the issues are discussed in general terms in this report. The details are available and can be provided upon request.

**Table 1.31    FRAAP Management Summary Report Visual**

| Risk Level | Number of Similar Threats | Description of Threat Scenario |
|:---:|:---:|:---|
| A | 4 | Physical intrusion |
| A | 2 | Power failure |
| B | 10 | Information handling and classification |
| B | 4 | Password weakness or sharing |
| B | 4 | People masquerading as customers |
| B | 3 | Firewall concerns |
| B | 2 | Computer viruses |
| B | 2 | Workstations left unattended |
| B | 2 | Employee training |
| B | 27 | Individual threats identified |

In the movie *The Big Chill,* Jeff Goldblum plays a writer for *People* magazine named Michael Gold. When asked what he wrote, he answered that it didn't matter what he wrote, he just had to make certain that the length of the article was "about the same time the average person spends in the bathroom." Here is a hint about the length of your management summary report: it should be no longer than the average time an executive will spend in the restroom. That is probably where it is going to be read, so you need to be prepared.

The management summary report shown in Table 1.31 is put together in a format that I use. The components of the report will be consistent for the most part, but the order of things may change based on the culture and standards of the organization. I use the following format:

■ Title page
■ Table of contents
■ Attendee list
■ Scope statement summary
■ Assessment methodology used
■ Summary of assessment findings
■ Where to obtain full documentation
■ Conclusions

After the standard title page and the table of contents, I like to establish right away who was part of the FRAAP. This is a result of my early training in the business world when typically the first question from management was about exactly who had been part of this process. NIST Special Publication 800-30, Risk Management Guide for Information Technology Systems, recommends that the attendee list be attached in an appendix to the report. Neither style is right nor wrong, they are both correct based on the specific culture of the organization.

When you prepare the management summary report, be certain to abide by the norms of the organization.

One more thing about the attendee list makeup. I have no qualms about identifying individuals who had been invited but did not attend. This again is a cultural issue that must be explored and researched before attempting to include in the report.

A summary of the risk assessment scope statement is discussed next. This should be two or three paragraphs at a maximum and should contain a high-level overview of what the assessment was. Include when and where the risk assessment was conducted. If there was a compelling reason to conduct the assessment at this time, that should be identified here. Be sure to include any assumptions and constraints that you feel impacted the process.

A brief description of the actual risk assessment methodology needs to be part of the documentation. Spend a few brief paragraphs creating a picture of how the team reached the conclusions that it did. The full-blown documentation will provide the intricate details; here an overview will be sufficient.

In the summary of assessment findings, I like to take the top high-level risks and present them to management in a brief description and a visual to reinforce the discussion. This discussion will give a brief synopsis of the key high-level risks and the actions to be taken to reduce the risks to acceptable levels (Table 1.31).

In our example the risk assessment identified five key areas of concern:

1. Restricted physical access areas should be considered throughout GLBA.
   *Action plan:* A physical security risk assessment will be conducted to determine if there is a need to create restricted access areas and increase physical access controls.
2. Power failure could cause corruption of information or prevent access to the system. *Action plan:* Network UPS may not be adequate for a power outage out of regular business hours. Install a backup domain controller at Ualena Street and connect it to the Ualena Street UPS.
3. Information classification scheme is incomplete. *Action plan:* GLBA has created a draft Information Classification Policy that addresses five categories: public, internal use, restricted, confidential, and classified. The new policy requirements are to be disseminated to the GLBA staff and will become part of the new employee orientation and the annual employee awareness program.
4. Concern that the weakness of passwords for some information systems user accounts could allow compromise of the password and permit unauthorized access to GLBA systems and information. *Action plan:* The GLBA Passwords Policy is to be modified to require strong passwords. GLBA information systems department (ISD) will investigate software solutions to enforce a strong password requirement.
5. Someone could impersonate a customer to corrupt or access bank records or accounts. *Action plan:* Concern to be addressed in GLBA employee awareness program and new employee orientation.

Finally, there is the Conclusions section. Here you can wrap up the overall process and tell management that the issues of risk are being addressed, and you can identify those risks that the owner decided to accept. This is also the place where any constraints that impacted the results of the risk assessment process should be identified.

Sometimes issues that are beyond the scope of the assessment under review rise to the surface during the risk assessment process. The Conclusions section offers a vehicle to identify and address these issues.

As you complete the management summary report, you will be faced with the question of whether or not the report needs to be published. This again is a cultural issue. Two corporations that I have worked for required only that the report be published and not actually signed by anyone.

The risk assessment report and documentation is a lot like an audit report. Typically, both sides work together to uncover deficiencies and to establish a mutually acceptable solution. When putting together the report documentation, the facilitator works directly with the owner and project lead to determine the best course of action and the time frame for compliance. In cases where both sides work together, the publication of the report may not require a signature. Check with management to ensure that the proper protocol is followed.

## 1.8.1 Complete the Action Plan

When last we left the FRAAP action plan, the worksheet contained the information shown in Table 1.32 and table 1.33. The final elements that must be determined is who will be responsible for the implementation of the new or enhanced controls and when the task will be completed. The establishment of the time frame for implementation will take a bit of work. This information needs to be entered into the worksheet. I typically use an Excel® worksheet, which gives me the flexibility I need to enter all of the information into one document (Table 1.34).

The risk assessment is not complete until the paperwork is done. The action plan must have the threats identified, the risk levels established, and the controls selected. Once the controls have seen selected, the action plan must identify who will implement the controls and by what date. If the management owner decides to accept the risk, this decision must be identified in the action plan and the management summary report.

Like all important tasks, the proof of how well it went lies in the documentation that supports the process. Remember the results of a risk assessment will be used twice, once when a decision must be made and again when something goes wrong. By having complete documentation, management will be able to show when a decision was made, who was involved in the process, what was discussed, and what alternatives were considered.

**Table 1.32 Post-FRAAP Worksheet Section 1**

| Business Attribute | Threat | Existing Controls | Probability/ Impact | Risk Level | Acceptable (Yes/No) |
|---|---|---|---|---|---|
| Integrity | Data stream could be intercepted. | Vacant ports are disconnected. | L/M | Low | Yes |
| | Faulty programming could (inadvertently) modify data. | Programs are tested before going into production, and change management procedures are in place. Fred's Information Technology Policies & Procedures Manual No. 5-11, ISD Documentation; Test Plan and Test Analysis Report Standard. | L/L | Low | Yes |
| | Written or electronic copies of reports could be diverted to unauthorized or unintended persons. | | M/M | Moderate | No |

**Table 1.33   Post-FRAAP Worksheet Section 2**

| Business Attribute | Threat | Existing Controls | Risk Level | New or Enhanced Control | Probability/ Impact | Risk Level | Acceptable Level (Yes/No) |
|---|---|---|---|---|---|---|---|
| Integrity | Data stream could be intercepted. | Vacant ports are disconnected. | Low | | | | |
| | Faulty programming could (inadvertently) modify data. | Programs are tested before going into production, and change management procedures are in place. GLBA's Information Technology Policies & Procedures Manual No. 5-11, ISD Documentation; Test Plan and Test Analysis Report Standard. | Low | | | | |
| | Written or electronic copies of reports could be diverted to unauthorized or unintended persons. | | Moderate | Information classification policy in place. Information handling standards are being developed. | L/M | Low | Yes |

**Table 1.34   Post-FRAAP Worksheet Section 3**

| Business Attribute | Threat | New or Enhanced Control(s) | Probability/ Impact | Risk Level | Acceptable Level (Yes/No) | Responsible Entity | Compliance Date |
|---|---|---|---|---|---|---|---|
| Integrity | Written or electronic copies of reports could be diverted to unauthorized or unintended persons. | Information classification policy in place. Information handling standards are being developed. | L/M | Low | Yes | Information security team | Third quarter this year |

## 1.9   Conclusion

Capturing the threats and selecting controls is important, but the most important element in an effective risk assessment process is establishing the risk levels. Before any organization can decide what to do, it must have a clear picture of where the problems are (Table 1.35). As you will see in the next chapter, there are any numbers of ways to modify the risk assessment process to meet the organization's needs. The process requires the facilitator to be flexible and to work with the owner to establish needs before the risk assessment process begins.

When the risk level is to be determined, it will be vital for the team to understand how each of the threats is to be judged. Is the team going to factor-in existing controls or will the team establish a baseline for the implementation of a standard set of controls? In the next chapter, we will discuss risk analysis (also known as project impact analysis). Chapter 3 will address a pre-screening methodology that will help the organization determine whether a full-blown risk assessment or business impact analysis (BIA) will be required. We will also discuss the gap analysis process that is used to help organizations determine the level of completeness presented by the current security program. The last item we will discuss is the BIA process.

In addition to these discussions, the appendices contain additional helpful information. Appendix G contains the two threat checklists we discussed. Appendix H contains various examples of probability and impact and the supporting risk -level determination matrix. In Appendix M, we have included sample controls lists. We have also included lists where we have mapped various controls to one another. For example, we have taken ISO 27002 and mapped its standards to HIPAA, GLBA, and SOX. We include mappings of many of the standards, laws, and regulations that you will find in Appendix D.

**Table 1.35 Sample Summary Sheet**

| Threat[a] | Risk Level[b] | Recommended Control[c] | Action Priority[d] | Selected Planned Control[e] | Required Resources[f] | Responsible Team/Person[g] | Completion Data[h] | Maintenance Requirements[i] |
|---|---|---|---|---|---|---|---|---|
| User can add peer-to-peer sharing of resources | High | Implement desktop policy; use active directory or third-party product | High | Disallow unauthorized install of software; turn on deep packet inspection to circumvent p2p sharing | 10 hours to develop policy; 20 hours to research and implement packet inspection | Policy: information security Packet inspection: network admin | Policy: 1 May 08 to 1 Sep 08 Packet: 1 June 08 to 30 June 08 | Annual review of both controls |

[a] The risks are the output results from the risk assessment process.
[b] The associated risk level of each identified risk is the output of the probability/impact process of risk assessment.
[c] Recommended controls are selected in the risk assessment process.
[d] Action priority is determined based on risk levels and available resources.
[e] Planned controls selected from the recommended controls for implementation.
[f] Resources required for implementing the selected planned controls.
[g] List of teams and persons who will be responsible for implementing the new or enhanced controls.
[h] Start date and project end date for implementing the new or enhanced controls.
[i] Maintenance requirement for new or enhanced controls after implementation.

# Chapter 2

# Risk Analysis (Project Impact Analysis)

## 2.1 Overview

Risk management is a process that provides management with the balance of meeting business objectives or missions and the need to protect the assets of the organization cost effectively. In this period of increased external scrutiny due to the myriad questionable management decisions and the corresponding legislative backlash, risk management provides management with the ability to demonstrate actively due diligence and how they are meeting their fiduciary duty. In this chapter we will examine how risk analysis helps managers meet their due diligence requirement.

## 2.2 The Difference between Risk Analysis and Risk Assessment

When we examine the business process development cycle (BPDC) (also known as the system development life cycle [SDLC]), we see that there are phases in which certain activities are scheduled to be performed. In the BPDC that I am familiar with, the first phase is the analysis process. This is the time when the case for a new project is created. The risk analysis, or project impact analysis (PIA), is used to document and demonstrate the business reasons why a new project should be approved. When the PIA is complete, the formal documentation is presented to the executive management committee for review, assessment, and possible approval. If approved by the committee, the proposal is then registered and becomes a "project."

Once a project has been approved, early in the next phase of the BPDC, the design phase, a risk assessment must be performed to identify the threats presented by this new project to the organization's mission or business objectives. The risk assessment allows the development team and the business stakeholders to identify potential threats, prioritize those threats into risks, and identify controls that can reduce the risks to acceptable levels. Knowing the control requirements in the design phase will help reduce costs when work begins on the project in the construction or development phase.

## 2.3  Risk Analysis and Due Diligence

Risk analysis is the process that allows management to demonstrate that it has met its obligation of due diligence when making a decision about moving forward with a new project, capital expenditure, investment strategy, or other such business process.

Due diligence has a number of variant definitions based on the industry that is being discussed. Typically, the consensus these definitions address is the measure of prudent activity, or assessment, as is properly to be expected from, and ordinarily exercised by, a reasonable and prudent person under the particular circumstances. Due diligence is not measured by any absolute standard but depends on the relative facts of each case.

In brief, the risk analysis or PIA examines the factors that come into play when trying to determine if a project should be approved. The PIA examines the tangible impacts (e.g., capital outlay, development costs, and long-term costs such as continued operations and maintenance). The risk analysis also addresses intangible impacts, such as customer connivance or regulatory compliance.

When the risk analysis is complete, the results are presented to a management oversight committee that is charged with reviewing new project requests and deciding whether or not to move forward. If the request is approved, the project is registered and a risk assessment is scheduled for early in the design phase of the BPDC or SDLC. The documentation is retained for a period of time and then can be used by the organization if ever there are any questions about why a project was or was not approved.

## 2.4  Risk Assessment and Fiduciary Duty

Because many organizations do not know what the threats and risks are to operate in the changing business environment, a formal risk assessment process must be conducted early in the design phase. Risk assessment provides a process to identify threats systematically and then determine risk levels based on a specific methodology designed for the organization conducting the assessment. After establishing a risk level, the project under development can then look to identify control measures that will reduce the risk to acceptable levels.

Risk assessment has four key deliverables:

1. Identify threats to the organization's mission
2. Prioritize those threats into risk levels
3. Identify mitigating controls or safeguards
4. Create an action plan to implement those mitigating controls

The output from the risk analysis and risk assessment processes will generally be used twice. The first time will be when decisions are made: for the risk analysis, that means deciding whether or not to proceed on a new project; for the risk assessment, that means identifying the types of controls or safeguards that need to be implemented. For risk assessment, the output will identify what countermeasures should be implemented or document that management has determined that the best decision is to accept the risk.

The other time the results will be used is when the "spam hits the fan." That is, when a problem arises and the organization must show the process it used to reach the decisions that it did. The documentation created in the risk management processes will allow the organization to show who was involved, what was discussed, what was considered, and what decisions were made.

By implementing risk analysis and risk assessment, an organization has the tools in place to make informed business decisions. By integrating these processes across the entire enterprise, the organization can take back control of its activities from outside interference. With an effective risk assessment process in place, only those controls and safeguards that are actually needed will be implemented. An enterprise will never again face having to implement a mandated control to "be in compliance with audit requirements."

## 2.5   Performing a Risk Analysis

Risk analysis is a process used to identify and assess factors that may jeopardize the success of a project or achieving a goal. Another term for this process is project impact analysis (PIA). It will require an in-depth cost–benefit analysis to be conducted. The process gives organization management the opportunity to examine and assess a proposal before it becomes a live project. This examination should not only determine whether the project should be approved but it should also establish key objectives or impacts.

The risk analysis process is conducted in the analysis phase of the SDLC. Here the interested parties are charged with building their case and presenting the

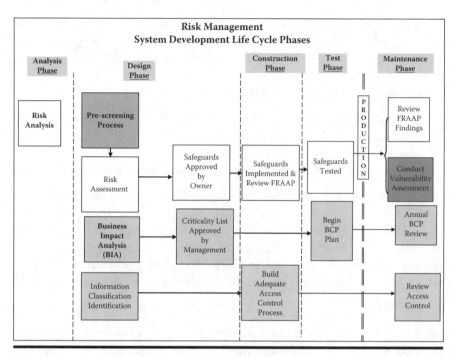

**Figure 2.1  System development life cycle (SDLC) chart.**

proposal to the management review committee for approval and initial funding (Figure 2.1).

The goal of the risk analysis process is to present to the management approval team the business reasons the proposal should become a project and then become part of the production environment. In addition to the pros and cons of accepting the proposal, the risk analysis will allow the team to establish the project goals and objectives, the risks and critical success factors, and the organization and implementation of the approved project.

The risk analysis process can take as little as a week or may take several months to complete depending on the size and scope of the project. Early on, the project proposal team will want to identify all the stakeholders or those individuals with a vested interest in the project. These individuals will help the proposal team examine and meet the risk analysis objectives.

Once the risk analysis is complete, the champion and the project lead take the document to the executive committee that reviews and approves new projects. This process could take more than one meeting with the committee. If the committee turns the proposal down, this process must be documented and the report filed away. Unsuccessful proposal reports should be kept for a period of five to seven years. The retention period will depend on the requirements identified by the records-management program of the organization.

If the proposal is successful, the champion and the project lead next visit the project management office to register the project. Part of this process will be the requirement to complete the pre-screening process (this process is discussed in detail in Chapter 3). The pre-screening process asks a few questions that will help determine whether this project will require a full risk assessment or business impact analysis. The only other element required early on in the SDLC is for the project team to classify the data to be found and used with the project.

## 2.6 Risk Analysis Elements

Part of the risk analysis will examine the costs of the project. When researching costs, the team will establish any costs for procurement of the project and any development costs. Although these costs are important, they do not represent the actual or total cost of the project. In your project proposal, it will be beneficial to have a chart similar to the one shown in Table 2.1.

Probably the lowest part of the overall cost for any project is the actual procurement or development costs. The costs that I find have the most impact include operations and maintenance. In the mid-1990s, as companies began to deploy to the Internet, the need for security was reinforced in the risk assessment process. One of the solutions was to implement a firewall. One electrical utility began the implementation in August 1995. The head of information security was told that there would be a need for a firewall to protect the organization as it connected to the Internet. The security professional was not initially concerned because the firewall was hardware and as such was a capital expenditure, which would be part of the Operations department's budget. That part of the implementation was true; however, what he didn't know about was the need for a firewall administrator. This

**Table 2.1   Risk Analysis Table 1**

| Description | Hours | Cost — "Cost" |
|---|---|---|
| 1.  Product procurement cost | | |
| 2.  Enhancements to code (contract) | 82 hours @ $75 per | $6,150 |
| 3.  Deployment and configuration management | 40 hours | |
| 4.  Conversion/migration costs | | |
| 5.  Daily operation costs (added staff requirements) | 1 additional headcount | |
| 6.  Maintenance (monthly/yearly) | | $10K annual |
| 7.  Infrastructure training | 4 hours per employee | |
| 8.  User training and documentation | 1 hour training per user | |
| 9.  Upgrades | TBD | |

added cost was compounded when the total number of firewalls was going to be fifteen, and that administration was a 24/7 operation, so there was going to be a need for more than one administrator

When working through the risk analysis process, it is always important to consider the impact of converting to a new process or having to migrate processes or data over to the new structure. During a recent class on risk management, a fellow security professional shared with the class that a former PeopleSoft company had just converted to SAP. We decided to use this project to walk through the components of the risk analysis process. We discussed the nine key components examined in the risk analysis table (Table 2.1). When we got to the discussion on conversion and migration, the discussion took a scary turn. It was related to the class that the conversion process was a most-formidable exercise. The process took over a year and many employees, including IT, financial, and HR, worked long hours. We discussed where one could go to find such information on conversion impact. We thought about user groups or asking fellow professionals or the vendor. We did a quick search of the Internet and found a number of articles that helped the class fill in the needed figures.

During our investigation, we found the following in a very interesting article titled "The Great PeopleSoft Migration" by Joab Jackson in *Government Computing News:*

> If all goes according to schedule, the Defense Department will complete the Defense Integrated Military Human Resources System — estimated to be the world's largest human resources program — in 2013. Unfortunately, 2013 is also the year DIMHRS will become a legacy system, because that's the year Oracle Corp. plans to end support for PeopleSoft applications, the platform DIMHRS will run on.
>
> Last December, when database vendor Oracle purchased PeopleSoft Inc., agency heads faced a tough decision. Should they stick with Oracle as the company migrated PeopleSoft users over to its own e-business platform? Or would the upgrade be so arduous, the new features so underwhelming, that making the switch would be untenable?*

Spending all of that time to implement a process only to discover that it will be running a non-supported legacy system is an issue that should have been uncovered in the risk analysis process.

## 2.7 Other Considerations

Although it is important to consider all of the elements of cost in deciding to move forward, the outlay of capital expenditures is just part of the risk analysis process.

---

* Joab Jackson, "The Great PeopleSoft Migration," *Government Computing News,* March 7, 2005.

What must also be considered is the cost of not moving forward with a project. What would be the impact to the enterprise if it was decided to delay or not approve the project? How would not moving forward impact the competitive advantage of the organization? How would this decision impact the ability to meet the mission of the enterprise? How would strategic business partners, suppliers, vendors, and other stakeholders be impacted?

In the late 1980s, many big organizations decided to convert from a paper-based order entry system to an e-commerce process. This foray into electronic data interchange (EDI) caught a number of suppliers off guard. EDI is the process of using telecommunications to exchange documents between companies. Orders, purchase agreements, shippers, and the like were going to be converted to electronic format. These small suppliers were concerned that they would not be able to meet the aggressive implementation deadline established by the big vendors. One manufacturer established a compromise for the handling of paper-based documents. They vendor would charge the supplier a one-dollar-per-page handling fee for each sheet of paper submitted. This handling fee would be automatically deducted from the amount owed the supplier.

When conducting a risk analysis, it is vital that as many factors as possible be uncovered. This is why the risk analysis should have access to the stakeholders and those with a vested interest in the project. Asking questions and exploring options is vitally important. Later in this chapter we will review a sample set of questions that can be used to improve the risk analysis process.

Another important factor to consider in this process is the impact of regulatory compliance issues. The new project should, whenever possible, enhance regulatory requirements. In Chapter 5, we discuss the gap analysis process. Gap analysis provides the organization with the ability to identify all of the regulatory laws and regulations and map them against the industry standards that the organization is using as its baseline security controls. The organization then maps their policies, procedures, and standards to the all-inclusive set of standards. This allows the organization to identify any areas where it needs to improve for regulatory compliance.

Any time a risk analysis is preformed, it will be important to review the gap analysis to ensure that the new project does not impact the compliance issues.

Sometimes a new idea or concept is drafted by a department such as Marketing, and it gains support and then management acceptance before the infrastructure, budget, or security personnel have an opportunity to perform a formal risk analysis. A number of years ago we were hired to perform a network vulnerability assessment on a utility company located in the Southwest. The technical team was running a port scan of the firewall and my technician came running in to inform us that there were some ports open that were major security issues. We went to the firewall administrator and asked why the ports were open. The firewall administrator told us senior management had requested that they be opened so that local high school students could have access to the Internet. Our investigation discovered that Marketing had approached the utility's management and indicated that it would be a good public service to provide Internet access to the students. When we presented the security hole to management, we were informed that no one was told what ports were opened, so there should be no security risk!

Once when performing a physical security review, we found a UNIX server located in an office area. We could not find the server on any list of hardware provided by the IT department. We went back to the user department with the lead IT auditor and the information security officer. When we asked about the server, we were informed that it had been purchased as "filing" equipment and a contractor had been hired to develop a new bill-paying program for them. They had tested the program and were just getting ready to contact IT to have their server connected to the network.

The tangible way to measure success is to see a lower bottom line for cost. Risk assessment can assist in this process by identifying only those controls that are needed to be implemented. Organizations are not implementing controls because they think they are needed. Only those actions that are actually required are being implemented. For risk analysis, the metric is that only those projects that show a true business need are being implemented.

Another way that the success of a risk analysis and risk assessment is measured is if there is a time when management decisions are called into review. By having a formal process in place that demonstrates the due diligence of management in the decision-making process, this kind of inquiry will be dealt with quickly and successfully.

## 2.8   When to Conduct a Risk Analysis

Whenever money or resources are to be spent, a risk analysis should be conducted. This process will provide the business reasons that should be used to justify the decision to move forward with a new project or capital expenditure. The documentation of this process can be used by management to demonstrate that they have been performing their due diligence responsibilities.

Typically, the output from a risk analysis will be used twice. The first time will be when the organization decides whether or not to move forward with a development or capital project. The other, and often the most important time is when the organization is being examined by some third party and they are looking to management to find out why the project was approved. This documented process will provide the necessary material to defend any decision.

## 2.9   Final Words

For risk analysis and project impact analysis, the need to demonstrate due diligence is an important output of the process. However, the overriding reason to conduct these processes is that it makes good business sense. The organization proceeds on certain paths based on need and the ability of the organization to meet those specific business or mission needs. The risk analysis process provides management with a consistent tool to be used to determine where the organization's limited resources will provide the best return on investment.

## 2.10  Sample Risk Analysis Questionnaire

It is important to establish a set of questions that will help the team present the best set of options for the approval process. When I am working on putting together such a report, I examine each of these questions with the champion and the project lead to ensure that the objectives are firmly established in business need. It will be necessary to include all of those individuals with a vested interest in the project or stakeholders (Table 2.2).

## 2.11  Sample Risk Analysis Report Outline

1. Name of project and brief description
2. Project champion/owner
3. Business reason or need for project
4. Estimated cost of project
    - a. Money
    - b. Time
    - c. Resources
5. Regulatory impact
6. Infrastructure impact
7. Maintenance cost
8. Time line

Items 3, 4, 5, 6, and 7 should have a minimum of one paragraph of supporting material. In item 4, the estimated cost of the project, it is often best to use a visual like the one provided in Table 2.2.

**Table 2.2   Project Impact Analysis Questionnaire**

| Issue | Applicable (Yes/No) | Comments |
|---|---|---|
| Identify any existing requirements in the baseline that conflict with the proposed change. | | |
| Identify any other pending requirement changes that conflict with the proposed change. | | |
| What are the consequences of not making the change? | | |
| What are possible adverse side effects or other risks of making the proposed change? | | |
| Will the proposed change adversely affect performance requirements or other quality attributes? | | |
| Will the change affect any system component that affects critical properties such as safety and security, or involve a product change that triggers recertification of any kind? | | |
| Is the proposed change feasible within known technical constraints and current staff skills? | | |
| Will the proposed change place unacceptable demands on any computer resources required for the development, test, or operating environments? | | |
| Must any tools be acquired to implement and test the change? | | |
| How will the proposed change affect the sequence, dependencies, effort, or duration of any tasks currently in the project plan? | | |
| Will prototyping or other user input be required to verify the proposed change? | | |
| How much effort that has already been invested in the project will be lost if this change is accepted? | | |
| Will the proposed change cause an increase in product unit cost, such as by increasing third-party product licensing fees? | | |
| Will the change affect any marketing, manufacturing, training, or customer support plans? | | |
| Identify any existing requirements in the baseline that conflict with the proposed change. | | |

# Chapter 3

# Pre-Screening

## 3.1 Introduction

Not every application, business process, or system needs to have a formal risk assessment process or a business impact analysis conducted for it. What is needed is an enterprisewide, formal methodology that allows for a "pre-screening" of applications and systems to determine needs. By using the processes learned in qualitative risk assessment, your organization will be able to develop a quick pre-screening methodology that could save time and money.

In addition to the methodology, it is necessary to create a standard set of baseline controls that will be used as part of the pre-screening process. These baseline controls can be used with the pre-screening methodology or when there is a problem with an owner stepping up to take responsibility for protecting information resources. We will also be using a baseline set of controls during the process to establish risk levels. It is, therefore, very important for your organization to identify all of the standards, regulations, and laws that support your organization's ability to meet its business objectives or its mission. Table 3.1 is a baseline set of controls using the Health Insurance Portability and Accountability Act (HIPAA) as its basis.

When developing a pre-screening methodology, it is best to start with a clear understanding of what the business objective or mission of the enterprise is. Using this information as a base, you can then develop a set of questions that can be completed by the project lead and the business manager during the pre-FRAAP meeting. These questions allow the facilitator and owner to determine whether a formal risk assessment or business impact analysis must be completed.

**Table 3.1    HIPAA Control Requirements**

| Control | Classification | HIPAA Control Description |
| --- | --- | --- |
| Risk analysis | Required | Conduct an accurate and thorough assessment of the potential risks and vulnerabilities to the confidentiality, integrity, and availability of Electronically Protected Health Information (EPHI). |
| Risk management | | Implement security measures sufficient to reduce risks and vulnerabilities to a reasonable and appropriate level. |
| Sanction policy | | Apply appropriate sanctions against workforce members who fail to comply with the security policies and procedures of the covered entity. |
| Information system activity review | | Implement procedures to review records of information systems activity regularly. |
| | | Identify the security official responsible for the development and implementation of the policies and procedures. |
| Privacy officer | | Identify a single person responsible for the development and implementation of the policies and procedures supporting HIPAA compliance. |
| | | Implement policies and procedures to ensure that all members of its workforce have appropriate access to EPHI, and to prevent those workforce members who are not authorized to have access under the Information Access Management standard from obtaining access to electronic health information. |
| Isolate healthcare clearinghouse functions | | If a Covered Entity (CE) operates a healthcare clearinghouse, it must implement policies and procedures to protect the EPHI maintained by the clearinghouse from unauthorized access by the larger organization. |
| | | Implement policies and procedures to address security incidents. |

**Table 3.1 (continued)   HIPAA Control Requirements**

| Control | Classification | HIPAA Control Description |
|---|---|---|
| Response and reporting | | Identify and respond to suspected or known security incidents; mitigate to the extent practicable harmful effects of the security incidents that are known to the CE; and document security incidents and their outcomes. |
| | | Establish (and implement as needed) policies and procedures for responding to an emergency or other occurrence that damages systems that contain EPHI. |
| Data backup | | Establish and implement procedures to create and maintain retrievable exact copies of EPHI. |
| Disaster recovery plan | | Establish (and implement as needed) procedures to restore any loss of data. |
| Emergency mode operations plan | | Establish (and implement as needed) procedures to enable continuation of critical business processes to assure access to EPHI and to provide for adequate protection of EPHI while operating in emergency mode. |
| | | Implement policies and procedures that specify the proper functions to be performed, the manner in which those functions are to be performed, and the physical attributes of the surroundings of a specific workstation or class of workstation than can access EPHI. |
| Workstation security | Standard | Implement physical safeguards for all workstations that access EPHI to restrict access to authorized users. |
| Device and media control | | Implement policies and procedures that govern the receipt and removal of hardware and electronic media that contain EPHI into and out of a facility, and the movement of these items within a facility. |
| Disposal | Required | Implement policies and procedures to address the final disposition of EPHI and/or the hardware or electronic media on which it is stored. |

*continued*

**Table 3.1 (continued)   HIPAA Control Requirements**

| Control | Classification | HIPAA Control Description |
|---|---|---|
| Media re-use | | Implement procedures for removal of EPHI from electronic media prior to re-use. |
| Accountability | Addressable | Maintain a record of the movement of hardware and software and any person responsible for movement. |
| Data backup and storage | | Create a retrievable, exact copy of EPHI, when needed, prior to moving equipment. |
| Unique user identification | Required | Assign a unique name and/or number for identifying and tracking user identity. |
| Emergency access procedure | | Establish (and implement as needed) procedures for obtaining necessary EPHI during an emergency. |
| Audit controls | Standard | Implement hardware, software, and/or procedural mechanisms that record and examine activity in information systems that contain or use EPHI. |
| Integrity | | Implement policies and procedures to protect EPHI from improper alteration or destruction. |
| Authentication | | Implement procedures to verify that a person or entity seeking access to EPHI is the one claimed. |
| Transmission security | | Implement technical security measures to guard against unauthorized access to EPHI that is being transmitted over an electronic communications network. |
| Business associate (BA) contracts | | The contract between the CE and its BA must meet the [following] requirements, as applicable: a CE is not in compliance if it knew of a pattern of activity or practice of the BA that constituted a material breach or violation of the BA's obligation under the contract, unless the CE took reasonable steps to cure the breach or end the violation, and if such steps were unsuccessful to (1) terminate the contract, if feasible; or (2) report the problem to the Secretary of HHS, if not. |
| | | Implement reasonable and appropriate policies and procedures to comply with the standards, implementation specifications, and other requirements. |

**Table 3.1 (continued)  HIPAA Control Requirements**

| Control | Classification | HIPAA Control Description |
|---|---|---|
| Time limit | Required | Retain the documentation required by the Security Rule for six years from the date of its creation or the date when it was last in effect, whichever is later. |
| Availability | | Make documentation available to those persons responsible for implementing the procedures to which the documentation pertains. |
| Updates | | Review documentation periodically, and update as needed, in response to environmental and operational changes affecting the security of the EPHI. |

We will examine different approaches to the pre-screening process. First, we will examine an impact analysis process that is used by a financial institution, and then we will review a process used by a major information systems service provider.

## 3.2  Background

In Chapter 2, we discussed risk analysis or project impact analysis (PIA). Risk analysis is a technique used to identify and assess factors that may jeopardize the success of a project or the achievement of a goal. This process requires a cost–benefit analysis to be conducted. The cost–benefit process should incorporate the features and benefits of the application, system, project, or capital expenditure being considered.

Part of the review examines the total cost of the project. Costs include procurement, development, and operation and maintenance costs such as documentation development, user and infrastructure support training, and possible upgrades. Other costs that must be factored into the analysis are conversion or migration costs. All costs are examined both in dollars and staffing implications. Once the PIA is complete, it is typically presented to the project approval committee. If approved, the request is logged into the system and becomes a project.

The very first process to be undertaken when registering a new project is to complete the pre-screening questionnaire. This questionnaire determines whether the new project needs to complete a formal risk assessment or business impact analysis (BIA). If the project is non-critical or non-sensitive, then an implementation of the baseline set of controls should be sufficient.

### 3.2.1  Pre-Screening Example 1

The first pre-screening example examines the impact of new project on two selected elements of a financial institution: the sensitivity of the data involved and the

**Table 3.2    Pre-Screening Example 1 Table 1**

| Project Cost | Total Approved Budget | Conduct Formal Risk Assessment and BIA? |
|---|---|---|
| High | $1.5 million or more | Yes |
| Medium | $500,001 to $1.5 million | Yes, if sensitivity level/criticality impact medium or high |
| Low | $500,000 or less | No, implement baseline controls |

resource impact. Resource impact includes financial (internal and external) and customer impact.

The project lead and the business owner are required to complete the questionnaire online to assess the project's level of impact to the enterprise and the type of technology to be used by the project. If the project is considered low sensitivity and low impact, then an implementation of a baseline set of controls is all that is required. If the project comes back as "low" but the business owner does not want the baseline controls, then a formal risk assessment must be conducted.

For those projects identified as high impact or high sensitivity, a formal risk assessment and business impact analysis must be scheduled. It is the responsibility of the business owner to complete the pre-screening questionnaire and to schedule any additional follow-up risk assessment and business impact analysis as required.

The project lead and business owner are asked three sets of questions. The first question is a policy issue and reflects the need for oversight on projects that exceed certain expenditure levels (Table 3.2).

The second set of questions helps determine the sensitivity level of the information contained or available through access to the project. Table 3.3 gives an example of how the questions might look. The questions for sensitivity level are based on the information classification policy for the company and provide the project lead and business owner with three levels of impact: high, medium, and low. Once the sensitivity level of the data has been determined, the questionnaire requests the project lead and business owner to answer three questions related to the criticality of the project to the mission of the enterprise.

The next four questions all have a financial twist to them. The first is looking for a project cost in the total budget approved. When you are developing your pre-screening questions, the values plugged into these tables will reflect your enterprise (Table 3.4). The first question relates to a company policy that requires all projects that have an estimated expenditure of $1.5 million or more to conduct a risk assessment and business impact analysis. The second question relates to the sensitivity level of the information processed or accessible due to the project. As you can see, the information sensitivity level is different from the project's criticality impact, but both impact each other. The final three questions lead directly to the mission criticality of the project and the need to perform a formal BIA, which will ultimately establish the contingency planning requirements for this project.

**Table 3.3   Pre-Screening Example 1 Table 2**

| Sensitivity Value | Information Sensitivity | Conduct Formal Risk Assessment? |
|---|---|---|
| High | Extreme sensitivity; restricted to specific individual need-to-know; its loss or compromise may cause severe financial, legal, regulatory, or reputation damage to the company. | Yes |
| Medium | Moderate sensitivity; used only by specific authorized groups with legitimate business need; may have significant adverse impact; possible negative financial impact. | Yes, if criticality impact medium or high |
| Low | Low sensitivity; information for internal business use within the company; it may have little adverse impact/negligible financial impact. | No, implement baseline controls |

**Table 3.4   Pre-Screening Example 1 Table 3**

| Impact Value | Financial Impact: Daily Dollar Amount of Transactions Processed | Customer Impact: Number of Customers Impacted | Regulatory/ Compliance Impact | Conduct Formal BIA? |
|---|---|---|---|---|
| High | $50 million or more | 10,000 or more | Substantial financial penalties | Yes |
| Medium | $1 to $49 million | 1,000 to 9,999 | Limited financial penalties | Yes, if sensitivity level is medium or high |
| Low | $1 million or less | Less than 1,000 | No regulatory or compliance issues | No, implement baseline business continuity plan |

## 3.2.2   Pre-Screening Example 2

Another example of application/system pre-screening was developed for a major service provider. This one examines two key elements: sensitivity of the information being handled, and the mission criticality of the project.

**Table 3.5   Pre-Screening Example 2 Table 1**

| Impact Value | Information Classification Level | Description | Longest Tolerable Outage |
|---|---|---|---|
| 5 | Top secret | Information which, if disclosed, could cause severe impact to the company's competitive advantage or business strategies. | 24 hours or less |
| 4 | Confidential | Information which, if disclosed, could violate the privacy of individuals, reduce competitive advantage, or damage the company. | 25–72 hours |
| 3 | Restricted | Information which is available to a specific subset of the employee population when conducting company business. | 73 hours–5 days |
| 2 | Internal use | Information which is intended for use by all employees when conducting company business. | 6–9 days |
| 1 | Public | Information which has been made available to the public through authorized company channels. | 10 days or more |

Where the first example used low, medium, and high, this pre-screening methodology uses five values. This specific number was selected because the company has five levels of information classification in their policy and the contingency planning team happened to have five categories of recovery windows (Table 3.5).

If the project lead and business owner select impact values of four or five as the appropriate answer to either or both questions, then a formal risk assessment and business impact analysis must be conducted. If the answer to both questions is a one, two, or three, then the project lead and business owner are asked to select the appropriate answer from one more set of questions (Table 3.6). If the owner selects a four or five as the correct answer to either or both of these questions, then a formal risk assessment and business impact analysis must be conducted. If the answer to both questions is a one, two, or three, then the requirement is to implement the baseline set of controls.

The key to the pre-screening process is to get input from the department that understands the threshold levels and impacts to the enterprise. This process, if properly established, allows the business units to bypass unneeded control mechanisms while still providing an appropriate level of security.

Being able to build on the information that has gone before allows you to create a risk management program that will be cost effective and acceptable to the user

**Table 3.6    Pre-Screening Example 2 Table 2**

| Impact Value | Disclosure | Contractual Obligation |
|---|---|---|
| 5 | National or international press coverage | Unable to meet external obligations |
| 4 | State or local press coverage | Delay in meeting external obligations |
| 3 | Incident known throughout the company | Unable to meet internal obligations |
| 2 | Incident known only at the division or department level | Delay in meeting internal obligations |
| 1 | Little or no impact | Little or no impact |

community. Nothing will cause you to succeed faster than by implementing processes that are easy to do and that cut down on the number of controls.

## 3.2.3    Pre-Screening Example 3

As I was working with the first two examples of pre-screening, I continued to get the feeling that there was something missing. Example 2 requires the owner to select for a sensitivity category (the classification of data levels) and a criticality or availability category (longest tolerable outage). Selecting a four or five in either category requires the owner to schedule both a risk assessment and a business impact analysis. I felt that a more-efficient pre-screening methodology could be developed to identify whether a risk assessment or a business impact analysis or both were required. By using the model established in the various qualitative risk assessment methodologies we have discussed, I came up with the following example for a pre-screening methodology.

When registering a new project, the project lead and business owner examine two sets of questions to determine what needs to be completed for a particular project. The questions address sensitivity of data or information and the criticality of the system or business process. The project lead and business owner select the category that most closely matches the project's qualities. This first set of categories relate to the information sensitivity level (Table 3.7).

The owner selects the most-appropriate category that describes the data or information that is handled, processed, or retained by the asset that is scheduled to undergo the risk assessment review. The impact level is entered on the pre-screening worksheet. We will select the category "Information is of such a nature that its unauthorized disclosure would cause media attention, customer negative response" or high (Table 3.8).

The owner selects the category that most closely matches the asset's qualities. This first set of categories relate to the information criticality level (Table 3.9).

**Table 3.7   Pre-Screening Example 3 Table 1**

| Disclosure Impact Level (DIL) | Definition | DIL Points |
|---|---|---|
| High | Information is of such a nature that its unauthorized disclosure would cause media attention, customer negative response. | 3 |
| Medium | Information is of such a nature that its unauthorized disclosure might cause media attention, customer negative response. | 2 |
| Low | Information is of such a nature that its unauthorized disclosure would have little or no impact to the organization. | 1 |

**Table 3.8   Pre-Screening Example 3 Worksheet 1**

| Category | Impact Level | Matrix Score | Requirement |
|---|---|---|---|
| Disclosure | High | | |
| Criticality | | | |
| Total | | | |

**Table 3.9   Pre-Screening Example 3 Table 2**

| Criticality Impact Level | Definition |
|---|---|
| High | Information is of such a nature that its unauthorized modification or destruction would cause media attention, customer negative response. |
| Medium | Information is of such a nature that its unauthorized modification or destruction might cause media attention, customer negative response. |
| Low | Information is of such a nature that its unauthorized modification or destruction would have little or no impact to the organization. |

The owner selects the most-appropriate category that describes the mission criticality of the asset that is scheduled to undergo the risk assessment. The impact level is entered on the pre-screening worksheet. We will select the category "Information is of such a nature that its unauthorized modification or destruction would have little or no impact to the organization" or low (Table 3.10).

The owner then looks to the pre-screening matrix and finds the intersection of the two levels and enters the number in the matrix score box of the worksheet. Using the scoring table (Table 3.11), we can get a better picture of what is recommended by the pre-screening process.

**Table 3.10   Pre-Screening Example 3 Worksheet 2**

| Category | Impact Level | Matrix Score | Requirement |
|---|---|---|---|
| Disclosure | High | | |
| Criticality | Low | | |
| Total | | | |

**Table 3.11   Pre-Screening Example 3 Scoring Table**

| Criticality | Disclosure | | |
|---|---|---|---|
| | High (3) | Medium (2) | Low (1) |
| High (3) | 3 + 3 = 6 | 3 + 2 = 5 | 3 + 1 = 4 |
| Medium (2) | 2 + 3 = 5 | 2 + 2 = 4 | 2 + 1 = 3 |
| Low (1) | 1 + 3 = 4 | 1 + 2 = 3 | 1 + 1 = 2 |

Any category that is selected as high gets a value of three for that specific category. In our example, the disclosure level was high, therefore on the matrix we select a three. The criticality value was determined to be low, so we select the intersection of high disclosure (a three) and low criticality (a one) for a total of four or a medium pre-screening score.

The disclosure category addresses the issue of the sensitivity of the data or information. The appropriate action for any asset with a disclosure or sensitivity score of medium (a two) or higher is to conduct a risk assessment.

The criticality category addresses the issue of required availability of the system and data. The appropriate action for any asset with a criticality factor of medium (a two) or higher is to conduct a business impact analysis.

In our example, the disclosure level is high, so we know we have to conduct a risk assessment. However, the criticality level is low. The requirement here is to implement the baseline set of controls for continuity and disaster recovery planning; a BIA is not required. The owner should review these baseline standards, and if the owner determines that the baseline does not meet their needs, then they can request a BIA. In a later chapter, we will discuss how to conduct a business impact analysis using qualitative risk assessment skills and tools (Table 3.12).

If the scoring results are high disclosure and low criticality, as in the example, then the recommended action is to conduct a risk assessment to examine threats, establish risk levels, and select possible mitigating controls. The business impact analysis recommendation is to classify the system criticality as a low priority and have it restored when the non-mission critical systems, applications, and business processes are recovered. One additional point here: it will be necessary to identify any systems, applications, or business processes that are dependent on the one under review. If any mission-critical resource is dependent on the asset under review, then a BIA must be scheduled.

**Table 3.12  Pre-Screening Example 3 Recommended Action**

| Criticality | Disclosure | | |
|---|---|---|---|
| | *High (3)* | *Medium (2)* | *Low (1)* |
| High (3) | BIA and risk assessment | BIA and risk assessment | BIA and baseline controls |
| Medium (2) | BIA and risk assessment | BIA and risk assessment | Baseline BIA and controls |
| Low (1) | Risk assessment and BIA baseline | Baseline BIA and controls | Baseline BIA and controls |

If the impact values selected are a low in disclosure, then only the baseline set of information protection standards need to be implemented. If the criticality is high, therefore giving an impact value of four, then a BIA must be scheduled.

With a basic understanding of qualitative risk assessment, it will be possible to create a process that will improve the workflow of your organization. As part of a misunderstood group, security, audit, and risk management professionals are often viewed by the rest of the organization as overhead to the enterprise. One way to overcome this misconception is to implement processes such as pre-screening that streamline control-review requirements and possibly eliminate the need to perform some functions.

### 3.2.4  Pre-Screening Example 4

The final example we will discuss takes the basic information presented by using charts and combines it with a management-endorsed concept of using a heat map. A heat map is a graphical representation of data where the values taken by a variable in a two-dimensional map are represented as colors. Typically, management likes red, yellow, and green.

Just as in the past, begin with an appropriate set of questions similar to the ones in Table 3.13. Once the owner has selected the appropriate answer to each question, the results will be plotted on the matrix shown in Table 3.14. These values can then be interpreted into a severity color by the use of a heat map similar to the one shown in Table 3.15. A value key should be included with the heat map so that management will be able to understand what each box and color represents (Table 3.16).

## 3.3  Summary

With a basic understanding of qualitative risk assessment, it is possible to create a process that will improve the workflow of your organization. As part of a misunderstood group, security, audit, and risk management professionals are often

**Table 3.13   Pre-Screening Example 4 Questions**

| Disclosure | Value | Criticality |
|---|---|---|
| Legal/regulatory sanctions; national/international press coverage | 5 | Unable to meet enterprise mission or business objectives; total loss of public confidence and reputation |
| Possible legal/regulatory sanctions; state/local press coverage | 4 | >5-day delay in meeting enterprise mission or business objectives; long-term blemish on company image |
| Some regulatory penalty possible; incident is known companywide | 3 | 2–4-day delay in meeting enterprise mission or business objectives; temporary blemish on company image |
| Highly unlikely legal or regulatory penalty; incident known at business unit department level | 2 | 1-day delay in meeting enterprise mission or business objectives; limited to company business unit or department image |
| Little or no impact | 1 | <1-day delay in meeting enterprise mission or business objectives; little or no image impact |

**Table 3.14   Pre-Screening Example 4 Results Matrix**

| Disclosure | Criticality | | | | |
|---|---|---|---|---|---|
| | 1 | 2 | 3 | 4 | 5 |
| 5 | 5 + 1 = 6 | 5 + 2 = 7 | 5 + 3 = 8 | 5 + 4 = 9 | 5 + 5 = 10 |
| 4 | 4 + 1 = 5 | 4 + 2 = 6 | 4 + 3 = 7 | 4 + 4 = 8 | 4 + 5 = 9 |
| 3 | 3 + 1 = 4 | 3 + 2 = 5 | 3 + 3 = 6 | 3 + 4 = 7 | 3 + 5 = 8 |
| 2 | 2 + 1 = 3 | 2 + 2 = 4 | 2 + 3 = 5 | 2 + 4 = 6 | 2 + 5 = 7 |
| 1 | 1 + 1 = 2 | 1 + 2 = 3 | 1 + 3 = 4 | 1 + 4 = 5 | 1 + 5 = 6 |

viewed by the rest of the organization as overhead to the enterprise. One way to overcome this misconception is to implement processes, such as pre-screening, that streamline control-review requirements and possibly eliminate the need to perform some functions.

**Table 3.15  Pre-Screening Example 4 Heat Map**

| Disclosure | Criticality | | | | |
| --- | --- | --- | --- | --- | --- |
| | 1 | 2 | 3 | 4 | 5 |
| 5 | Risk assessment — baseline BCP | Risk assessment — baseline BCP | Risk assessment & BIA | Risk assessment & BIA | Risk assessment & BIA |
| 4 | Risk assessment — baseline BCP | Risk assessment — baseline BCP | Risk assessment and BIA required | Risk assessment & BIA | Risk assessment & BIA |
| 3 | Baseline controls & BCP | Risk assessment — baseline BCP | Risk assessment and BIA required | Risk assessment and BIA required | Risk assessment & BIA |
| 2 | Baseline controls & BCP | Baseline controls & BCP | Baseline controls — BIA required | Baseline controls — BIA required | Baseline controls — BIA required |
| 1 | Baseline controls & BCP | Baseline controls & BCP | Baseline controls & BCP | Baseline controls — BIA required | Baseline controls — BIA required |

**Table 3.16  Pre-Screening Example 4 Heat Map Key**

| | |
| --- | --- |
| Risk assessment and BIA | Process requires formal risk assessment and business impact analysis |
| Risk assessment and BIA required | See specific requirements |
| Baseline controls and BCP | Process requires baseline controls and baseline BCP only |

# Chapter 4

# Business Impact Analysis

## 4.1  Overview

The principal objective of the business impact analysis (BIA) is to determine the effect mission-critical information system failures have on the viability and operations of enterprise core business processes. By using all of the techniques discussed in this book, you can create a facilitated process for BIA. Once the critical resources are scored, the organization can then identify appropriate controls to ensure the business continues to meet its objectives or mission.

Just as we looked at scoring tables that were developed with the assistance of other departments, the BIA will work the same process. The enterprise will have to determine what elements are important and then develop a process to score those elements. The BIA will use those tables to examine the business processes and establish their priorities and what other processes are dependent on them.

There are a number of tangible and intangible elements that should be considered in the BIA process. In Chapter 3, we examined tables that addressed corporate embarrassment, value to competitor, legal implications, cost of disruption, and financial loss. The BIA produces similar types of tables and modifies them to meet requirements of the business.

Part of the BIA process comes from the risk analysis process itself. When reviewing system and application availability, the results from this process will lead the business manager to see the need for a BIA. The process will review the business areas for vulnerabilities, such items as cash flow, telecommunications systems, computer operations, or critical dependencies.

## 4.2 BIA versus Risk Assessment

How does risk assessment fit into the BIA process? These two processes complement one another and provide additional security from a proactive and a reactive perspective. Often I am asked if it is necessary to do both a risk assessment and a BIA on an application or other asset. The quick answer is yes. The standard security risk assessment examines each asset by looking for impacts based on confidentiality, integrity, and availability. In the risk assessment we assess each threat and assign a risk value to that threat. If the risk level is too high, then a compensating control is selected. For availability threats the controls are typically backups, tighter access control, continuity plans, and similar control measures. The risk assessment process allows us to establish compensating controls that might include the development of a business continuity plan or a disaster recovery plan.

The outcome of a BIA is to establish at what point in the recovery cycle this process will be needed. In disaster recovery planning there are three key phases to the disaster recovery process: response, recovery, and restoration. The response phase addresses issues such as ensuring the safety of on-site personnel and accounting for everyone. During the response phase the issues of securing the area and preventing further damage are addressed. Once the environment and people are secure, a damage assessment team examines the site and reports their findings to the crisis management team. If the situation is severe enough, the crisis management team will declare a disaster and the next phase begins.

The results of the BIA process are put to use in these phases. During the recovery phase the organization will concentrate on bringing mission-critical services back online. The sequence of recovery order has been predetermined by the results of the BIA process. In addition to establishing recovery time objectives (RTO) the BIA has identified lines of dependency. A number of years ago we conducted a BIA for an organization and identified the customer credit file as a tier-3 application that would be brought up in the third wave of recovery systems. This would be three to five days after the event. When we ran a test of the disaster recovery plan we found out that customer order and customer shipping were dependent on the customer credit file. Customer order and shipping were tier-1 applications and came up in the first wave. Customer credit had to be reclassified to support the business process.

The third phase is called restoration. This is the process where the organization moves into its restored primary site or has moved to a new primary site. Here the organization initially recovers the remaining processes, restores the high-priority processes, and deactivates the recovery site.

The BIA process allows an organization to establish a RTO for each application, system, or business process. The risk assessment will help establish those controls that will allow the organization to recover the business of the organization (Figure 4.1).

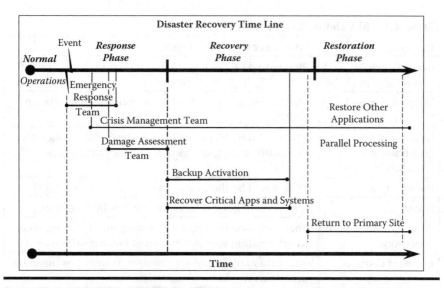

**Figure 4.1   Disaster recovery time line**

## 4.3   Creating a BIA Process

The results of the BIA process will be used by an organization to determine how critical a specific application, system, business process, or other asset is relative to all of the other assets in the organization. The BIA results are submitted to the senior management oversight committee, typically the information security steering committee, for review and approval.

The BIA process begins with the creation of a set of definitions of possible impacts to the business or mission of the organization (see Table 4.1). From these definitions a set of impact tables should be created to identify the impact thresholds for the various categories. The BIA team will work with the specific departments to establish the criticality thresholds. We discussed the development of these types of tables in Chapter 2.

A set of impact tables is established to be used by the organization to establish the RTO for each application, system, or business process. The impact table shown as Table 4.2 is actually five separate tables. When examining each application or system, there are five questions that need to be answered. When you use a table like this, the team filling out the worksheets must understand that there is no corollary between the columns. The columns are to be read vertically only. There is no corollary between dollars lost and health/safety, and no corollary between dollars lost and production outage. Each is a factor that must be examined individually.

The impact value number process sometimes causes concern; after all, five is a larger number than one. For all of the years I have been in disaster planning we have discussed bringing up tier-1 applications first, tier-2 next, and so forth.

**Table 4.1 BIA Definitions Table**

| Category | If the Asset Was Unavailable: |
|---|---|
| Competitive disadvantage | What would be the impact to our competitive standing? |
| Direct business loss | What would be the impact to our business revenues or profits? |
| Loss of public confidence or reputation | What would be the impact to our customer confidence, our public image, shareholder or supplier loyalty? |
| Poor morale | What would be the impact to our employee morale |
| Fraud | What level of goods, services or funds be diverted? |
| Wrong management decisions | What would be the impact to management having access to information to make informed business decisions? |
| Business disruption | What other applications, programs, systems, or business processes would be impacted? |
| Legal liability | Could the organization be in breach of legal, regulatory, or contractual obligations? |
| Privacy loss | Could our customers, clients, or employees suffer loss of personal privacy information? |
| Safety risk — "Risk" | What would be the impact to our customers, clients, and employee's health and safety? |

However, if this numbering process causes confusion, simply invert the numbers. Perhaps instead of numbers you could assign terms.

## 4.4 Creating the Financial Impact Table

The financial staff is interviewed to determine how much is enough. To assist in this process, a financial impact worksheet is developed. There are some problems with the figures that this will generate.

The worksheet takes into account the effects of outages during the most critical time of the business cycle for each business process. So the "value" figure that is obtained from the review includes loss of sales in addition to other costs of doing business in an outage situation. The total business impact from each of these sheets can add up to more than the revenue generated in annual sales by the enterprise. Although this figure may be correct, it will probably require some detailed explanation on your part to make management understand that an outage of only ten days can lead to losses beyond the annual gross income. Be very careful how you use the figures generated from a worksheet like the one shown in Table 4.3.

**Table 4.2  BIA Impact Table**

| Impact Value | Intangible Loss (Dollar Loss Difficult To Estimate) | | | | Tangible Loss |
| | Health/Safety | Interruption of Production Impact | Public Image | Environmental Release | Financial ($) |
| --- | --- | --- | --- | --- | --- |
| 1 | Loss of life or limb | 1 week | Total loss of public confidence and reputation | Permanent damage to environment | More than 10M |
| 2 | Requires hospitalization | 3 days | Long-term blemish of company image | Long-term (1 year or more) damage to environment | 1,000,001 to 10M |
| 3 | Cuts, bruises requiring first aid | 1–2 days | Temporary blemish of company image | Temporary (6 months to 1 year) damage | 100,001 to 1M |
| 4 | Major exposure to unsafe work environment | 1 day | Company business unit image damaged | Department non-compliant | 50,001 to 100K |
| 5 | Little or no negative impact Minor exposure to unsafe work environment | <4 hours | Little or no image impact | Little or no impact | 0 to 50K |

**Table 4.3   BIA Financial Impact Worksheet**

| Type of Impact — "Impact" | Estimated Dollar Loss If Asset Were Unavailable Just beyond the Longest Tolerable Outage |
|---|---|
| Loss of sales | |
| Regulatory fines | |
| Legal fines | |
| Cost — "Cost" of money (e.g., revenue collection delayed) | |
| Loss of competitive advantage | |
| Loss of investor confidence | |
| Loss of customer confidence | |
| Adverse public opinion | |
| Reporting delay (financial reports, etc.) | |
| Cost — "Cost" of disruption to business | |
|   Replacement of employees | |
|   Elimination of work backlog | |
|   Use of alternate procedures | |
|   Loss of productive time | |
|   Replacement of lost information | |
|   Equipment repair or replacement | |
|   Decreased employee morale | |
|   Operating delay | |
| Total estimated loss | |

I recommend that the first value you present to management for one day's outage be something along the line of the total gross revenue divided by 264 (the typical number of working days in a year). So if your enterprise has an annual gross income of $50 million, then the first day's losses would equal $50,000,000/264 = $190,300.69. First you must establish that you understand the annual revenues. Then you can discuss the increasing costs of being out of business.

## 4.5   Working the BIA Process

Once the values for each element are determined for each business process affected by the application or system, those figures are plugged into a table like the one shown as Table 4.4. What you want the project leader and business owner to do is to examine each time frame. If the system was down for less than twenty-four hours, what would be the impact level? What would be the impact level from a one- to three-day outage, and so forth? What you want to see is where the high impact values begin to appear.

**Table 4.4   BIA Worksheet Example**

| If the Asset User Review Were Unavailable For: | Using the Provided BIA Impact Table, What Would Be the Impact To: | | | | |
|---|---|---|---|---|---|
| | Health/ Safety | Interruption of Production | Public Image | Environmental Release | Financial |
| <24 hours | | | | | |
| 24–72 hours | | | | | |
| 73 hours–5 days | | | | | |
| 6–9 days | | | | | |
| 10 days or more | | | | | |

**Table 4.5   Purchasing BIA Example**

| If the Asset User Review Were Unavailable For: | Using the Provided BIA Impact Table, What Would Be the Impact To: | | | | |
|---|---|---|---|---|---|
| | Health/ Safety | Interruption of Production | Public Image | Environmental Release | Financial |
| <24 hours | N/A | | | N/A | |
| 24–72 hours | | | | | |
| 73 hours–5 days | | 3 | 4 | | 4 |
| 6–9 days | | | | | |
| 10 days or more | | | | | |

**Table 4.6   Accounts Payable BIA Example**

| If the Asset User Review Were Unavailable For: | Using the Provided BIA Impact Table, What Would Be the Impact To: | | | | |
|---|---|---|---|---|---|
| | Health/ Safety | Interruption of Production | Public Image | Environmental Release | Financial |
| <24 hours | N/A | | | | |
| 24–72 hours | | 2 | 4 | 3 | 3 |
| 73 hours–5 days | | | | | |
| 6–9 days | | | | | |
| 10 days or more | | | | | |

A typical BIA process looks at a program, system, business process, or application and the worksheet is filled in based on what the business unit believes is the longest tolerable outage. Table 4.5 is an example of what an impact table might look like for a purchasing department that has determined that five days is their impact level. The worksheet for an accounts payable department that has determined at year-end that two days is its longest tolerable outage might look like Table 4.6.

The purchasing business process is categorized as a tier-3 recovery level (three to five days) and the accounts payable process is a tier 2.

Business impact analysis is an example of what can be done once the basics of qualitative risk analysis are mastered. The only limit is what you can think of to use the process for.

## 4.6   Additional Examples

Recently I ran across a different take on the BIA process. This one used two basic security concerns: disclosure and criticality. Tables 4.7 through 4.9 are examples of what is being down now; they are neither right nor wrong, just examples of what is working in today's environment. In Table 4.7, the department selects which category most directly reflects their organization, then plot the answers on a heat chart (Table 4.8). Once the application or process owner selects the appropriate impact category and plots the results on the BIA scoring matrix, the key in Table 4.9 is used to determine when the application or process will be scheduled for recovery in the event of an emergency.

This next example is quite good and is currently being used at a university. It allows the BIA team to establish a finite score for each application, system, or business process. You will note in the summary chart (Table 4.10) that there is a weighted scale for each category. The university felt that the health and safety of the students was the most important element to be considered. For that reason health

**Table 4.7   BIA Example 2**

| Disclosure | Value | Criticality — "Criticality" |
|---|---|---|
| Legal and regulatory sanctions; national/international press coverage | 5 | Unable to meet enterprise mission or business objectives; total loss of public confidence and reputation |
| Possible legal/regulatory sanctions; state/local press coverage | 4 | >5-day delay in meeting enterprise mission or business objectives; long-term blemish of company image |
| Some regulatory penalty possible; incident is known companywide | 3 | 2–4 day delay in meeting enterprise mission or business objectives; temporary blemish of company image |
| Highly unlikely legal or regulatory penalty; incident known at business unit department level | 2 | 1- day delay in meeting enterprise mission or business objectives; limited to company business unit or department image |
| Little or no impact | 1 | <1-day delay in meeting enterprise mission or business objectives; little or no image impact |

**Table 4.8 BIA Example 2 Scoring Matrix**

| Disclosure | Criticality | | | | |
| --- | --- | --- | --- | --- | --- |
| | 1 | 2 | 3 | 4 | 5 |
| 5 | Moderately critical; restore in third wave | Highly critical; restore directly after mission critical | Highly critical; restore directly after mission critical | Mission critical; restore first | Mission critical; restore first |
| 4 | Important; restore after moderately critical | Moderately critical; restore in third wave | Highly critical; restore directly after mission critical | Mission critical; restore first | Mission critical; restore first |
| 3 | Important; restore after moderately critical | Moderately critical; restore in third wave | Moderately critical; restore in third wave | Highly critical; restore directly after mission critical | Mission critical; restore first |
| 2 | Support systems; nice to have, restore when possible | Important; restore after moderately critical | Moderately critical; restore in third wave | Moderately critical; restore in third wave | Highly critical; restore directly after mission critical |
| 1 | Support systems; nice to have, restore when possible | Support systems; nice to have, restore when possible | Important; restore after moderately critical | Moderately critical; restore in third wave | Highly critical; restore directly after mission critical |

**Table 4.9   BIA Example 2 Scoring Key**

| Color | Ranking |
|---|---|
| Red | Mission critical; restore first |
| Orange | Highly critical; restore directly after mission critical |
| Yellow | Moderately critical; restore in third wave |
| Green | Important; restore after moderately critical |
| Blue | Support systems; nice to have, restore when possible |

and safety were assigned the highest weighting. The selection in each category is entered into Table 4.11 and a specific number in calculated for each application, system, or business process.

This BIA process is one that seems to have a lot of possibilities. I like that you are able to weigh each category. A number of years ago we attempted to work the same weighing process into a facilitated BIA process that we were using. The worksheet looked like Figure 4.2. This was the prototype we used to begin to develop more sophisticated BIA processes. We tried to figure out what the weight for each category might be. We knew that some were more important than others, but we could not agree on the breakdown, so we assigned twenty percent to each category. Note in this example we asked what the longest tolerable outage is during peak periods. This is actually what a BIA is trying to determine. This issue drove us to create some of the examples cited previously.

With the scoring process discussed earlier I recommend that you begin the BIA rollout by conducting awareness sessions to explain what the process is and why it is important to have it completed on every system, application, and business process. These awareness sessions can usually be presented during a regularly scheduled department or staff meeting. Prepare a fifteen-minute overview of the process and give an example or two to reinforce the message. Once a number of the awareness sessions have been conducted it will be time to facilitate a BIA.

I like to send out a one-page overview prior to the meeting with a copy of the materials we will be using. Then either in group or individual meetings I am able to help the customers complete the worksheets. When working under a deadline and with the strong support of management this process can be completed within a matter of two or three weeks.

There are two basic approaches to gathering information for a BIA: the one-on-one interview and the group session. Conducting individual BIA interview sessions is popular, but organizational size and location issues sometimes make conducting such sessions impossible. Table 4.12 highlight the pros and cons of these two approaches. Either process can work; even a combination of the processes can be beneficial to most organizations. What need to be established are the goals and objectives of the BIA process.

**Table 4.10  BIA Example 3 Definitions**

| | Category | Image | Regulatory Compliance | Revenue (All Sources) | Expense | Health/Safety |
|---|---|---|---|---|---|---|
| 5 | Severe | Significant, sustained negative international or national media exposure<br>Funding sources are threatened<br>Threat — "Threat" of loss of accreditation | Criminal penalties or fines greater than $10M<br>Major regulatory sanctions, criticism, actions | Irrevocable direct loss of endowment or operating revenue from tuition, grants, donations greater than $10M | Increase in costs (i.e., maintenance, labor, supplier fees, etc.) greater than $10M | Multi-campuswide infectious disease epidemic<br>Loss of life or limb |
| 4 | Major | Ongoing negative regional or national media exposure<br>Loss of key research partners (e.g., NIH)<br>Loss of students or faculty | Penalties or fines of $2M to $10M | Irrevocable direct loss of endowment or operating revenue $2M to $10M | Increase in costs (i.e., maintenance, labor, supplier fees, etc.) $2M to $10M | Single campuswide infectious disease epidemic<br>Severe injuries requiring hospitalization |
| 3 | Moderate | Ongoing (less than 2 weeks) negative local media exposure<br>Disruption of educational or research activities | Penalties or fines of $500K to $2M | Irrevocable direct loss of endowment or operating revenue $500K to $2M | Increase in costs (i.e., maintenance, labor, supplier fees, etc.) $500K to $2M | Significant local outbreak of infectious disease<br>Cuts and bruises requiring first aid |

*continued*

**Table 4.10 (continued)  BIA Example 3 Definitions**

| | Category | Image | Regulatory Compliance | Revenue (All Sources) | Expense | Health/Safety |
|---|---|---|---|---|---|---|
| 2 | Minor | Degradation in quality of education or research<br>Limited negative local media exposure | Penalties or fines of $50K to $500K | Irrevocable direct loss of endowment or operating revenue $50K to $500K | Increase in costs (i.e., maintenance, labor, supplier fees, etc.) $50K to $500K | Major exposure to unsafe classroom, dormitory, workplace, or lab environment<br>Spike in cases of infectious disease |
| 1 | Nuisance | Reputation inconsistent with desired image<br>No press coverage | Penalties or fines of less than $50K | Irrevocable direct loss of revenue less than $50K | Increase in costs (i.e., maintenance, labor, supplier fees, etc.) less than $50K | Minor exposure to unsafe classroom, dormitory, workplace, or lab environment<br>Little or no negative impact |

**Table 4.11    BIA Example 3 Scoring Table**

| Category | Weight | Grade | Score |
|---|---|---|---|
| Impact — "Impact" to employee or student health and safety | 5.0 | 0  1  2  3  4  5 | |
| Impact — "Impact" to university image | 4.5 | 0  1  2  3  4  5 | |
| Impact — "Impact" to operations, education, or research | 4.0 | 0  1  2  3  4  5 | |
| Financial impact — "Impact" | 4.0 | 0  1  2  3  4  5 | |
| Legal/regulatory compliance impact — "Impact" | 3.0 | 0  1  2  3  4  5 | |
| | | BIA — "BIA" rating | |

## 4.7    Objectives of the BIA

The overall goal of the BIA is to review the organization's critical needs including applications, systems, processes, functions, and personnel. The initial BIA process should be conducted without reference to any particular scenario. This "scenario-neutral" step will allow the interviewees to concentrate on the critical business processes and to prevent confusion during the interviews. When done in conjunction with BCP or DRP activities the subsequent BIAs should include specific threat scenarios.

Table 4.13 lists the objectives that the BIA is designed to document. Regardless of the BIA process used the objectives remain the same. Let us look at using questionnaires for the BIA process.

## 4.8    Using Questionnaires for a BIA

The BIA questionnaire is made up of three different types of questions:

1. Quantitative questions ask the interviewee to consider and describe the economic or financial impacts of a potential disruption.
2. Qualitative questions ask the participants to estimate potential loss impact in terms of their emotional understanding or feelings. These intangible issues often lead to shorter recovery time windows.
3. Specialized questions are customized to the organization because it is especially important to make sure that both economic and operational impacts (lost customers, cost of money, reputation, etc.) are stated in such a way that each interviewee will understand the intent and measurement.

Interview candidates should be selected initially at a relatively high level such as payroll, human resources, accounting, IT, etc.). Subsequent BIAs can be conducted at a more-detailed level. Once the level has been established the participants should be chosen based on their knowledge of the process they will review and how it interacts with the rest of the organization.

| Key Business Processes or Business Functions Supported by the Application/System (Name) | Time Sensitivity | | | Business Loss Impact Value | | | |
|---|---|---|---|---|---|---|---|
| | Peak Activity Period (Day of wk, wk of mo, mo of yr) | Longest Tolerable Outage Period During Peak (Impact Value)* | Is It Likely That an Outage Can Delay Installation, Delivery, Restoration, or Interrupt Service? (Yes=1, No=0) | Health & Safety (Impact Value) | Customer Satisfaction (Impact Value) | Embarrassment (Impact Value) | Financial (Impact Value) |
| 1 | | | | | | | |
| 2 | | | | | | | |
| 3 | | | | | | | |
| 4 | | | | | | | |
| 5 | | | | | | | |
| | Weight = | | | | | | |
| | Minimum Impact Score = | | | | | | |
| | | Interrupt Service? | NO | | | Total Impact Score = | 0.00 |

**Figure 4.2 BIA sample worksheet**

**Table 4.12   BIA Methodology Pros and Cons**

| Individual Interviews | Group Sessions |
| --- | --- |
| The separate interview with organizational representatives is the preferred manner in which to gather BIA — "BIA" information | Pro — can be very efficient in ensuring that a lot of data is gathered in a short period of time |
| Pro — ability to watch and observe the individual during discussions | Pro — can speed up the BIA — "BIA" process |
| Pro — the interviewer will get a great deal of verbal and visual information concerning the topic at hand | Con — if not conducted properly it can result in a number of meetings where little information is obtained |
| Pro — a personal rapport can be established | Con — requires a greater amount of time from each participant |
| Pro — this rapport can be beneficial during the BCP and DRP development phases | |
| Con — can be very time consuming | |
| Con — can impact the BIA — "BIA" timeline | |

**Table 4.13   BIA Objectives**

| | |
| --- | --- |
| Identify critical business processes | Identify the minimum number of staff required to recover each process |
| Establish the sequence of recovery based on criticality | Determine the space required for the recovery staff |
| Identify specialized equipment needed | Identify special forms or supplies needed |
| Generate workaround procedures if IT facilities are unavailable | Impact — "Impact" from common recovery sites serving multiple lines of business or departments |
| Identify critical external relationships and dependencies | Identify the impact on the organization in terms of losses and legal and regulatory requirements |

Interviews should be scheduled to allow sufficient time to discuss the business process at an appropriate level of detail. The interview should be conducted at the participants' location. This will allow them to have access to supporting material.

# 4.9   Data Collection and Analysis

As the BIA information is gathered, considerable tabular and written information begins to accumulate quickly. This information needs to be collated and analyzed.

By staying on top of the materials when issues arise, you will be able to go back to the participant and clarify the data quickly.

Even as the initial BIA interviews are being scheduled and completed, it is a good idea to begin preparation of the BIA findings and recommendations. There are two key reasons for keeping up with the work. The first is that if you wait until the end of the process to start formally documenting the results, it is going to be more difficult to recall details that should be included. Second, as the report begins to evolve, there will be issues that will require you to conduct further investigations. By doing this work right away, you will have the time to ensure the process is as thorough as possible.

Another practical technique is to document each BIA interview with its own BIA summary sheet. The information from the summary report can be directly loaded into the final report and it can also be sent back to the participant to verify the results. The BIA summary sheet can contain any verbal information that was shared. By giving the participant the opportunity to review the preliminary findings, you will continue to build consensus for the project. You may want to consider a formal sign-off on the summary findings.

Table 4.14 is an example of a BIA summary sheet. In Appendix H is a sample BIA questionnaire created for use at a university.

## 4.10  Prepare Management Presentation

Presentation of the results of the BIA to concerned management should result in no surprises for them. If you are careful to ensure that the BIA findings are communicated and adjusted as the process has unfolded, then the management review process should really become more of a formality in most cases. The final presentation meeting with the senior management group is not the time to surface new issues and make startling results public for the first time.

As you near the time for the final BIA presentation, it is sometimes a good idea to conduct a series of one-on-one meetings with selected senior management representatives to brief them on the results and gather their feedback for inclusion in the final deliverables. In addition, this is a good time to begin building grassroots support for the final recommendations that will come out of the BIA process and at the same time give you an opportunity to practice making your points and discussing the pros and cons of the recommendations.

Senior management-level presentations most often are better prepared in a brief and focused manner. It will undoubtedly become necessary to present much of the background information used to make the decisions and recommendations, but the formal presentation should be in bullet-point format, crisp, and to the point. Copies of the report, which have been thoroughly reviewed, corrected, bound, and bundled for delivery, can be distributed at the beginning or the end of the presentation depending upon circumstances.

**Table 4.14   BIA Sample Summary Report**

| *Business Activity:* *Activity Owner:* *Weight Assigned?* | | | | |
|---|---|---|---|---|
| *No.* | *Application (See #2 Below)* | *Does Application Support Mission Critical Activity? (See #3 Below)* | *Does Application Contain Confidential Information?* | *Acceptable Downtime Period (Hours, Days, Weeks, Etc.)? (See #4 Below)* |
| 1 | | | | |
| 2 | | | | |
| 3 | | | | |
| 4 | | | | |
| 5 | | | | |
| 6 | | | | |
| 7 | | | | |
| 8 | | | | |

In addition, copies of the bullet-point handouts can also be supplied so attendees can make notes and for reference at a later time.

The BIA process should end with a formalized agreement on management's intentions with regard to maximum permissible downtimes so that business unit and support services managers can be guided accordingly. It is here that that formalized agreement should be discussed and the mechanism for acquiring and communicating it determined.

## 4.11   Final Thoughts

When formal agreement of maximum permissible downtime has been achieved, communicate the information from the BIA to the manager responsible for maintenance of the information technology recovery plans. The manager should review the maximum permissible downtime and the computer applications and systems for each business process. The manager responsible for maintenance of information technology recovery plans must ensure that the recovery plans show that the computer applications and systems needed to support each business application will be available to facilitate the recovery of the business applications within the maximum permissible downtime. If that is not the case, then the manager should initiate updates to the information technology recovery plans.

# Chapter 5

---

# Gap Analysis

---

## 5.1 Introduction

Gap analysis consists of comparing the present state to the desired or "target" state. In the later stages of problem solving, the aim is to look at ways to bridge the gap defined and this may often be accomplished by backward-chaining logical sequences of actions or intermediate states from the desired state to the present state. In other words, asking the questions:

What must be in place to be compliant?
What is currently in place?
What needs to be done to become compliant?

Gap analysis alone, however, is not adequate for all problem situations as goals may evolve and emerge during the course of problem solving. "What ought to be" can be a highly variable target. Also, some problems have many alternative solutions, in which case backward-chaining search strategies will have little practical use.

## 5.2 Background

A gap analysis process coupled with mapping legal and regulatory requirements allows an organization to establish a number of important issues. Typically, I begin the process by establishing which standard will be used by the organization or

**Table 5.1  Sample International Standards**

| International Standard | Formal Title |
|---|---|
| CobiT — "CobiT"® — "CobiT" | Control Objectives for Information and related Technology — "Control Objectives for Information and related Technology" |
| ISO 27002 — "ISO 27002" | Code of Practice for Information Security Management |
| ITIL — "ITIL" | Information Technology Infrastructure Library |
| NIST 800-53 | Recommended Security Controls for Federal Information Systems |

which one is most appropriate. Any of the standards listed in Table 5.1 will do as a starting point.

Before determining whether or not the organization is compliant with the selected standard, I will map to other legal and regulatory issues. Appendix M gives a number of examples of mapping controls lists. To begin the process, it will be necessary to determine which laws and regulations apply. For example, you might want to consider those listed in Table 5.2.

For the remainder of this chapter we will first examine the gap analysis process and then discuss two variations on the theme.

## 5.3  GAP Analysis Process

Obtain a copy of all of the regulations with which your organization must comply. This may seem to be a daunting task, but the Internet is a great source of much of this information. Many of our fellow professionals have taken the time to condense the requirements down to manageable sizes. It will be necessary for you to assemble the policies, procedures, standards, and controls already in place in your organization. By selecting an industry standard to compare your current state of compliance, you will have selected a structure that can be used to assemble your organization's materials.

As with any project it will be necessary to define the scope of the analysis. There are a couple of ways to approach this requirement. For some organizations a simple review of local documents is conducted to determine whether there is a match for each requirement established by the industry standard. This process will provide the organization with a quick overview of what is on the books and what is missing.

The first gap analysis I performed was back in the very early 1980s. I was able to get a copy of the audit guide that was used by the corporate, divisional, and local audit staffs when they conducted audits of my organization. The first process I did was to make a list of everything that they could or would look for. I created a special standards and procedures document, titled "Computer Security Audit and

**Table 5.2  Possible Laws and Regulations**

| Law and Regulations | Description |
|---|---|
| Model Business Corporation Act — "Model Business Corporation Act" | A model act originally developed by the American Bar Association (ABA) in the 1980s to encourage uniformity within the corporation laws of each U.S. state. |
| The Foreign Corrupt Practices Act — "Foreign Corrupt Practices Act" (FCPA) | Requires publicly held companies to have adequate internal controls. |
| Sarbanes–Oxley Act (SOX — "SOX") | Requires certification of financial statement by the CFO and CEO and they must attest that internal controls are adequate. |
| Gramm–Leach–Bliley Act (GLBA — "GLBA") | Primary purpose is to provide privacy of customer information by financial service organizations; comprehensive data protection measures are required. |
| Health Insurance Portability — "Portability" and Accountability Act (HIPAA — "HIPAA") | The law has been expanded to include strict rules for privacy and security of health information, giving individuals more control over how their health information is used. The law covers the information in whatever form it is seen or heard and applies to the information in whatever manner it is to be used. |
| Code of Practice for Information Security Management ISO 27002 — "ISO 27002" (formerly ISO 17799 — "ISO 17799") | An international set of standards established to improve information security management. |
| National Institute of Standards and Technology (NIST) Special Publications 800 series | NIST has published over fifty documents to assist the security professional in selecting effective controls and standards. |
| California SB 1386 — "SB 1386" | Requires an agency, person, or business that conducts business in California and owns or licenses computerized "personal information" to disclose any breach of security. |
| Senate Bill 1408 (proposed) | A covered entity will develop, implement, maintain, and enforce a written program for the security of sensitive personal information the entity collects, maintains, sells, transfers, or disposes of, containing administrative, technical, and physical safeguards. |

*continued*

**Table 5.2 (continued)    Possible Laws and Regulations**

| Law and Regulations | Description |
|---|---|
| Code of Federal Regulations Title 21 Part 11 — "Title 21 Code of Federal Regulations Part 11" (FDA Part 11) | Requires Federal Drug Administration (FDA)-regulated industries to implement controls, validation systems, audit trails, electronic signatures, and documentation for software and systems processing many forms of data as part of business operations and product development. |
| The Federal Trade Commission (FTC — "FTC") Act | The FTC — "FTC" Act prevents unfair competition and unfair or deceptive acts that may affect business commerce. Violations of the FTC Act are usually proven by showing bad faith, fraud, oppression, or a violation of public policy. |

Inventory." In this document I established standards and procedures to address each item that an auditor might request or examine during an audit.

If there was a requirement to conduct an inventory of the physical electronic media, I prepared two sets of procedures. The first was for the security team to know when to send a notice to the Operations department that the inventory was due. Part of this procedure was the retention period to keep the inventory results. The other procedure, created with the tape librarian, was the steps to be followed to conduct an inventory and what the report should look like.

The interesting part of this exercise was that initially there was no examination of the quality of the procedures and standards. The first two or three audits focused on what we had and whether it met the basic audit guide requirements. This was a type of gap analysis that concentrated on simple compliance and not on quality of actions.

When establishing your gap analysis scope, it will be important to determine whether or not the analysis will examine simple compliance or will it determine quality of response. Later in this chapter we will review a gap analysis that goes beyond simple compliance.

Once your scope has been established it will be necessary to collect all of the relevant documents that describe your current practices. This will include privacy policy, security procedures, comptroller's letters, chairman's letters, standards, practices, guidelines, and hardware and software documentation. Make certain that this process is as thorough as possible.

I wrote the Information Protection Policies and Practices (IPP&P) manual for a Fortune 50 organization. As I was doing my research to establish what the organization was already requiring the company to be compliant with, I uncovered a president's letter dated 1939 that addressed protection of confidential information and was still in effect. Although I found this to be interesting the letter next to this one was of even more interest to me. It discussed this company's objectives as it prepared for possible war. Sometimes in your research you will uncover very interesting items.

Once you have assembled all of the relevant documents it will be necessary to organization them into a logical order. I recommend that you take your selected industry standard and compile the documents into that basic structure.

Before beginning the analysis process, conduct a number of interviews to find out what policies and procedures the employees actually know about and use. Although there may be a formal set of documents that the organization spent money to create, you may find that these documents are too complicated and the employees have created a usable set of procedures.

For some of the basic concepts such as classification of company assets I like to talk to a number of non-IT executives to get their view on what the classification levels are and who is responsible for performing these processes. Typically, I have three questions that I ask an executive:

1. Do you have any information that is confidential?
2. What is the most important process that you run or require?
3. What is one thing that IT does or doesn't do that keeps you up at night?

These simple questions provide a wealth of information that can be used when conducting a gap analysis. During this phase you may want to consider taking a physical inventory of the systems and the facility.

Examine your systems for proper implementation of security measures, you will want to play close attention to common problem areas such as inadequate use of the change management process.

Once everything is in place you will want to compare the current practices and tools against the expected standards and procedures. This will allow you to identify where areas of non-compliance may occur. Not all issues have the same level of concern so it will be important to prioritize the gaps you have found and identify remedies.

## 5.3.1 Gap Analysis Example 1

One of the first gap analysis projects I worked on took place when the business units were given the tasks of conducting internal reviews. I had been on a vacation and when I returned I was told that the company had gotten rid of the auditors. After an initial bit of confusion I discovered that the external audit team (Dewey, Cheatum, and Howe) we retained as well as the corporate audit staff and the divisional and local auditors had been replaced with internal control review coordinators and that instead of audits they would ensure that Internal control review questionnaires were completed. This process consisted of a number of questions that addressed the issues that were important to the organization. The questionnaire looked similar to Table 5.3.

**Table 5.3   Gap Analysis Example 1**

| Control | Compliant (Yes/No) | Comment |
|---|---|---|
| A corporate information security officer (CISO) or equivalent executive-level authority has been named and is responsible for implementing and maintaining an effective organizationwide information protection (IP) program. | | |
| The CISO has a team or department with dedicated job responsibilities to IP activities within the organization, including security administration, awareness and training, research, and incident investigations. | | |
| The IP program supports the business objectives/mission statement of the organization. | | |
| An enterprisewide IP policy has been implemented and is championed or sponsored by executive management. | | |
| Comprehensive IP policies, procedures, standards, and guidelines have been created and disseminated to all employees and third parties with access to the network/non-public organization information. | | |
| The IP program is an integral required element of the organization's overall management practices. | | |
| IP is identified as a separate and distinct budget item (minimally 5–8 percent of the overall information systems operations budget). | | |
| Executive management is aware of the business need for an effective IP program and demonstrates commitment to support the IP program success. | | |
| A formal risk analysis process has been implemented to assist management in identifying potential threats — "threats," probability of threat occurrence, and possible countermeasures, and is part of every systems development process. | | |

**Table 5.3 (continued)   Gap Analysis Example 1**

| Control | Compliant (Yes/No) | Comment |
|---|---|---|
| The purchase and implementation of IP tools and controls are based on cost–benefit analysis utilizing the risk analysis input. | | |
| IP responsibilities and accountability for all employees and business associates are explicit and well publicized. | | |
| Each business unit, department, agency, etc., has designated an individual responsible for communicating IP policies and implementing the IP program for the organization. | | |
| The IP program is integrated into all areas of the company, both within and outside the computer security field. | | |
| An ongoing IP awareness program has been implemented for all organization employees and business associates. | | |
| A positive, proactive relationship between IP and auditing has been established and regular communications occur between the two. | | |
| Employees and business associates are made aware that their activities may be monitored. | | |
| An effective program to monitor and measure the effectiveness of IP program-related activities has been implemented. | | |
| Employee compliance to IP-related issues is an annual appraisal element. | | |
| The system development life cycle addresses IP requirements during all phases, including the initiation or analysis (first) phase. | | |
| The IP program is reviewed at least annually and modified where necessary. | | |

In this process each question was followed by a reference to the corresponding policy, standard, procedure, or regulation that required the level of compliance. The business unit or department reviewed each question and entered responded either yes or no. Yes responses had to be explained (see Table 5.4).

If there was a question that the unit was noncompliant with, they would fill out the form as shown in Table 5.5.

**Table 5.4   Gap Analysis Example 1 Completion Process**

| Control | Compliant (Yes/No) | Comment |
|---|---|---|
| A corporate information security officer (CISO) or equivalent executive-level authority has been named and is responsible for implementing and maintaining an effective organizationwide information protection (IP) program. | Yes | Lawrence E. Degg was named CISO on 31 January 2007. |
| The CISO has a team or department with dedicated job responsibilities to IP activities within the organization, including security administration, awareness and training, research and incident investigations. | Yes | CISO mission statement and charter were published 1 April 2007. |

**Table 5.5   Gap Analysis Example 1 Noncompliance Sample**

| Control | Compliant (Yes/No) | Comment |
|---|---|---|
| A formal risk analysis process has been implemented to assist management in identifying potential threats — "threats," probability of threat occurrence, and possible countermeasures, and is part of every systems development process. | No | A risk management team has been identified and they are in the process of establishing the FRAAP — "FRAAP" as the risk assessment process of choice. Task to be completed by 15 August 2008. |

This form of gap analysis was very effective because it identified the policies, standards, practices, and regulations that supported each question. The audit team examined the questionnaires when they performed their formal feature audits of the unit. I found it was easy to sell the process to management by pointing out that if we did a thorough job of honestly addressing our current status and create a compliance plan, we would have control of our own destiny.

## 5.3.2   Gap Analysis Example 2

When ISO 17799 came onto the scene many of the security professionals felt that an industry standard that had the support of the international community was an excellent step in the right direction. Using the concepts established above a self-assessment questionnaire was soon developed. For the security professionals it

**Table 5.6   Gap Analysis Example 2**

| 1 SCOPE |
|---|
| This international standard establishes guidelines and general principles for initiating, implementing, maintaining, and improving information security management in an organization. |

| 2 TERMS AND DEFINITIONS |
|---|
| For better understanding, ISO 27002 identifies and defines key information security terms. |

| 3 STRUCTURE OF THIS STANDARD |
|---|
| This standard contains (11) chapters containing 38 control areas. |

| 4 RISK ASSESSMENT AND TREATMENT |
|---|
| The information security risk assessment should have a clearly defined scope. |

| 5 SECURITY POLICY<br>*Note:* ISO17799 Sections 1, 2, and 3 are non-action items, and are not included as checklist items. | | |
|---|---|---|
| 5.1 Information Security Policy | Management direction and support for information security must be clearly established. | Y ___<br>N ___ |
| 5.1.1 Information Security Policy Document | Has an information security policy been approved by management? | Y ___<br>N ___ |
| | Has an information security policy been implemented? | Y ___<br>N ___ |
| | Has an information security policy been communicated to all employees? | Y ___<br>N ___ |
| 5.1.2 Review of the Information Security Policy | Has the Information security policy been assigned an owner? | Y ___<br>N ___ |
| | Has a policy review process been established? | Y ___<br>N ___ |

gave a clear direction for their program. By using a questionnaire similar to the one shown in Table 5.6, each organization could score their compliance level based on an international standard.

## 5.3.3   How to Use the Self-Assessment Checklist

The checklist (Table 5.6) is designed to assist you in taking "snapshots" of your organization's security status. Answer each question, checking Y or N. The blank column is designed for comments. When you have finished each section, add one point for each question answered Y. Finally, total all scores (sections 4 through 14).

| Superior: | >95 "yes" answers |
|-----------|-------------------|
| Fair: | 82–95 "yes" answers |
| Marginal: | 68–81 "yes" answers |
| Poor: | 54–67 "yes" answers |
| At risk — "Risk": | <54 "yes" answers |
| Score (number of questions answered Yes): \_\_\_\_ | |

Appendix L has a number of different gap analysis examples. In these examples you will see where the requirement is addressed as a Yes or No response, and there is either proof of the findings for the Yes responses or an action statement for compliance in the comment section.

A third example of a gap analysis is a bit more formal. It combines the mapping along with the analysis piece. Here the security professional took the base ISO 27002 and then mapped in the Payment Card Industry Data Security Standard (PCI DSS). Using these two standards the assessment then examined the company's existing policies and standards. This is an excellent way to ensure that management understands that all issues (legal and regulatory) are addressed in the security program (Table 5.7).

## 5.4 Summary

The gap analysis process provides a snapshot of the organization's current level of compliance with industry standards and legal and regulatory requirements. A well-executed gap analysis can provide the organization with a road map to compliance. It will establish what is complete, what needs to be addressed, and with some work a prioritized list of next steps can be created.

**Table 5.7  Gap Analysis Example 3**

| 5 – Security policy | | | | |
|---|---|---|---|---|
| 5.1 – Information security policy | | | | |
| To provide management direction and support for information security in accordance with business requirements and relevant laws and regulations. Management should set a clear policy direction in line with business objectives and demonstrate support for, and commitment to information security through the issue and maintenance of an information security policy across the organization. | | | | |
| *Class* | | *Control Description* | *PCI – "PCI" DSS* | | *Big Company* |
| 5.1.1 | Information security policy document | An information security policy document should be approved by management, and published and communicated to all employees and relevant external parties. | 12.1 | Establish, publish, maintain, and disseminate a security policy. | UXED IT SP&S Section I IT Policy and Standards Statement. |
| 5.1.2 | Review of the information security policy | The information security policy should be reviewed at planned intervals or if significant changes occur to ensure its continuing suitability, adequacy, and effectiveness. | 12.1.3 | Include a review at least once a year and update when the environment changes. | UXED IT SP&S Section VIII Maintenance — all policies and standards will be periodically reviewed and updated by "Big IT Security." |

# Appendix A

# Facilitator Skills

Facilitation of a FRAAP requires the use of a number of special skills. These skills can be improved by attending special training and by facilitating. The skills required include the ability to:

- *Listen.* Having the ability to be responsive to verbal and non-verbal behavior of the attendees. In today's society the ability to listen is a lost art. Instead of a dialogue we participate in parallel monologues. The best way to picture how we function is to imagine the world as a big token ring. When someone has the token, they speak. While they are speaking the rest of us are in quiet mode. It looks like we are listening, but we are really preparing to receive the token and start talking.

  Recently I heard an interview on National Public Radio where an author was discussing this very activity. He used the following example: a worker sits down at the lunch table and tells his co-workers that his wife is dying of cancer. Another employee responds, "I had an aunt that died of cancer." This is not dialogue, this is a parallel monologue. The second worker did not respond to the first; he opened a second line of discussion.

  It is like when you are talking to your teenage son. You may be explaining that if he continues to do something of which you disapprove, you will ground him until he's thirty-five. As soon as you stop talking, your son looks at you and asks, "So do I get the car for tonight or not?" That is a true parallel monologue.

  As a facilitator it will be necessary to give each team member your undivided attention when they begin to discuss a specific threat. As a facilitator you will generally be thinking ahead to remember who the next speaker is and other questions will run through your mind. You will have to fight this natural tendency and concentrate on what is being said to you.

As a personal example, I worked for a company where one of my peers would ask a question of someone during a meeting, and halfway through the answer she would say, "Can you start over? I wasn't paying attention." She wasn't paying attention because she was busy preparing her next question.

By paraphrasing the threat responses you will be better able to concentrate on the team member's comment and this will help the scribe capture the threat description.

■ *Lead.* Getting the FRAAP session started and encouraging discussion while keeping the team focused on the topic at hand.

We have all been in meetings when someone other than the discussion leader took over. Make sure that as the facilitator you do not relinquish the role of leader. The owner has asked you to lead the session and to keep it on track. By being prepared to do the job, there will be little chance for someone else to take over the risk assessment session.

■ *Reflect.* Repeating ideas in fresh words or for emphasis. This will allow two things to occur. First, the facilitator will be better able to concentrate on the threat being discussed. Repeating the comment in different words requires the facilitator to understand what is being said and to put the comment into precise phrases. Second, this process will assist the scribe in gathering the comments correctly.

■ *Summarize.* Being able to pull themes and ideas together. Many times the team members will give long explanations of the issue that they believe warrants investigation. They will embellish the information as they search for the correct words. By being able to weed out the extraneous information and summarizing the remarks into one or two sentences the FRAAP will move along more efficiently.

■ *Confront.* Being able to feed back opinions, reacting honestly to input from the team, and being able to take harsh comments and turn them into positive statements. As with any meeting, some people come with an agenda. It could be that they believe that they are too busy and don't have time for such foolishness or that someone on the team may have wronged them recently. Whatever the cause, some team members will be caustic and acerbic. Do not get sucked into their state of mind. Try to remind them that the team owner asked for them to attend because they had knowledge that will help the owner make intelligent decisions. If all else fails, at the break discuss the situation with the owner and if necessary tell the person that they can leave.

■ *Support.* Creating a climate of trust and acceptance. This was to make everyone feel they are important and part of the team. As the FRAAP facilitator, this will be your job.

■ *Intervene during crisis.* Helping to expand a person's vision of options or alternatives and to reinforce action points that can help resolve any conflict or crisis. Some team members will not understand what is going on and what all of these negative threats is going to do to the overall project. Even after the FRAAP or whatever risk assessment process you will use has become part of your business culture, some employees may not be aware of what it is intended to do.

At the beginning of each FRAAP session, remind the team that the project impact analysis (risk analysis) was completed and that the project has been approved. The risk assessment is conducted to identify threats to the successful implementation of the project and to identify safeguards or countermeasures that will provide an acceptable level of risk.

■ *Center.* Helping the team to accept others' views and build confidence for all to respond and participate. Some team members might preface a remark with "this may be really off target" or "this may seem stupid" and then give their threat concern. Make certain that you reinforce the concept that during a brainstorming session no threat is insignificant. Each threat will be examined by the team during the process to establish risk levels. Whatever the team establishes as the probability of occurrence and the impact to the business objectives will determine the relative value of the comment.

■ *Solve problems.* Gathering relevant information about the issues at hand and helping the team establish an effective control objective. By ensuring that all deliverables from the ore-FRAAP are complete, the team will have the tools needed to complete the risk assessment process. Although it is important to keep the FRAAP session moving, do not compromise thoroughness for speed. Take the time to get the correct information.

■ *Change behavior.* Look for those that appear not to be part of the process and bring them into active participation. I was conducting a FRAAP on Long Island a while back and there were 35 team members. Up toward the front on my right-hand side sat a gentleman named Clevon. As the process went through its first round, when we got to Clevon, he passed. On the second round, he again passed. As we got halfway through the third round, I went over to Clevon and said, "Clevon, get ready. We're coming toward you." When we got to him, he was ready and had a threat. He just needed time to see how the process worked and that no one was ridiculed because of their response.

I make sure I am in the room for the FRAAP as the team members come in. I watch to see if the team members know each other. As the first matter of business, I have them introduce themselves. I request that their introduction includes their name, department, location, and reason for being there. If I feel it would be appropriate, I have a number of ice-breaker quizzes and personality tests that I can administer if I feel the group needs help to become a team.

Basic facilitation rules must be observed by all facilitators if the FRAAP is to be successful. FRAAP leaders must observe carefully and listen to all that the team says and does.

- *Recognize all input and encourage participation.* There are two basic personality types: introverts and extroverts. I consider myself an outspoken introvert. It is easy to identify the extroverts; they will appear to be self-confident and unafraid to put forth their ideas. The introvert, however, may require nurturing before participating. Be aware of this need and make sure you bring the introverts into the process.
- *Be observant for non-verbal responses.* If someone flashes you half of a peace sign, then you might examine how well things are going. Look for body language. If a male team member folds his arms across his chest, it usually means he has had enough. If a woman does that, it normally means she is cold. If she crosses her legs and her foot starts to bob, then she has had enough. Watch for people that back away from the table. These are signs that the team has reaching the end of their concentration level.
- *Do not lecture; listen and get the team involved.* Remember that you are the facilitator. The team members are the subject matter experts (SMEs). It is their expert opinions that the risk assessment process needs.
- *Never lose sight of the objective.* Keep the project scope statement posted in the room during the session. If the team moves away from the objective, pull them back and direct their focus on the mission at hand.
- *Stay neutral (or always appear to remain neutral).* As a security, audit, or risk management professional, you have ideas on how things should be done. When you are the facilitator, you must keep those opinions to yourself.
- *Learn to expect hostility, but do not become hostile.* Remember that this isn't personal. You are there to assist the owner in performing their due diligence. Sometimes rude or disparaging remarks are made in the heat of the discussion process. Frustration can boil over and cause the team members to act or say things that are inflammatory. For instance, many employees know that the quickest way to get at the network administration group is to say something like "the network is running a little slow today." Here they are just baiting the network administrators, sometimes as a "joke" and other times to be mean. Watch out for these kinds of comments and help defuse the situation.

  I once did six FRAAPs in a week. By the time I got to numbers four through six, I was not as sweet and nice as I was in earlier sessions. The FRAAP is a physically and mentally demanding process. Try to schedule them so that you can have at least one off day between each FRAAP.
- *Avoid being the "expert authority."* The facilitator's role is to listen, question, enforce the process, and offer alternatives. As stated earlier, the team is made up of SMEs; the facilitator's job is to ensure that the team stays on focus and completes the FRAAP in a timely and efficient manner.

■ *Adhere to time frames and be punctual.* Welcome to my pet peeve. The best way to show respect is to start and finish on time. The FRAAP is not a one-time activity. The members of the team may be called on by other owners to participate in other FRAAPs. By starting on time, starting back up on time after the break, and stopping no later than the scheduled finish time, the SMEs are more likely to participate in other FRAAPs.

■ *Be on the lookout for the "mercy" page or phone call.* This activity is a variation on the old blind-date technique where a half hour into the date, you have scheduled someone to call you. If the date is going badly, you say it's the babysitter and you have to go home. Employees will get a page or phone call within twenty minutes of starting a meeting, announce that there is an emergency, and then leave. I have commented at the beginning of a session that those of you expecting your "mercy" page should probably take it now so as not to disrupt the FRAAP.

■ *Use breaks to free a discussion.* If a discussion veers off point and gets some team members bogged down, try to move the discussion item to the deferred issues list. If that fails to break the discussion, call for a short break (ten minutes maximum). Meet with the discussion group and try to reach resolution. It may be necessary for them to take the discussion offline at a later time.

■ *The facilitator is there to serve the FRAAP team.* The goal of the facilitator is to be a part of a process that focuses on the team and their contributions to the risk assessment process. I have had two facilitators work for me that saw this as their chance to do stand-up comedy. This is not the true role of the facilitator. The process comes first; the opinions of the facilitator should never come up.

■ *Stop the FRAAP if the group is sluggish and difficult to control.* In this book we examine the pre-screening process. This is conducted as the first deliverable of the pre-FRAAP meeting and can identify whether the asset in question needs a complete risk assessment or business impact analysis (or both). This process will save time by not conducting risk assessments on those applications, systems, business processes, or platforms that have no urgent need for a thorough examination at this time.

■ *Beware of external sources that might impact the results of the FRAAP.* One time I was hired to go to Richmond, Virginia, to conduct a FRAAP training session and then conduct a FRAAP on a specific business application. I was scheduled to be there Monday through Thursday; on Wednesday and Thursday I would be working with the team to conduct a FRAAP and then help them prepare the documentation. By Tuesday I was trying to figure out what was wrong with the training session. The attendees were nice enough to me, but they did not offer any comments and had no questions. During lunch, there one of the attendees told me that all of the members of the team being trained had been told the previous Thursday that they were redundant and that they would be discharged in two weeks.

I went to my contact to verify the facts and was told that these people would be there on Wednesday to participate in the FRAAP. Well, it was one of those times when I went through a FRAAP and no one attended.

Another time I was in San Francisco conducting a FRAAP and every twenty minutes or so one of the team members would leave. Some would come back and some didn't. At the break I asked the contact what was happening. I was told that the day of the FRAAP was also the day the company scheduled reduction-in-force meetings. Those who came back were still employed, the others weren't.

When conducting a FRAAP be aware of outside influences. For some departments it could be a critical time in their calendar such as end-of-month or end-of-quarter. Make sure that the FRAAP is scheduled to meet the needs of the owner and the team best.

# Appendix B

# FRAAP Team Members

## Introduction

For the best chance for success, the risk assessment team must consist of representatives from the various stakeholder groups. In addition to having the right groups represented, it will be necessary to have subject matter experts (SMEs) a part of the team.

Recently, a client asked if I could help them understand why the risk assessment process had failed. I am always interested in gaining new insights, so I asked the client to explain why they felt the process was not working. For the next twenty minutes the client described the process that was followed in the pre-risk assessment process. The client had established a scope statement, which was to perform a risk assessment on the information technology network backbone. The client described in more detail the components that made up the backbone and stated that they had created a visual model. Threats to the backbone had been examined based on natural, environmental, and human elements. The client briefly walked me through the brainstorming process that had been used, and explained how risk level had been assigned to the identified threats. Then the client discussed how they selected controls that would help mitigate the open high-level risks. All of the correct steps had been followed, and I asked the client where the process had failed. The client told me that the user community was balking at funding the intrusion detection system (IDS) identified as the best solution to detect possible intruders into the network backbone.

I walked back through the process in my mind and asked a few questions. Nothing seemed to be out of line and then I wrote down the seven deliverables from the pre-risk assessment meeting. We had not discussed the team membership. The client told me that the risk assessment had the facilitator and scribe (both from information security), the network owner (from information technology), and the lead IT auditor. That was the team.

I asked the client what had happened to including those areas that would have a vested interest in the results of the risk assessment process. I was told that the client did not want to include the user community because they might learn how vulnerable the network really was. The problem with this thinking was that now the client wanted the disenfranchised to contribute a portion of their tight budget to fund a project to procure, implement, and maintain an IDS. The user community had no understanding of the need, the threat, the risk, or the exposure; all they were being told was that it was needed and they had to pay.

The risk assessment process worked fine, the client had failed to include the stakeholder in the decision-making process.

## The Risk Assessment Team

During the pre-FRAAP meeting, the business owner and project lead will need to identify who should be part of the FRAAP session. The ideal number of participants is between seven and fifteen. It is recommended that representatives from all of the affected areas be invited.

To start with, we will examine who might be included in the team membership in a generic new application development process (Table B.1) and then we will address each example.

There are no hard-and-fast rules as to who should attend, but to be successful it will be necessary for the functional business owner and system users to be part of the FRAAP. However, there may be concern about the actual business owner being part of a discovery process. Let us take a few minutes to discuss the pros and cons of each possible team member.

■ The business owner needs to be represented on the risk assessment team mainly because it is their project that will be reviewed and it will be important that they be part of the process.

Howsever, as we discussed in Chapter 1, the business owner is the executive of the department that will be responsible for the implementation and protection of the project. An executive can have an interesting effect on the free flow of ideas and discussions by their mere presence in a meeting. As an example, I worked for a company that held a monthly off-site meeting for the managers and directors of an information technology organization. The object of the meeting was that each manager would give a ten-minute presentation on the project, issue, or concern that their team was working on that month. After the presentation there would be a five-minute period of input

**Table B.1    Risk Assessment Team Members Example 1**

| Possible FRAAP Team Member | Crucial | Support |
|---|---|---|
| Business owner | Yes | |
| System users | Yes | |
| Systems analysts | Yes | |
| Applications programming | Yes | |
| Database administration | Yes | |
| Auditing (if appropriate) | | Yes |
| Physical security | | Yes |
| Facilities management | Yes | |
| Telecommunications | Yes | |
| Network administration | Yes | |
| Legal (if necessary) | | Yes |
| Regulatory affairs | | Yes |
| Corporate communications | | Yes |
| Human resources | | Yes |
| Labor relations | | Yes |
| Processing operations management | Yes | |
| System administrator | Yes | |
| Systems programming | Yes | |
| Information security | Yes | |

from the gathered peers. This input was designed to help the manager see different perspectives and solutions. This sounds like a laudable concept.

In reality the sessions were the most non-productive waste of time for nearly forty managers and directors. The key reason was that the number-one game in the IT organization was cutthroat politics. Instead of constructive dialogue, the presenter would face an onslaught of negative comments about the real objective of the project discussed and how the presenter lacked the intellect to manage such a project effectively.

This kind of negative discussion continued until the CIO arrived. At that point all of the invectives ceased; it was as if all joined hands and sang, "It's a Small World After All." They were a team and as such there was no issue so large that they could not solve together. This behavior continued until the CIO left for his next meeting. Then the hands dropped, the fists came back up, and the disparaging words returned.

The CIO impacted the interaction with the team. Although this is an extreme case, the same could happen in the risk assessment threats identification process. What we would do in a case like this was to invite the business owner to open the meeting, thank the team for assembling, review the scope statement, and then leave. There would be a representative of the business owner there, but usually not the actual executive.

■ The users need to be part of the process because they have a different perspective on how the processes work than do the infrastructure support members.

■ The systems analysis group is made up of those bilingual individuals that speak fluent business and information technology. This skill set can be vital in ensuring that what is spoken at a risk assessment is understood by all parties.

■ Applications programming is the individual that will either create the new application or will customize existing application or third-party software to meet the functional owner's needs. This is different than a project lead; this is usually the actual code developer.

■ The database administrators are the technical individuals that understand how the mechanics of the database work and are often responsible for ensuring that database security mechanisms are working properly.

■ The audit staff is a group that can offer some good ideas, but they often impact the free flow of information. Unless you have a very good working relationship with the audit staff, it is recommended that they not take part in the risk assessment session. The audit team will see the results of the risk assessment later and will probably use the output when they conduct an audit of the resource.

Some organizations that I have helped implement a risk assessment process will have a representative from the audit team as part of the risk assessment process. This individual will not be the auditor responsible for conducting formal audits of the project or process. Because of the confidentiality classification of the information discussed in the risk assessment meeting, there can be an expectation that issues presented in the risk assessment process will not be divulged outside of the session.

■ Physical security or someone from facility engineering should be part of the team. They will bring a perspective of viewing concerns from the physical operations of the environment. In many organizations facilities management is charged with maintaining the business continuity plan (BCP).

■ If the resource under review is going to access the network or other telecommunications devices, representatives from those areas must be part of the process.

■ Any Web-based applications will require representatives from the Internet support organization, including the Webmaster and the firewall administrator.

■ The legal staff is normally too busy for every risk assessment. However, if there is a resource under review that has a major impact on the enterprise, it will probably be appropriate to extend an invitation to them. I recommend that you meet with the legal staff and discuss what the risk assessment is, as we discussed earlier, and attempt to establish a guideline when they need either to be part of the process or to see specific risk concerns.

■ Another group that can provide invaluable insight into a number of issues is the regulatory affairs group. They are charged with keeping current on what the various regulations government agencies and industry groups require.

■ Corporate communications is responsible for communicating with the public and other entities. If the asset under review impacts customers or business partners, then this group needs to be part of the team.

■ Any issues that impact the employees will require the attendance of a representative from human resources. If union-represented employees are impacted by the risk assessment, then labor relations should be invited.

■ The operations group is responsible for maintaining the production environment on the various platforms. Their input into how the data center disaster recovery plan works and how it will support the asset under review will be vital in discussing service level agreements.

■ The system(s) group is also an important pat of the risk assessment team. The system administrator, who has had some training in the new application or system, is normally found in the user department and is the initial point of contact for users when they have problems.

■ The system programming group is made up of individuals that support the platforms and ensure that the current operating environment is working and properly configured.

■ Information security should have a representative as part of the risk assessment team. Many FRAAPs are facilitated by someone from information security, but this is often a conflict of interest. The facilitator is to have an aura of neutrality about them.

This list is not all-inclusive nor does it represent the correct mix of players if the risk assessment moves away from the traditional information security risk assessment. The key here is to understand that to be successful, the risk assessment team must be made up of representation from a wide spectrum of employee groups.

## Risk Assessment Team Example 1

Let us take the following as an example of an application development project that has been approved and the pre-screening process has determined that a risk assessment must be conducted. We have a remote time entry system (RETS) that will allow remote-based employees to enter their hours directly. This information will be passed along to the payroll system that will issue bi-monthly paychecks. The following information is what will be used for this new RETS:

- Using third-party software
- Client/server application
- UNIX based
- Accessed through the corporate WAN
- Remote access will be required
- Information is time sensitive
- Possible Internet connection for input/output

Using this as our system under risk assessment review, let us take the list of possible risk assessment team members and establish our team in Table B.2. The business owner may or may not be payroll. To be certain, the time entry organization must be part of the risk assessment process as does the payroll group. Although this may not be their project, it does ultimately impact their product.

The system users need representatives from the various types of facilities. The team should include representation from each location that has a significantly different mode of operation. For example, there may be remote locations that have

**Table B.2   Risk Assessment Team Members Example 2**

| Possible Risk Assessment Team Member | Crucial | Support |
|---|---|---|
| Business owner | Yes | |
| System users | Yes | |
| Systems analysts | Yes | |
| Applications programming | N/A | |
| Vendor support | Yes | |
| Database administration | N/A | |
| Auditing | Yes | |
| Physical security | | No |
| Facilities management | Yes | |
| Telecommunications | Yes | |
| Network administration | Yes | |
| Legal (if necessary) | | No |
| Regulatory affairs | | No |
| Corporate communications | | No |
| Human resources | Yes | |
| Labor relations | Yes | |
| Processing operations management | Yes | |
| System administrator for RETS | Yes | |
| Systems programming | | No |
| Information security | Yes | |

VPN access to the backbone network, and there may be locations that require dial-in or Internet access.

Let us quickly review the others:

- The system analysts we discussed earlier.
- Application development may not be involved because the RETS is going to use third-party software. There will be a need to have a representative from the vendor present to answer questions and present issues.
- Database administration is not currently involved in this project.
- Auditing is always welcome, but physical security is not needed this time.
- Facilities management is needed because of their role in the BCP.
- Telecommunications and network administration are required.
- Legal, regulatory affairs, and corporate communications are not required.
- IT operations always is needed and a help desk or system administrator must be part of the team.
- System programming is probably not needed, but information security is always part of this type of project.

The important element is to ensure that all stakeholders are properly represented on the risk assessment team. It is always better to err on the side of having too many than it is to leave those with a vested interest off the team.

The representatives from these groups must also possess the knowledge and experience to ensure that the risk assessment process identifies as many threats as possible and then categorizes them into proper risk levels. This means that the seasoned veterans of the organization should be called to active duty.

## Conclusion

The quality in qualitative risk assessment relies a great deal on the team that is assembled. It is important to have all of the areas with a vested interest in the project to be represented by individuals with knowledge of the workings of the organization. When I am assembling a team, I look for those individuals who have been around long enough to understand how the organization works. I look for people who know which controls work and which ones do not. I look for people that typically push the limits of controls to see what would happen.

When I was putting together one of my first risk assessment teams, I wanted a certain individual but I did not know her name. I asked my staff who that woman was at the previous briefing who had expressed strong opinions on how information security functioned. I had only been on the job a couple of weeks and we were still feeling the effects of the previous manager. My staff told me who this she was and warned me that she was very negative and would disrupt any process that information security offered.

What my team failed to understand was that this person just wanted to be heard. She had the ear of certain management types and they listened to her. What I needed was for her to become part of the information-gathering process so that she could advise us during this phase. What had traditionally occurred was that she was excluded from this development process and only had opportunity to express her opinions and concerns after a project was in development.

When you are assembling your risk management team, be sure to look for those who have the ear of management and make them part of the team. Those individuals whom you might label as "curmudgeons" must be heard. What they want is to be part of the solution. If they are not included in the process, they will become part of the problem of getting the risk assessment results accepted and implemented.

# Appendix C

# Project Scope Statement

## Overview

For any project to be successful there must be an establishing of the boundaries relating to that specific project. It will be important to describe in detail what process is to be managed, what resources are required, and what deliverables constitute completion. For any project to be successful the development of the project scope statement must be as thorough as possible. It will be difficult to complete a project if all of the team members do not have the same vision of what is to be accomplished

During this initial step in the project life cycle, typically the team lead, the customer or owner, and a facilitator meet to complete the project scope statement. The key here is to establish the boundaries of what is to be accomplished. Most failed projects come to grief because the scope of the project was poorly defined to begin with or because the scope was not managed well and was allowed to "creep" until it was out of control. If you are going to manage any project, then the purpose of the project must be captured into the contents of the scope statement. All of the elements that go into writing a successful scope statement should be used to define the asset. We will examine those elements shortly.

As with any project, the deliverable from the asset definition step is to reach agreement with the owner on what the assessment is to review and all relevant parameters. The objective here is to put in writing a risk assessment statement of opportunity that consists of two elements: project statement and specifications.

For the project statement, identify the desired outcome. For example:

> The team will identify potential threats to the asset under review and will prioritize those threats by assessing the probability of the threat occurring and the impact to the asset if the threat happened. Using the prioritized list of risks, the team will identify possible controls, countermeasures, and/or safeguards that can reduce the risk exposure to an acceptable level.

This will become the risk assessment scope statement and provide the focus for the specifications.

Take enough time during the scope statement development to discuss and clarify the parameters of the project. Although these parameters will vary from project to project, the following items should be considered each time:

- *Purpose:* Fully understand the purpose of the project. What is the need driving the project? If the purpose is to correct a problem, identify the cause of the problem. The bulk of the supporting information should be found in the documentation generated from the project impact analysis (PIA) or risk analysis that was completed in the analysis phase of the system development life cycle (SDLC). A PIA has been performed that has decided that the project is to move forward. Review the results of this process to understand better the project's purpose. (More details on the PIA and risk analysis processes can be found in Chapter 2.)
- *Customer:* Your customer is the person or unit that has the need that this project is meant to fill. Determine who the real customer is and note other stakeholders. Typically, the stakeholders will become members of the project team. They will be assigned various tasks throughout the SDLC.
- *Deliverables:* These are specific things that are to be delivered to the customer. This is the statement that defines when a project is complete. For example, in a risk assessment the deliverables typically are (1) threats have been identified, (2) risk levels have been established, and (3) possible controls have been identified.
- *Resources:* Here the team wants to identify which of the following resources will be required to accomplish the project:
  - *Money:* Typically, we don't have "money," but we will need budget for the project.
  - *Personnel:* This is where the identification of stakeholders comes into play. We also need to identify the infrastructure support requirements for the project.
  - *Equipment:* Here is where the need for hardware, software, firmware, or anything else will be identified.

- *Supplies:* The team involved in the project may need to be housed together and the materials they need to support the project need to be identified.
- *Services:* As with equipment, there may be a need for services from other groups or third-party providers.

■ *Constraints:* Identify those activities that could impact the deliverables of the project. Consider such things as:

- *Laws:* It is very important that any project be developed with an understanding of the legal and regulatory climate currently impacting the organization. One of the team members should be from legal and regulatory affairs.
- *Policies:* Every organization should have a basic set of policies that discuss the expected conduct of the employees, business units, and organization. All new projects should have completed the PIA process. During the PIA, the team specifically addresses policy compliance.
- *Procedures:* Basic operating procedures ensure that the organization is able to function in a consistent manner. Even the development process must follow the development methodology procedures; included in this review is adherence to the change management procedures.

■ *Resource limitations:* Another key constraint is the impact of resources being unavailable. This includes hardware, software, firmware, and wetware. An example of a constraint that impacted a risk assessment project I was working on turned out to be an added-on front-end authenticator. The application was developed to be used by third parties that accessed the resources through the Internet. To provide some level of security, the team had developed a front-end authentication program. This program had never gone through the change management process and had not been subject to the development methodology requirements. Therefore, the results of the application risk assessment were skewed pending a risk assessment of the authenticator program.

■ *Assumptions:* Identify those things that the project team believes to be true or complete. Assumptions are ways to document what the team believes is the current operating environment. The following are examples of assumptions:

- An infrastructure risk assessment has been completed and that industry-accepted standards of control have been implemented.
- The project has gone through the PIA and has been registered as a formal project with an active budget code.

The work of the PIA process also addresses the viability of the vendor supplying the service or product. Without this due diligence process, vendor viability could be either a constraint or an assumption.

■ *Criteria:* Agree specifically on how the customer will evaluate the success of the project. What are the customer's criteria to determine that the deliverables were presented on time? Within budget? With quality?

Criteria should be relevant and valid measures of how well the project accomplishes its stated purpose. You may need to help the customer clarify their true needs to assure that the criteria to be used are valid indicators of project success.

The most difficult will be the quality issue. When creating a new program, we look to the requirements gathered in the analysis and design phases of the SDLC. If these key indicators are met and the application or system is developed according to the development methodology and was subject to the requirements of the change management process, then there is a good chance the quality issue will be satisfied.

For a project such as risk assessment, the quality issue is often resolved by the use of industry-accepted standards of control. An organization would select industry-accepted standards such as the following:

| International Standard | Formal Title |
| --- | --- |
| CobiT® | Control Objectives for Information and related Technology |
| ISO 27002 | Code of Practice for Information Security Management |
| ITIL | Information Technology Infrastructure Library |
| NIST 800-53 | Recommended Security Controls for Federal Information Systems |

Once the organization has selected the appropriate industry standard, the laws and regulations that impact the organization will have to be identified (see Appendix D for a list of laws, standards, and regulations). Once this list is created, then the organization would perform a gap analysis (see Chapter 5) to determine their current compliance level. The results of the gap analysis will be a compliance program that will provide the risk assessment process with a level of expected quality.

## Summary

When Christopher Columbus headed off in 1492, he didn't know where he was going. When he got there, he didn't know where he was, and when he got home he didn't know where he had been. Although this project plan may work for fifteenth-century explorers, it is a bad model for twenty-first-century business and industry.

To run a successful project the boundaries of what is to be accomplished must be identified and agreed upon. This process must be documented and approved by the interested parties. An effective project scope statement provides for a solid road map to success.

# Appendix D

# Laws, Standards, and Regulations

| Law and Regulations | Description |
|---|---|
| Model Business Corporation Act | Originally developed by the American Bar Association (ABA) in the 1980s to encourage uniformity within the corporation laws of each U.S. state. |
| The Foreign Corrupt Practices Act (FCPA) | Requires publicly held companies to have adequate internal controls. |
| Sarbanes–Oxley (SOX) | Requires certification of financial statement by the CFO and CEO and they must attest that internal controls are adequate. |
| Gramm–Leach–Bliley Act (GLBA) | Primary purpose is to provide privacy of customer information by financial service organizations and comprehensive data protection measures are required. |
| Health Insurance Portability and Accountability Act (HIPAA) | The law has been expanded to include strict rules for privacy and security of health information, giving individuals more control over how their health information is used. The law covers the information in whatever form it is seen or heard and applies to the information in whatever manner it is to be used. |

*continued*

| Law and Regulations | Description |
|---|---|
| Code of Practice for Information Security Management ISO 27002 (formerly ISO 17799) | An international set of standards established to improve information security management. |
| National Institute of Standards and Technology (NIST) Special Publications 800 series | NIST has published over fifty documents to assist the security professional in selecting effective controls and standards. |
| California SB 1386 | Requires an agency, person, or business that conducts business in California and owns or licenses computerized "personal information" to disclose any breach of security. |
| Senate Bill 1408 (proposed) | A covered entity will develop, implement, maintain, and enforce a written program for the security of sensitive personal information the entity collects, maintains, sells, transfers, or disposes of, containing administrative, technical, and physical safeguards. |
| Title 21 Code of Federal Regulations Part 11 (FDA Part 11) | Requires industries regulated by the Federal Drug Administration (FDA) to implement controls, validation systems, audit trails, electronic signatures, and documentation for software and systems processing many forms of data as part of business operations and product development. |
| The Federal Trade Commission (FTC) Act | The FTC Act prevents unfair competition and unfair or deceptive acts that may affect business commerce. Violations of the FTC Act are usually proven by showing bad faith, fraud, oppression, or a violation of public policy. |

# Frequently Asked Questions about Risk Management

## Introduction

Risk management is a process that provides management with the balance of meeting business objectives or missions and the need to protect the assets of the organization cost effectively. In this period of increased external scrutiny due to myriad recent legislation requirements, risk management provides management with the ability to actively demonstrate due diligence and how they are meeting the fiduciary duty.

In this appendix, we will examine frequently asked questions relating to the key elements of risk management.

## Is There a Difference between Risk Analysis and Risk Assessment?

The short answer to this question is yes. When we examine the business process development cycle (BPDC; also known as the system development life cycle), we see that there are phases in which certain activities are scheduled to be performed. In the BPDC that I am familiar with, the first phase is the analysis process. This is the time when the case for a new project is created. The risk analysis, or project impact analysis (PIA), is used to document and demonstrate the business reasons why a new project should be approved.

Once a project has been approved, early in the design phase a risk assessment must be performed to identify the threats to the organization's mission or business objectives presented by this new project. The risk assessment allows the development team and the business stakeholders to identify potential threats, prioritize those threats into risks, and identify controls that can reduce the risks to acceptable levels. Knowing the control requirements in the design phase will help reduce costs when work begins on the project in the construction or development phase.

## Why Should a Risk Analysis Be Conducted?

Risk analysis is the process that allows management to demonstrate that they have met their obligation of due diligence when making a decision whether or not to move forward with a new project, capital expenditure, investment strategy, or other such business process.

Due diligence has a number of variant definitions based on the industry that is being discussed. Typically, the consensus of these definitions address the measure of prudence, activity, or assessment, as is properly to be expected from, and ordinarily exercised by, a reasonable and prudent person under the particular circumstances; it is not measured by any absolute standard but depends on the relative facts of the special case.

In brief, the risk analysis or PIA examines the factors that come into play when trying to determine whether a project should be approved. The PIA examines the tangible impacts, such as capital outlay, and intangible impacts, such as customer connivance or regulatory compliance.

When the risk analysis is complete, the results are presented to a management oversight committee that is charged with reviewing new project requests and deciding whether or not to move forward. The documentation is retained for a period of time and then can be used by the organization if ever there are any questions as to why a project was or was not approved.

## When Should a Risk Assessment Be Conducted?

Because many organizations do not know what the threats and risks are to operate in the changing business environment, risk assessment provides a process to identify threats systematically and then assign risk levels based on the specific organization conducting the assessment. By establishing a risk level or a prioritization of the threats, an organization can best use its limited resources to meet its greatest need.

Risk assessment has four key deliverables. It will identify threats to the organization's mission, prioritize those threats into risk levels, identify mitigating controls or safeguards, and publish an action plan.

The output from the risk analysis and risk assessment processes will generally be used twice. The first time will be when decisions are made; for the risk analysis that means deciding whether or not to proceed on a new project and for the risk assessment, what types of controls or safeguards need to be implemented. For risk assessment, the output will identify what countermeasures should be implemented or that management has determined that the best decision is to accept the risk.

The other time the results will be used is when the "spam hits the fan." That is, when a problem arises and the organization must show the process it used to reach the decisions that it did. The documentation created in the risk management processes will allow the organization to show who was involved, what was discussed, what was considered, and what decisions were made.

A risk management process also lets an enterprise take control of its own destiny. With an effective risk assessment process in place, only those controls and safeguards that are actually needed will be implemented. An enterprise will never again face having to implement a mandated control to "be in compliance with audit requirements."

## Who Should Conduct the Risk Assessment?

Speaking as a consultant, it should be conducted by consultants — no. Who knows your organization better than any other entity in the world? Your own employees, that's who. An external consultant can lead a risk assessment, but to get a true grasp on and understanding of how current controls are working, the employees are an excellent resource for this knowledge.

If your organization is fortunate enough to have a project management office, then the facilitators from this group would be perfect for conducting the risk management processes. There are some groups that, because of their charters and responsibilities, would find a conflict of interest to lead or facilitate these processes. Applications development is a group that could have an impact on both risk analysis and risk assessment. Their job is to create applications and systems as quickly and efficiently as possible. So there could be an appearance of conflict of interest.

The audit staff and systems operations are two other groups that have charters of responsibility that would give an appearance of conflict of interest.

## How Long Should a Risk Assessment Take?

It should be completed in days, not weeks or months. To meet the needs of an enterprise, the risk management process must be able to complete it quickly with a minimum of impact on the employees' already-busy schedule. We currently offer a class in "how to complete a risk assessment in five days or less." This class has been very popular and the process is field-tested every month to ensure that the five-day time limit is attainable.

Time is a very precious commodity and processes such as risk management must be structured to be fast and efficient. As you will see, if there is more time available, then there is no end to the different things that can be done. Most organizations, however, have little enough time to spare.

## What Can a Risk Analysis or Risk Assessment Analyze?

Risk assessment can identify to the enterprise what the threats are and which threats pose the greatest risk to the organization. By identifying the areas of greatest risk, management can concentrate on addressing the areas of risk. Because resources are limited, the risk-identification process will allow management to use its current resources to its best advantage. The goal of risk assessment is not to eliminate all risk. It is a tool to be used by management to reduce risk to an acceptable level.

The greatest benefit of a risk analysis is whether it is prudent to proceed. It allows management to examine all currently identified concerns, to prioritize the level of vulnerability, and then to select an appropriate level of control or to accept the risk.

## Who Should Review the Results of a Risk Analysis and Risk Assessment?

A risk analysis is rarely conducted without a senior management sponsor. The results are geared to provide management with the information they need to make informed business decisions. Typically, the results of the risk analysis or PIA are shared with the senior management team responsible for reviewing and deciding whether or not to proceed with a proposed project. The information is normally categorized as internal use only (restricted).

The results of a risk assessment are normally classified as confidential and are provided only to the sponsor and to those deemed appropriate by the sponsor. When working the risk assessment processes, it will be necessary to remind all employees that the information discussed in the process is classified as confidential and may not be shared outside the risk management forum. For any third party taking part in the process, it will be necessary to execute a non-disclosure or confidentiality agreement to ensure the protection of information discussed.

## How Is the Success of the Risk Analysis Measured?

The tangible way to measure success is to see a lower bottom line for cost. Risk assessment can assist in this process by identifying only those controls that need to be implemented.

Another way that the success of a risk analysis is measured is if there is a time when management decisions are called into review. By having a formal process in place that demonstrates the due diligence of management in the decision-making process, this kind of inquiry will be dealt with quickly and successfully.

## Summary

The risk management process is a business process that supports management in its decision making. It provides the management owners of the assets to perform their fiduciary responsibility of protecting the assets of the enterprise in a reasonable and prudent manner. The process does not have to be a long, drawn-out affair. To be effective, risk analysis and risk assessment must be done quickly and efficiently.

# *Appendix F*

# Risk Analysis versus Risk Assessment

## Overview

Risk management is a process that provides management with the balance of meeting business objectives or missions and the need to protect the assets of the organization cost effectively. In this period of increased external scrutiny due to myriad recent questionable management decisions and the corresponding legislative backlash, risk management provides management with the ability to demonstrate due diligence and how they are meeting the fiduciary duty.

In this article we will examine how risk analysis helps manager's meet their due diligence requirement and how risk assessment fulfills the fiduciary duty requirement.

## The Difference between Risk Analysis and Risk Assessment

When we examine the business process development cycle (BPDC; also known as the system development life cycle), we see that there are phases in which certain activities are scheduled to be performed. In the BPDC that I am familiar with, the first phase is the analysis process. This is the time when the case for a new project is created. The risk analysis, or project impact analysis (PIA), is used to document and demonstrate the business reasons why a new project should be approved. When the PIA is complete, the formal documentation is presented to the executive management committee for review, assessment and possible approval. If approved by the committee, the proposal is then registered and becomes a "project."

Once a project has been approved, early in the design phase a risk assessment must be performed to identify the threats to the organization's mission or business objectives presented by this new project. The risk assessment allows the development team and the business stakeholders to identify potential threats, prioritize those threats into risks, and identify controls that can reduce the risks to acceptable levels. Knowing the control requirements in the design phase will help reduce costs when work begins on the project in the construction or development phase.

## Risk Analysis and Due Diligence

Risk analysis is the process that allows management to demonstrate that they have met their obligation of due diligence when making a decision whether or not to move forward with a new project, capital expenditure, investment strategy, or other such business process.

Due diligence has a number of variant definitions based on the industry that is being discussed. Typically, the consensus of these definitions address is the measure of prudent activity, or assessment, as is properly to be expected from, and ordinarily exercised by, a reasonable and prudent person under the particular circumstances; it is not measured by any absolute standard but depends on the relative facts of each case.

In brief, the risk analysis or PIA examines the factors that come into play when trying to determine whether a project should be approved. The PIA examines the tangible impacts, such as capital outlay, development costs, and long-term cost such as continued operations and maintenance. The risk analysis also addresses intangible impacts, such as customer connivance or regulatory compliance.

When the risk analysis is complete, the results are presented to a management oversight committee that is charged with reviewing new project requests and deciding whether or not to move forward. If the request is approved, the project is registered and a risk assessment is scheduled for early in the design phase of the DPDC or SDLC. The documentation is retained for a period of time and then can be used by the organization if ever there are any questions as to why a project was or was not approved.

## Risk Assessment and Fiduciary Duty

Because many organizations do not know what the threats and risks are to operate in the changing business environment, a formal risk assessment process must be conducted early in the design phase. Risk assessment provides a process to identify threats systematically and then determine risk levels based on a specific methodology designed for the organization conducting the assessment. By establishing a risk level the project under development, an organization can then look to identify control measures that will reduce the risk to acceptable levels.

Risk assessment has four key deliverables. It will identify threats to the organization's mission, prioritize those threats into risk levels, identify mitigating controls or safeguards, and create an action plan to implement those mitigating controls.

The output from the risk analysis and risk assessment processes will generally be used twice. The first time will be when decisions are made; for the risk analysis that means deciding whether or not to proceed on a new project and for the risk assessment, what types of controls or safeguards need to be implemented. For risk assessment, the output will identify what countermeasures should be implemented or that management has determined that the best decision is to accept the risk.

The other time the results will be used is when the "spam hits the fan." That is, when a problem arises and the organization must show the process it used to reach the decisions that it did. The documentation created in the risk management processes will allow the organization to show who was involved, what was discussed, what was considered, and what decisions where made.

By implementing risk analysis and risk assessment, an organization has the tools in place to make informed business decisions. By integrating these processes across the entire enterprise, the organization can take back control of its activities from outside interference. With an effective risk assessment process in place, only those controls and safeguards that are actually needed will be implemented. An enterprise will never again face having to implement a mandated control to "be in compliance with audit requirements."

## Conducting a Risk Assessment

No one knows better about your organization than your own employees. An external consultant can lead a risk assessment, but to get a true grasp of and understanding on how current controls are working, where the threats are, and what risks these threats present requires the input from your own employees. Your employees are an excellent resource for this knowledge.

If your organization is fortunate enough to have a project management office, then the facilitators from this group would be perfect for conducting the risk management processes. There are some groups that, because of their charters and responsibilities, would be in a conflict of interest to lead or facilitate these processes. Applications development is a group that could have an impact on both risk analysis and risk assessment. Their job is to create applications and systems as quickly and efficiently as possible. So there could be an appearance of conflict of interest.

The audit staff and systems operations are two other groups that have charters of responsibility that would give an appearance of conflict of interest.

## Risk Assessment Timetable

It should be completed in days, not weeks or months. To meet the needs of an enterprise, the risk management process must be able to complete it quickly with a minimum of impact on the employees' already-busy schedule. We currently offer a class in "how to complete a risk assessment in five days or less." This class has been very popular and the process is field-tested every month to ensure that the five-day time limit is attainable.

Time is a very precious commodity and processes such as risk management must be structured to be fast and efficient. As you will see, if there is more time available, then there is no end to the different things that can be done. Most organizations, however, have little enough time to spare.

## Risk Assessment and Risk Analysis Results

Risk assessment can identify to the enterprise what the threats are, and which threats pose the greatest risk to the organization. By identifying the areas of greatest risk, management can concentrate on addressing the areas of risk. Our resources are limited and the risk identification process will allow management to deploy these limited resources to where they can be most advantageous. The goal of risk assessment is not to eliminate all risk but to reduce risk to an acceptable level.

The greatest benefit of a risk analysis is to determine whether or not it is prudent to proceed with a new project. It allows management to examine existing tangible and intangible issues and then decide if moving forward with a project makes sound business sense.

## Risk Management Metrics

The tangible way to measure success is to see a lower bottom line for cost. Risk assessment can assist in this process by identifying only those controls that are needed to be implemented. Organizations are not implementing controls because they *think* they are needed. Only those actions that are *actually* required are being implemented.

For risk analysis the metric is that only those projects that show a true business need are being implemented.

Another way that the success of a risk analysis and risk assessment is measured is if there is a time when management decisions are called into review. By having a formal process in place that demonstrates the due diligence of management in the decision-making process this kind of inquiry will be dealt with quickly and successfully.

## Summary

The risk management process is a business process that supports management in its decision-making process. Risk analysis ensures that those projects that are needed by the business are screened, approved, funded, and implemented. The risk assessment process provides management with the tools needed to perform their fiduciary responsibility of protecting the assets of the enterprise in a reasonable and prudent manner. These processes do not have to be a long, drawn-out affairs. To be effective, risk analysis and risk assessment must be done quickly and efficiently.

# *Appendix G*

# Sample Threat Checklist

For years I have worked to establish a sample list of threats that could be used by risk management professionals to expedite the risk assessment process. A few years ago when I was doing a class in Brazil a student gave me a URL that has helped the threat identification process. A German organization, IT-Grundschutz, has established two important lists for the risk management professional. The organization's aim is to achieve a security level for IT systems that is reasonable and adequate to satisfy normal protection requirements and that can also serve as the basis for IT systems and applications requiring a high degree of protection. This is achieved through the appropriate application of organizational, personnel, infrastructural, and technical standard security safeguards.

The threats catalog contains 426 pages of threats in detail. The threats are divided into five categories:

| Threat Category | Number of Threats |
|---|---|
| Force majeure | 15 |
| Organizational shortcomings | 101 |
| Human failure | 76 |
| Technical threat | 52 |
| Deliberate acts | 126 |

The URL to access the list of threats (Table G.2) is http//www.bsi/English/gshb/index.htm.

**Table G.1 Sample Threat Checklist**

| Threat | Applicable (Yes/No) |
|---|---|
| **Integrity** | |
| Data stream could be intercepted. | |
| Faulty programming could (inadvertently) modify data. | |
| Written or electronic copies of reports could be diverted to unauthorized or unintended persons. | |
| Data could be entered incorrectly. | |
| Intentional incorrect data entry. | |
| Use of outdated programs could compromise integrity of information. | |
| Faulty hardware could result in inaccurate data entry and analysis. | |
| Third parties could modify data. | |
| Files could be accidentally deleted. | |
| Hackers could change data. | |
| Internal users could launch unauthorized programs to access and or modify bank data. | |
| Reports could be falsified. | |
| Internal theft of information by employees could be modified and used later. | |
| Network sniffing could intercept user passwords and allow unauthorized modification of information. | |
| Information could be outdated. | |
| Hackers could obtain unauthorized access into network to corrupt system resources. | |
| Physical intrusion by unauthorized persons. | |
| Documents could be falsified to appear as official company documents. | |
| Unauthorized or fictitious sales could be approved. | |
| Information could be misinterpreted due to language barriers. | |
| Fraudulent programming could impact data integrity, e.g., hidden hooks. | |
| Computer viruses could modify data. | |
| Information could be misdirected. | |
| Transactions could be intentionally not run or misrouted. | |
| Newer or upgraded software could cause corruption of documents or files. | |

**Table G.1 (continued)   Sample Threat Checklist**

| Threat | Applicable (Yes/No) |
|---|---|
| Non-standard procedures could cause misinterpretation of information. | |
| Unauthorized persons may use an unattended workstation. | |
| Information to and from third parties could be corrupted in transmission. | |
| Account information may be shared. | |
| A power failure could corrupt information. | |
| Information could be submitted in a vague or misleading manner. | |
| Someone could impersonate a customer to corrupt records (identity theft). | |
| Information could be taken outside the company. | |
| Integrity of information could be compromised due to decay of information media. | |
| Someone could impersonate an employee to corrupt information. | |
| A terminated employee could intentionally corrupt information. | |
| Company could be targeted for system hacking by a dissatisfied customer. | |
| A default username and password for a network device could be exploited to gain access to system resources. | |
| Confidentiality | |
| Insecure e-mail could contain confidential information. | |
| Internal theft of information. | |
| Employee is not able to verify the identity of a client, e.g., phone masquerading. | |
| Confidential information is left in plain view on a desk. | |
| Social discussions outside the office could result in disclosure of sensitive information. | |
| Information could be salvaged by unauthorized persons from dumpsters or other waste receptacles. | |
| Information sent to third parties may be misused. | |
| Unattended computer could give unauthorized access to files. | |
| Passwords may not be required for all workstations. | |
| Mailing two or more different customer statements/documents in one envelope. | |
| Unauthorized people in confidential or restricted areas. | |

*continued*

**Table G.1 (continued)   Sample Threat Checklist**

| Threat | Applicable (Yes/No) |
|---|---|
| Confidential information may be left on the fax or copy machine granting unauthorized viewing of documents. | |
| Fraudulent or misrepresentation of individuals in phone conversations. | |
| Response to a fax request without verification. | |
| Documents sent out for authorization could be forged and then returned. | |
| Unauthorized access to information by viewing documents over the shoulder of an employee (shoulder surfing). | |
| Documents could be excessively duplicated. | |
| Employee passwords could be shared. | |
| Interoffice messengers may handle confidential information. | |
| Employee and messenger relationships could exchange sensitive or confidential information. | |
| Unauthorized disclosure of information by third parties. | |
| Not adequately destroying electronic media may leave information available to unauthorized persons. | |
| Inadequate firewall configuration could inadvertently allow disclosure of information. | |
| Actual client information could be used on templates causing disclosure of sensitive information. | |
| Employees may be overheard discussing confidential information outside the office. | |
| Documents could be inadvertently delivered to wrong person. | |
| Holding phone conversations when unable to verify identity. | |
| Company could be subjected to electronic eavesdropping. | |
| Terminated employees may be able to access the building or information. | |
| Cleaning crews may see confidential information. | |
| Rubbish could contain confidential information. | |
| Employees may not follow the dual control procedures. | |
| Temporary or new employees may be insufficiently trained. | |
| Restricted areas may be accessed by visitors. | |
| Use of the speaker phone may violate confidentiality. | |
| Information and files may be inappropriately accessed on company's systems. | |

**Table G.1 (continued)  Sample Threat Checklist**

| *Threat* | *Applicable (Yes/No)* |
|---|---|
| Data stored off site could be compromised. | |
| Employees may install illegal or unauthorized software. | |
| Consultants or other contracted help may view confidential information. | |
| Availability | |
| Files stored in personal directories may not be available to other employees when needed. | |
| Hardware failures could impact the availability of company resources. | |
| A failure in the data circuit could prohibit system access. | |
| "Acts of God": tornado, tsunami, hurricane. | |
| Upgrades in the software may prohibit access. | |
| Company system could be unavailable or down. | |
| Eating and drinking at a workstation could cause keyboard failure. | |
| An undersecured work area could jeopardize the confidentiality of customer information. | |
| A power failure could interrupt employee access. | |
| Software upgrades could affect other programs. | |
| Expired user access and/or insufficient employee training could disrupt the computer system. | |
| Availability of PCs shared by multiple users may be inadequate. | |
| Vendor or supplier support personnel may be unavailable due to the time zone differences. | |
| A communication failure could disrupt business operations. | |
| Employees may have incorrect or inappropriate file access. | |
| If a person is out (sick/absent) some critical files cannot be accessed. | |
| Issues with third-party support to fix problems would give access to confidential information. | |
| An absent person or tools could prevent backup if not available. | |
| Company could be subject to bombs or other acts of terrorism. | |
| Theft of equipment or other information. | |
| Insufficient cross-training of critical procedures could impact Fred's business processes. | |
| Availability of information resources controlled by third party could impact business processes. | |

*continued*

**Table G.1 (continued)    Sample Threat Checklist**

| Threat | *Applicable (Yes/No)* |
|---|---|
| Damaged or altered storage or hardware media. | |
| Not all workstations have all programs loaded. | |
| Users could lose or misplace files. | |
| In today's environment there is a risk of man-made threats. | |
| Geography and getting materials in, due to distance. | |
| Vandalism and sabotage could be attempted to the network. | |
| Number of software licenses could be Insufficient. | |
| Insufficient personnel resources could impact business processes | |
| A computer virus could be introduced via e-mail or disk. | |
| Denial-of-service attacks from malicious Internet users outside of Fred's. | |
| Employee causes a document to be inaccessible temporarily due to human error. | |
| Natural threat | |
| Electrical storm | |
| Ice storm | |
| Snowstorm/blizzard | |
| Major landslide | |
| Mudslide | |
| Tsunami | |
| Tornado | |
| Hurricane/typhoon | |
| High winds (70+ mph) | |
| Tropical storm | |
| Tidal flooding | |
| Seasonal flooding | |
| Local flooding | |
| Upstream dam /reservoir failure | |
| Sandstorm | |
| Volcanic activity | |
| Earthquake (2–4 on Richter scale) | |
| Earthquake (5 or more on Richter scale) | |
| Epidemic | |
| Human — Accidental | |

**Table G.1 (continued)   Sample Threat Checklist**

| *Threat* | *Applicable (Yes/No)* |
|---|---|
| Fire: Internal–minor | |
| Fire: Internal–major | |
| Fire: Internal–catastrophic | |
| Fire: External | |
| Accidental explosion — on site | |
| Accidental explosion — off site | |
| Aircraft crash | |
| Train crash | |
| Derailment | |
| Auto/truck crash at site | |
| Human error — maintenance | |
| Human error — operational | |
| Human error — programming | |
| Human error — users | |
| Toxic contamination | |
| Medical emergency | |
| Loss of key staff | |
| Human — deliberate | |
| Environmental | |
| Power flux | |
| Power outage — internal | |
| Power outage — external | |
| Water leak/plumbing failure | |
| HVAC failure | |
| Temperature inadequacy | |
| Telecommunications failure | |
| Toxic contamination | |

**Table G.2   Natural Security Threats List**

| Threat | Definition |
|---|---|
| 1. Terrorism | This issue concerns foreign power–sponsored or foreign power–coordinated activities that:<br><br>■ Involve violent acts.<br>■ Appear to be intended to intimidate or coerce.<br>■ Transcend national boundaries. |
| 2. Espionage | Foreign power–sponsored or foreign power–coordinated intelligence activity directed at the U.S. government or U.S. corporations, establishments, or persons, which involves the identification, targeting, and collection of U.S. national defense information. |
| 3. Proliferation | Foreign power–sponsored or foreign power–coordinated intelligence activity directed at the U.S. government or U.S. corporations, establishments or persons, which involves:<br><br>■ The proliferation of weapons of mass destruction to include chemical, biological, or nuclear weapons, and delivery systems of those weapons of mass destruction; or<br>■ The proliferation of advanced conventional weapons. |
| 4. Economic espionage | Foreign power–sponsored or foreign power–coordinated intelligence activity directed at the U.S. government or U.S. corporations, establishments, or persons, which involves:<br><br>■ The unlawful or clandestine targeting or acquisition of sensitive financial, trade, or economic policy information, proprietary economic information, or critical technologies; or<br>■ The unlawful or clandestine targeting or influencing of sensitive economic policy decisions. |
| 5. Targeting the national information infrastructure | Foreign power–sponsored or foreign power–coordinated intelligence activity directed at the U.S. government or U.S. corporations, establishments, or persons, which involves the targeting of facilities, personnel, information, or computer, cable, satellite, or telecommunications systems which are associated with the national information infrastructure. Proscribed intelligence activities include: |

**Table G.2 (continued)   Natural Security Threats List**

| Threat | Definition |
|---|---|
| | ■ Denial or disruption of computer, cable, satellite, or telecommunications services;<br>■ Unauthorized monitoring of computer, cable, satellite, or telecommunications systems;<br>■ Unauthorized disclosure of proprietary or classified information stored within or communicated through computer, cable, satellite, or telecommunications systems;<br>■ Unauthorized modification or destruction of computer programming codes, computer network databases, stored information, or computer capabilities; or<br>■ Manipulation of computer, cable, satellite, or telecommunications services resulting in fraud, financial loss, or other federal criminal violations. |
| 6. Targeting the U.S. government | Foreign power–sponsored or foreign power–coordinated intelligence activity directed at the U.S. government or U.S. corporations, establishments, or persons, which involves the targeting of government programs, information, or facilities, or the targeting or personnel of:<br><br>■ The U.S. intelligence community;<br>■ The U.S. foreign affairs, or economic affairs community; or<br>■ The U.S. defense establishment and related activities of national preparedness. |
| 7. Perception management | Foreign power–sponsored or foreign power–coordinated intelligence activity directed at the U.S. government or U.S. corporations, establishments, or persons, which involves manipulating information, communicating false information, or propagating deceptive information and communications designed to distort the perception of the public (domestically or internationally) or of U.S. government officials regarding U.S. policies, ranging from foreign policy to economic strategies. |
| 8. Foreign intelligence activities | Foreign power–sponsored or foreign power–coordinated intelligence activity conducted in the United States, or directed against the U.S. government, or U.S. corporations, establishments, or persons, that is not described by or included in the other issue threats. |

*Source:* http://www.ntc.doe.gov/cita/CI_Awareness_Guide/T1threat/Nstl.htm
(Department of Energy National Training Center).

# *Appendix H*

# Sample BIA
# Questionnaire

# Business Impact Analysis Checklist
## The Excellent University Business Impact Analysis Form
### (For Administrative Departments and the Administrative Support Functions and Staff within Schools and the Deans' Offices)

The purpose of the Business Impact Analysis (BIA) is to determine the criticality to the university of a given business process (e.g., student billing, accounts payable, admissions, grades and transcripts, HR functions, etc.) and the losses and/or risks which may be incurred if this process were not available for a given period of time. This questionnaire is designed to collect the information necessary to support the development of alternative processing strategies and solutions.

---

Respondent Information: Please complete one questionnaire for each business process performed by your department. Please note that all questions should be answered if applicable. Wherever possible, please provide additional information to qualify and clarify your answers. Please use the comments fields if the question seems to apply but the choices of answers seem not to. If a question is genuinely not applicable, that should be noted.

---

1. Process Name: _____

2. Participant Name/Title: _____

3. University Process Description:

_____
_____
_____
_____
_____

4. List all ITS systems, applications, or services which are critical to the performance of this function.

System or Application Name: _____

System or Application Name: _____

System or Application Name: _____

5. How long can this university process continue to function without its usual I/S support? Assume that loss of I/S support occurs during your busiest or peak period. Please check one only.

Less than 1 day _____    Up to 2 weeks _____
Up to 2 days _____    Up to 1 month _____
Up to 4 days _____    Up to 3 months _____
Up to 1 week _____    3 months or longer _____

Comments:

_____

_____

_____

**6. What was the longest time this university process was unable to function due to the loss or interruption of its usual I/S support in the last 5 years?**

Less than 1 day _____         Up to 1 week _____
Up to 2 days _____            Up to 2 weeks _____
Up to 4 days _____            Up to 1 month _____
            1 month or longer _____
Comments:

_____

_____

---

**7. How frequently is this university process performed?**

☐ **Hourly** ☐ **daily** ☐ **weekly** ☐ **monthly** ☐ **annually** ☐ **other (explain)**

Comments:

_____

_____

_____

**8. Indicate the peak and/or critical time of year and/or day of the week, if any, for this university process.**

| _____January | _____Monday | _____End of Week |
| _____February | _____Tuesday | _____End of Month |
| _____March | _____Wednesday | _____End of Quarter |
| _____April | _____Thursday | _____End of Fiscal Year |
| _____May | _____Friday | _____End of Calendar Year |
| _____June | _____Saturday | _____Other (please specify) |
| _____July | _____Sunday | |
| _____August | | |
| _____September | | |
| _____October | | |
| _____November | | |
| _____December | | |

**Please explain why**:

_____

_____

_____

_____

_____

**9. Interaction with / dependency on other systems, applications, or processes:**

_____

_____

_____

**10. Future System Changes:**

(Are there any major system changes scheduled and if so how will they affect the business function/process?)

_____

_____

_____

> **Respondent Information: The following questions attempt to measure and categorize the impact on your department and the university as a whole from and interruption to or the unavailability of this university business function. This is not an exact science, and you are not requested to do extensive cost analyses, for example. Use your judgment and knowledge to provide informed estimates.**

**11. Tangible (monetary) Impact:**

Y/N                                                              Impact: High (**H**), Medium (**M**), Low (**L**)

_____        Increased Costs/Expenses                          _____
_____        Reduced Income (all sources)                      _____
_____        Regulatory Penalties or Fees                      _____

Please give your best estimate of the actual cost to the University if this Business Process could not be provided?

_____ Less than $1,000                    _____ Between $100,000 to $499,999
_____ Between $1,000 to $9,000            _____ Between $500,000 to $9,999,999
_____ Between $10,000 to $99,000          _____ $1,000,000 or more

Please circle one:  Per Day of Outage    Per Week of Outage    Per Month of Outage

**Comments:**

_____

_____

_____

**12. Intangible Impact:**

Y/N                                                              Priority: High (**H**), Medium (**M**), Low (**L**)

_____        Damage to University Reputation                    _____
_____        Reduction in Service / Customer Dissatisfaction    _____

| | |
|---|---|
| _____ Loss of Student Trust/Confidence | _____ |
| _____ Loss of Competitive Edge in Recruiting, Grants, etc. | _____ |
| _____ Threat to Student/Employee/Public Health & Safety | _____ |
| _____ Regulatory/Statutory Penalties, Citations | _____ |

**Comments:**

_____

_____

_____

**13. Using the following labels, indicate the relative impact of the loss of this process for each of the time frame slots below. Assume the outage is continuous and occurs during a time of peak business activity.**

- CATASTROPHIC Out of business and/or endanger public safety
- SIGNIFICANT Major impact on the long-term financial status of the university, and/or major disruption of educational or research activities, and/or endanger public safety
- MODERATE Major impact on the short-term financial status of the university, and/or temporary disruption of educational or research activities
- MINOR No impact to the financial status of the university, no significant disruption of educational or research activities.

After:
- 1 Hour _____
- 8 Hours _____
- 48 Hours _____
- 72 Hours _____
- 1 Week _____
- 1 Month _____

Comments:

_____

_____

_____

**Information Processing**

> **Respondent Information: The following questions refer to use of IT systems for <u>this</u> university function in <u>your</u> department or unit, not the university as a whole.**
> **E.g., how many people in your office use Banner, not how many Banner users are there in the university.**

**14. System or application and number of local users**

_____ # of users _____

_____ # of users _____

_____ # of users _____

Comments:

_____

_____

_____

_____

**15. Major Input Documents (essential to this function)**
**15a. (If not internally generated, indicate how and from where they come to you.)**

_____

_____

_____

**16. Major Output Documents/Reports (essential to this function)**
**16a. (If not for internal use, indicate where or to whom you send them.)**

_____

_____

_____

_____

**17. Type of IT System Use:**      On-line Inquiry_____      On-line Update _____

    Data entry for batch update _____      Other _____

Comments:

_____

_____

_____

_____

**18. Frequency of IT System Use:**      Daily (# hrs) _____ Weekly (# hrs) _____

  Other (explain) _____

Comments:

_____

_____

_____

**19. Location of IT System Use:**      Office desktops _____ Mobile laptops _____

  Remote: Web (Public Terminals, other) _____      Home (GoToMyPC) _____

Comments:

_____

_____

_____

## USER DEPARTMENT COPING STRATEGIES

**19. ALTERNATE PROCESSING CAPABILITY** (to prevent/reduce impact):

A. Are there any documented manual procedures that could be used without I/S support:

B. When were the manual procedures last tested or used?

C. Additional supplies required: (tables, office supplies, desks, chairs)

Cost: _____

D. Additional hardware required: (workstations, check signers, modems, terminals)

Cost: _____

E. Additional personnel requirements: (office workers, runners, security personnel)

Cost: _____

F. At what percentage level would production drop, when utilizing alternate processing mode:

% drop = ____

G. What is the maximum length of time which this alternate process could be performed:

**20. Additional Comments**:

_____
_____
_____
_____
_____
_____
_____
_____
_____
_____
_____
_____
_____

**Interviewer:** _____     **Date:** _____

## BUSINESS IMPACT ANALYSIS

*Complete a copy of this form for each business activity.*
**For each business activity, identify the:**
a.) Systems upon which it relies to perform its necessary business function, and,
b.) Any systems that contain confidential information.

**Business Activity:**
**Activity Owner:**
**Weight Assigned:**

| No. | Application (See #2 below) | Does application support mission critical activity? (See #3 below) | Does application contain confidential information? | Acceptable downtime period? (hrs, days, wks, etc.) (See #4 below) |
|-----|------|------|------|------|
| 1 | | | | |
| 2 | | | | |
| 3 | | | | |
| 4 | | | | |
| 5 | | | | |
| 6 | | | | |
| 7 | | | | |
| 8 | | | | |

1. **Business Activity, Activity Owner,** and **Weight Assigned** should be obtained from the Form 1's.
2. Application or manual process upon which the **business activity** is dependent to produce its product(s) and/or service(s). [Note: All applications regardless of platform should be listed.]
3. Applications or manual processes that are relied upon to produce the **business activities'** mission critical product and/or service should be classified as critical. (Refer to output from Step 1 to determine the mission critical nature of the business activity.)
4. Since many applications are cyclical in nature, an acceptable downtime period may differ depending on the time of the year when an outage may occur. Responses should assume a "worst case" scenario when answering this question.

> Scope:
> Recovery of GLBA Bank business processes

The purpose of the Business Impact Analysis (BIA) is to determine the criticality to the company of a given business process (e.g., billing, accounts payable, marketing, customer support, HR, etc.) and the losses that may be incurred if this process were not available for a given period of time. This questionnaire is designed to collect the information necessary to support the development of alternative processing strategies and solutions.

Please note that all questions should be answered. Wherever possible, please provide additional information to qualify and clarify your answers. If a question is not applicable, it should be noted.

> Respondent Information: Please complete one questionnaire for each business process performed by your department

Name: _____

Title: _____

Department: _____

Business Process: _____

Phone Number: _____

> Business Process Description (one form for each)

Please provide a brief description of the business process as it relates to your department:

_____

_____

_____

_____

> Process Frequency

How frequently is/are the previously selected business process(es) performed?

☐ Hourly        ☐ Daily        ☐ Weekly        ☐ Monthly        ☐ Annually

Comments:_____

### Critical Time Periods

What are the most critical time periods for the previously selected business process(es)? Please explain if a particular hour(s), day, week, month, or quarter is more significant than another.

☐ Daily   ☐ End of Week   ☐ Month-end   ☐ Quarter-end   ☐ Year-end   ☐ Other _____

Comments:_____

_____

### Cyclical Processing

Identify cyclical processing periods in your department and whether important functions are involved in these fluctuations.*

|  | Jan | Feb | Mar | Apr | May | June | July | Aug | Sept | Oct | Nov | Dec |
|---|---|---|---|---|---|---|---|---|---|---|---|---|
| Extremely Busy | O | O | O | O | O | O | O | O | O | O | O | O |
| Slightly Busy | O | O | O | O | O | O | O | O | O | O | O | O |
| Normal | O | O | O | O | O | O | O | O | O | O | O | O |
| Slightly Slow | O | O | O | O | O | O | O | O | O | O | O | O |

* Please indicate what functions are generating above/below normal workloads, reasons these functions are cyclical, and how the department manages this workflow (overtime, temporary staff, re-prioritized functions, etc.)

Comments:_____

_____

### Outage Tolerance

What is the maximum timeframe that the business process(es) could be suspended in the event of a disaster?

☐ Immediately          ☐ 1 Business Day          ☐ 2 Business Days
☐ 7 Business Days       ☐ 15 Business Days        ☐ 30 Business Days
☐ Other (please specify)

Comments:_____

_____

| Financial Impact |
|---|

Quantifying the financial impact of losing a business process/function is key to the BIA. It is important that all costs (tangible and intangible, recoverable and irrecoverable) associated with a potential loss be identified. Costs may vary from day to day and vary over time (e.g., incremental penalty payments which increase daily). These costs may be incurred at different points as either daily or one-time costs.

What is the expected revenue loss/financial impact to *GLBA Bank* if this business process/function were not completed for the time periods indicated following a disaster? Please assume that a business disruption has occurred at your facility (e.g., a fire) and you cannot gain access to your normal work environment.

Immediately:     $_____
1 Day:              $_____
2-3 Days:          $_____
1 Week:            $_____
1 Month:          $_____

Comments:_____

_____

_____

Estimate what additional costs (fines, lost leases, canceled contracts, lost discounts, temporary help, etc.) *GLBA Bank* would incur if this business function were not restored in an appropriate time following an outage:

Immediately:     $_____
1 Day:              $_____
2-3 Days:          $_____
1 Week:            $_____
1 Month:          $_____

Comments:_____

_____

_____

**Non-Financial Impact**

Please rank the impacts that will occur if each business process is interrupted for the time periods stated below with one (1) having "No Impact" and five (5) having the "Greatest Impact."

*Internal Customer Needs*

If this business process(es) cannot be performed the ability for *GLBA Bank* to meet internal customer needs (i.e., other *GLBA Bank* business units/processes) will be adversely impacted. Where possible, identify in the space below those units that will be affected the most.

| | No Impact | | | | Greatest Impact |
|---|---|---|---|---|---|
| Instantly: | ☐ 1 | ☐ 2 | ☐ 3 | ☐ 4 | ☐ 5 |
| 1 Day: | ☐ 1 | ☐ 2 | ☐ 3 | ☐ 4 | ☐ 5 |
| 2 Days: | ☐ 1 | ☐ 2 | ☐ 3 | ☐ 4 | ☐ 5 |
| 3 Days: | ☐ 1 | ☐ 2 | ☐ 3 | ☐ 4 | ☐ 5 |
| 1 Week: | ☐ 1 | ☐ 2 | ☐ 3 | ☐ 4 | ☐ 5 |

Affected Units:_____

_____

_____

*Customer Service/External Needs*

Customer service would be impacted if the previously selected business process(es) were not completed following a disaster. Where possible, identify in the space below those entities that will be affected the most.

| | No Impact | | | | Greatest Impact |
|---|---|---|---|---|---|
| Instantly: | ☐ 1 | ☐ 2 | ☐ 3 | ☐ 4 | ☐ 5 |
| 1 Day: | ☐ 1 | ☐ 2 | ☐ 3 | ☐ 4 | ☐ 5 |
| 2 Days: | ☐ 1 | ☐ 2 | ☐ 3 | ☐ 4 | ☐ 5 |
| 3 Days: | ☐ 1 | ☐ 2 | ☐ 3 | ☐ 4 | ☐ 5 |
| 1 Week: | ☐ 1 | ☐ 2 | ☐ 3 | ☐ 4 | ☐ 5 |

External Entities: _____

_____

### Operating Efficiency

It would impact the operating efficiency of the business unit if the previously selected Business Process(es) were not available following a disaster.

| | No Impact | | | | Greatest Impact |
|---|---|---|---|---|---|
| Instantly: | □ 1 | □ 2 | □ 3 | □ 4 | □ 5 |
| 1 Day: | □ 1 | □ 2 | □ 3 | □ 4 | □ 5 |
| 2 Days: | □ 1 | □ 2 | □ 3 | □ 4 | □ 5 |
| 3 Days: | □ 1 | □ 2 | □ 3 | □ 4 | □ 5 |
| 1 Week: | □ 1 | □ 2 | □ 3 | □ 4 | □ 5 |

### Legal & Regulatory Requirements

Legal or regulatory requirements would not be met if the previously selected business process(es) were not available.

| | No Impact | | | | Greatest Impact |
|---|---|---|---|---|---|
| Instantly: | □ 1 | □ 2 | □ 3 | □ 4 | □ 5 |
| 1 Day: | □ 1 | □ 2 | □ 3 | □ 4 | □ 5 |
| 2 Days: | □ 1 | □ 2 | □ 3 | □ 4 | □ 5 |
| 3 Days: | □ 1 | □ 2 | □ 3 | □ 4 | □ 5 |
| 1 Week: | □ 1 | □ 2 | □ 3 | □ 4 | □ 5 |

### Industry Reputation & Image

If the business process(es) cannot be performed the ability to maintain *GLBA Bank's* corporate image will be adversely affected.

| | No Impact | | | | Greatest Impact |
|---|---|---|---|---|---|
| Instantly: | □ 1 | □ 2 | □ 3 | □ 4 | □ 5 |
| 1 Day: | □ 1 | □ 2 | □ 3 | □ 4 | □ 5 |
| 2 Days: | □ 1 | □ 2 | □ 3 | □ 4 | □ 5 |
| 3 Days: | □ 1 | □ 2 | □ 3 | □ 4 | □ 5 |
| 1 Week: | □ 1 | □ 2 | □ 3 | □ 4 | □ 5 |

**Employee Morale**

The Department Name will experience ill-will with the user community or suppliers if this previously selected business process(es) were not available following a disaster.

|  | No Impact | | | | Greatest Impact |
|---|---|---|---|---|---|
| Instantly: | ☐ 1 | ☐ 2 | ☐ 3 | ☐ 4 | ☐ 5 |
| 1 Day: | ☐ 1 | ☐ 2 | ☐ 3 | ☐ 4 | ☐ 5 |
| 2 Days: | ☐ 1 | ☐ 2 | ☐ 3 | ☐ 4 | ☐ 5 |
| 3 Days: | ☐ 1 | ☐ 2 | ☐ 3 | ☐ 4 | ☐ 5 |
| 1 Week: | ☐ 1 | ☐ 2 | ☐ 3 | ☐ 4 | ☐ 5 |

**Interdependencies**

An interdependency exists when a function must interact with another function or resource before it is performed or completed. Examples of interdependencies include receipt of inventory and order information before manufacturing planning begins, consolidation of division results before corporate results are posted, or distribution of actual expense summaries before yearly budget preparation.

**Interdepartmental Reliance**

Please select each department which your department relies upon to perform the previously described business process(es).

☐                                              ☐
☐                                              ☐
☐                                              ☐
☐                                              ☐
☐                                              ☐

Please describe the inputs and outputs associated with this business process(es). An input or output may be a feed from/to another department, a report, a statement, etc.

| Input(s) to the business process(es) | Output(s) of the business process(es) |
|---|---|
| (*Note: There is not necessarily a one-to-one relationship between inputs and outputs) | |
| 1. _____ | 1. _____ |
| 2. _____ | 2. _____ |
| 3. _____ | 3. _____ |
| 4. _____ | 4. _____ |
| 5. _____ | 5. _____ |

---

**External Interdependencies**

Please identify the external entities which your department relies upon to perform the previously described business process(es).

☐ Service 1 ☐
☐ Service 2 ☐
☐ " ☐
☐ " ☐
☐ " ☐

Please identify the non *GLBA Bank* inputs and outputs for the identified business process(es). This may include electronic media (i.e., data feeds) or other non-automated service (i.e., mail, reports, etc.). Once again, there does not have to be a one-to-one relationship between inputs and outputs.

| Input(s) to the business process(es) | Output(s) |
|---|---|
| 1. _____ | 1. _____ |
| 2. _____ | 2. _____ |
| 3. _____ | 3. _____ |
| 4. _____ | 4. _____ |
| 5. _____ | 5. _____ |

---

**Computer Applications**

Please complete the chart below as it relates to each application/system that this business process(es) requires. This table will facilitate the "mapping" of each application to identify whether or not it is housed in the same location as the business process(es) it is supporting. The recovery time objective should be the number of hours (or days) by which the application must be made available.

| Application Name | Type of Hardware/Platform | | | | | Processing Location | Recovery Time Objective |
|---|---|---|---|---|---|---|---|
| | Mainframe | Client Server | LAN/WAN | Local | Other | | |
| *A listing of apps* | O | O | O | O | | | |
| *should be included!!* | O | O | O | O | | | |
| | O | O | O | O | | | |
| | O | O | O | O | | | |
| | O | O | O | O | | | |

**Alternate Procedures**

**Alternate Procedures - Loss of Entire Facility**

What alternate procedures could be employed, either manual or automated, if this business process(es) could not be performed, in the event of a disaster, and at what point in time would these procedures need to be enacted?

Procedures (by business process):
1. _____
2. _____
3. _____
4. _____
5. _____
Add lines or pages as necessary

**Alternate Procedures - Loss of Centralized Computer Systems ONLY**

What alternate procedures could be employed, either manual or automated, if the computer systems in *Data Center Location* were unavailable for more than one day, and at what point in time would these procedures need to be enacted?

Procedures (by business process):
1. _____
2. _____
3. _____
4. _____
5. _____
Add lines or pages as necessary

Alternate Site(s)

Please identify if an alternate processing site has been selected for the above business process(es) and state whether it is an internal or external (i.e., hotsite) facility.

Site(s): _____

_____

Other Issues

Please specify any other issues, not mentioned above, which you consider relevant in evaluating the impact of the loss of this business function.

Comments:_____

_____

_____

**Resource Requirements**

Resources Staffing & Recovery Resource Requirements: Please list the current number of resources required for this business process(es). In your opinion, identify the minimum resources, in the event of a disaster, that should be available during the recovery process (when resources may be limited) to perform the previously described business process(es).

| Resources | Number Currently Available | Number Required for Recovery | Time Frame |
|---|---|---|---|
| Personnel | _____ | _____ | _____ |
| Telephones | _____ | _____ | _____ |
| Network PCs/ Workstations | _____ | _____ | _____ |
| Non-Networked PCs | _____ | _____ | _____ |
| Modems | _____ | _____ | _____ |
| Printer | _____ | _____ | _____ |
| Photocopier | _____ | _____ | _____ |
| Fax Machine | _____ | _____ | _____ |
| Hardcopy Files (yes/no) | _____ | _____ | _____ |
| Microfiche/Microfilm | _____ | _____ | _____ |
| Special Forms & Stationery (please list forms required for recovery) | _____ | _____ | _____ |

Other (please specify below):

_____
_____
_____

*Note*: At a later stage of the plan development process, it may be necessary to clearly identify some of the above items (i.e., report names, types of supplies, unique equipment, etc.).

**Overall Ranking**

Rank this business process(es) criticality to *your department* on a scale from 0 to 5 (0 being the least critical, 5 being the most critical):                   RANK _____

Rank this business process(es) criticality to *GLBA Bank* on a scale from 0 to 5 (0 being the least critical, 5 being the most critical):                   RANK _____

# Business Impact Analysis Report

9-May-06
Version: Draft

**GLBA Bank**
**Business Impact Assessment Report**

## Table of Contents

## GLBA Bank
### Business Impact Assessment Report

# Management Summary

### Introduction

A business impact analysis (BIA) has been conducted at the bank. As this is the first time a BIA has been conducted at the bank (and because the BIA was performed within strict time constraints), this initial BIA has been conducted at a relatively high level (payroll, special assets, mortgage, etc.). Subsequent BIAs will be conducted at more detailed levels. (See Next Steps/Recommendations.)

### Critical Processes

The attached report shows the bank's business processes ranked in various modes of criticality. The rankings show:
- o  Criticality (as assigned by the process owner)
- o  Recovery sequence
- o  Equipment requirements
- o  Workaround procedures
- o  Relationships and dependencies
- o  Recovery space requirements
- o  Special forms
- o  Business impact (financial)
- o  Business impacts (non-financial)
- o  Systems and applications required by each process

### Next Steps/Recommendations

1. This BIA report must be reviewed by the level of management immediately above the level that participated in the BIA interviews. That level of management must review the report to affirm the criticality and values assigned to each process and, where a question arises, the reviewer must discuss the question with the interviewee and — when appropriate, amend the entry. This action should be completed within one month of the release of this report.
2. The bank's Disaster Management Plan must be reviewed and, as part of that review, each department should undertake a Business Impact Analysis (BIA) led by the Vice President of Compliance. This second iteration of the BIA should examine each process at a lower level of detail and should form the basis for amendments to the banks Disaster Management Plan. This action should commence as soon as possible after the release of this report.
3. The owners of the bank's ISD recovery plan, Item Processing recovery plan and Network recovery plan must review this report after the first recommendation in this section is completed. The criticality of each business process and the recovery sequence for business processes must be compared to relevant entries in these recovery plans and, where necessary, these recovery plans must be amended. We recommend this step should be started as soon as possible after the first recommendation is completed.

**GLBA Bank**
**Business Impact Assessment Report**

## Background

A business impact analysis (BIA) is the first step in developing and testing a business continuity plan. The BIA:
- Identifies the potential impact – on business processes – of unforeseen events.
- Includes all of an organization's departments and business functions (rather than simply IT).
- Provides estimates of maximum allowable outage time for each process and the losses and other impacts associated with such outages.

The BIA allows bank management to establish recovery priorities for business processes and those recovery processes identify key personnel, essential technologies and other resources necessary for recovery (such as vital records and data, facilities, etc.). The BIA also considers the impact of legal and regulatory requirements such as required notifications to the bank's federal regulator.

As this is the first time a bankwide BIA has been conducted, this initial BIA has been conducted at a relatively high level (payroll, special assets, mortgage, etc.). Subsequent BIAs will be conducted at more detailed levels. (See Next Steps/Recommendations.)

When conducting this BIA (as it is the first pass through the BIA and to work within time constraints), the bank focused on those business processes owned by departments other than the technology departments (ISD, Item Processing and PC Services). For the purpose of ranking technology processes by criticality in relation to the business processes of the bank, the entries in the BIA Consolidated Table (Attachment 1 to this report) were made to show the technology processes as being of the highest criticality. BIA interview summaries form Attachment 2 to this report.

Other entries in the BIA Consolidated table were forced (shown in red in the table). For example, although the interviewee could put no financial impact figure on the loss of Branch Operations, common sense says that Branch Operations is the most critical process in the bank and so a high financial impact number was forced into the table for Branch Operations to ensure that it appears at the top of the list for criticality.

## Current State Assessment

The bank has not conducted a formal, bankwide BIA but has performed rankings of criticality for the recovery plans it has in place. ISD and Item Processing recovery plans have been tested and updated. Network recovery plans have been drafted and will be tested upon completion of this BIA.

Disaster management plans for non-technology departments of the bank have been drafted but are outdated (for example, many departments' disaster management plans cite Ualena Street Operations Center as their first alternate site and there is no space to accommodate them at Ualena Street Operations Center). (See Next Steps/Recommendations.)

**GLBA Bank**
**Business Impact Assessment Report**

## Time Critical Business Processes

The BIA Consolidated Table has four worksheets:

o Timing – which shows the peak processing criticality and critical time periods for each process
o Dependencies – which shows each process's dependency on other bank departments and outside vendors and the inputs and outputs for each process.
o Impacts – which shows the financial impact of the loss of each process and the impacts of the inability to continue each process on:
  - Internal customers
  - External customers
  - Operating efficiency
  - Legal and regulatory compliance
  - The reputation of the bank
  - Employee morale
o Recovery 1 – which shows the technology requirements to recover each process and the alternate arrangements made to continue each process in the event that normal operations are interrupted
o Recovery 2 – which shows the resources necessary to recover each process in the event that normal business operations are disrupted. Resources shown are:
  - Personnel
  - Phones
  - Networked PCs
  - Standalone PCs
  - Modems
  - Printers
  - Photocopiers
  - Fax machines
  - Hardcopy files
  - Microfilm
  - Special forms
  - Criticality – which is a worksheet containing data from the other worksheets and used to sort in order of criticality as described below

Each worksheet on the table shows the criticality assigned to each process by the process owner.

*Criticality*

In order to show time critical business processes in order of criticality, the Criticality worksheet was sorted. The first sort order was the criticality of the process assigned by the process owner. The second sort order was the process owner's estimate of the financial impact on the bank of the process being unavailable. The third sort order was the number of days the process owner estimated that the process could be suspended with no marked impact on the bank. (Note: Due to the Peak Periods (Timing worksheet) associated with processes, some of this last number is

**GLBA Bank**
**Business Impact Assessment Report**

relative to those peak periods and so, on the Criticality worksheet they will not necessarily appear in order.)

The time critical business processes, in order of criticality, are shown in Table 1 below.

| Process | Department | Owner | Criticality | |
|---|---|---|---|---|
| | | | Overall | Dept. |
| Branch Operations | Cashiers | | 5 | 5 |
| IS Services | ISD | | 5 | 5 |
| Item Processing | Cashiers | | 5 | 5 |
| Network | PC Services | | 5 | 5 |
| General Ledger | Accounting | | 5 | 5 |
| Payroll | Human Resources | | 5 | 5 |
| Payroll | Accounting | | 5 | 5 |
| Internet Banking | Cashiers | | 5 | 5 |
| Mortgage Servicing | Mortgage | | 4 | 5 |
| Mortgage Origination | Mortgage | | 4 | 5 |
| Benefits | Human Resources | | 4 | 4 |
| Financial Statements | Accounting | | 3 | 3 |
| Corporate Banking | Corp. Banking | | 3 | 5 |
| Charge Card Issue | Charge Cards | | 3 | 4 |
| Wire Transfer | Cashiers | | 3 | 4 |
| Fedline | Cashiers | | 3 | 4 |
| Loan Services | Loan Services | | 3 | 5 |
| Loan Approval | Loan Services | | 3 | 4 |
| Merchant Services | Charge Cards | | 3 | 5 |
| Terminations | Charge Cards | | 3 | 3 |
| Disputed Charges | Charge Cards | | 3 | 3 |
| Recruitment | Human Resources | | 3 | 3 |
| Card Reissues | Charge Cards | | 3 | 3 |
| Loan Collection | Special Assets | | 3 | 5 |
| Accounts Payable | Accounting | | 2 | 2 |
| Branch Support | Marketing | | 2 | 5 |
| Credit Administration | Loan Administration | | 2 | 5 |
| ATM Card Reissue | Cashiers | | 1 | 2 |
| Fixed Assets | Accounting | | 1 | 1 |
| Internal Communications | Marketing | | 1 | 5 |
| Recovery | Special Assets | | 1 | 3 |

**Table 1 – Time Critical Business Processes**

**GLBA Bank**
**Business Impact Assessment Report**

*Recovery Sequence*

As each business process is heavily dependent on technology, it is safe to say that none can be recovered without the use of technology – ISD Network and Item Processing. (It may be argued that some bank processes could be done manually but this is impractical over a period of more than a few hours.) However, if we take it as given that the first step in a recovery scenario would be to recover the technology on which the bank depends, then the remainder of the recovery sequence must stem from recovering Branch Operations. In order to show this, the Criticality worksheet was sorted once again. The first sort order – as before – was the criticality assigned to the process by the business owner. The second sort order was the number of days the process owner estimated that the process could be suspended with no marked impact on the bank and the third sort order was the process owner's estimate of the financial impact on the bank of the process being unavailable.

The recovery sequence, excluding technology recovery that must precede these processes, is shown in Table 2 below:

| Process | Department | Owner | Criticality | |
|---|---|---|---|---|
| | | | Overall | Dept. |
| Branch Operations | Cashiers | | 5 | 5 |
| General Ledger | Accounting | | 5 | 5 |
| Internet Banking | Cashiers | | 5 | 5 |
| Payroll | Human Resources | | 5 | 5 |
| Payroll | Accounting | | 5 | 5 |
| Mortgage Servicing | Mortgage | | 4 | 5 |
| Mortgage Origination | Mortgage | | 4 | 5 |
| Benefits | Human Resources | | 4 | 4 |
| Wire Transfer | Cashiers | | 3 | 4 |
| Fedline | Cashiers | | 3 | 4 |
| Loan Services | Loan Services | | 3 | 5 |
| Charge Card Issue | Charge Cards | | 3 | 4 |
| Loan Approval | Loan Services | | 3 | 4 |
| Merchant Services | Charge Cards | | 3 | 5 |
| Terminations | Charge Cards | | 3 | 3 |
| Disputed Charges | Charge Cards | | 3 | 3 |
| Recruitment | Human Resources | | 3 | 3 |
| Financial Statements | Accounting | | 3 | 3 |
| Card Reissues | Charge Cards | | 3 | 3 |
| Corporate Banking | Corp. Banking | | 3 | 5 |
| Loan Collection | Special Assets | | 3 | 5 |
| Accounts Payable | Accounting | | 2 | 2 |
| Branch Support | Marketing | | 2 | 5 |
| Credit Administration | Loan Administration | | 2 | 5 |
| ATM Card Reissue | Cashiers | | 1 | 2 |
| Fixed Assets | Accounting | | 1 | 1 |
| Internal Communications | Marketing | | 1 | 5 |

**GLBA Bank**
**Business Impact Assessment Report**

| Process | Department | Owner | Criticality | |
|---------|-----------|-------|-------------|---|
| | | | Overall | Dept. |
| Recovery | Special Assets | | 1 | 3 |

Table 2 – Recovery Sequence

*Equipment Requirements*

The Recovery 2 worksheet shows each process's recovery requirements for personnel and equipment. Table 3 (next page) shows the processes sorted alphabetically by process name and the recovery requirements for personnel and equipment for each process.

**GLBA Bank**
**Business Impact Assessment Report**

| Process | | Personnel | Phones | Networked PCs | Modems | Printers | Photocopiers | Fax | Hardcopy Files | Microfilm | Special Forms |
|---|---|---|---|---|---|---|---|---|---|---|---|
| | | | | | | **Recovery Resource Requirements** | | | | | |
| Mortgage Servicing | | 4 | 4 | 4 | 1 | 1 | 1 | 1 | 1Y | N | Y |
| Benefits | | 1 | 1 | 1 | 0 | 1 | 0 | 0 | 0Y | N | Y |
| Payroll | | 1 | 1 | 1 | 0 | 1 | 0 | 0 | 0Y | N | Y |
| Recruitment | | 1 | 1 | 1 | 0 | 1 | 0 | 1 | 1Y | N | Y |
| Accounts Payable | | 1 | 1 | 1 | 0 | 1 | 0 | 0 | 0Y | N | Y |
| Financial Statements | | 1 | 0 | 1 | 0 | 1 | 1 | 1 | 0Y | N | N |
| Fixed Assets | | 1 | 0 | 1 | 0 | 1 | 0 | 0 | 0Y | N | N |
| General Ledger | | 5 | 2 | 3 | 0 | 1 | 0 | 0 | 1Y | Y | N |
| Payroll | | 1 | 1 | 1 | 0 | 1 | 0 | 0 | 0Y | N | N |
| Charge Card Issue | | 1 | 0 | 1 | 0 | 1 | 0 | 0 | 0Y | Y | N |
| Disputed Charges | | 1 | 1 | 1 | 0 | 1 | 0 | 0 | 0Y | Y | N |
| Merchant Services | | 1 | 1 | 1 | 0 | 1 | 0 | 0 | 0Y | Y | N |
| Card Reissues | | 1 | 1 | 1 | 0 | 1 | 0 | 0 | 0Y | Y | N |
| Terminations | | 1 | 1 | 1 | 0 | 1 | 0 | 0 | 0Y | Y | N |
| Credit Administration | | 3 | 1 | 2 | 0 | 1 | 1 | 1 | 1Y | N | N |
| ATM Card Reissue | | 1 | 0 | 1 | 0 | 1 | 0 | 0 | 0N | N | N |
| Branch Operations* | | 6 | 3 | 5 | 1 | 2 | 1 | 1 | 1Y | Y | Y |
| Fedline | | 2 | 0 | 1 | 1 | 1 | 0 | 0 | 1Y | N | N |
| Internet Banking | | 1 | 0 | 1 | 0 | 1 | 0 | 0 | 1Y | N | N |
| Wire Transfer | | 2 | 1 | 2 | 0 | 1 | 0 | 0 | 1Y | N | N |
| Branch Support | | 1 | 1 | 1 | 0 | 1 | 0 | 1 | 0Y | N | N |
| Internal Communications | | 1 | 1 | 1 | 0 | 1 | 0 | 0 | 0Y | N | N |
| Loan Approval | | 16 | 16 | 13 | 0 | 3 | 0 | 0 | 1Y | Y | N |
| Loan Services | | 6 | 3 | 6 | 0 | 2 | 1 | 1 | 1Y | N | N |
| Mortgage Origination | | 4 | 3 | 3 | 1 | 1 | 1 | 0 | 1Y | N | Y |
| Loan Collection | | 3 | 3 | 3 | 0 | 1 | 1 | 1 | 1Y | N | N |
| Recovery | | 1 | 1 | 1 | 0 | 1 | 1 | 1 | 1Y | N | Y |
| IS Services | ** | | | | | | | | | | |
| Network | *** | | | | | | | | | | |

**GLBA Bank**
**Business Impact Assessment Report**

| Process | Personnel | Phones | Networked PCs | Modems | Printers | Photocopiers | Fax | Hardcopy Files | Microfilm | Special Forms |
|---|---|---|---|---|---|---|---|---|---|---|
| | | | | | | | **Recovery Resource Requirements** | | | |
| Item Processing **** | | | | | | | | | | |
| Corporate Banking * | 1 | 1 | 1 | 0 | 1 | 1 | 1N | | N | N |
| * Resources are per branch | | | | | | | | | | |
| ** See ISD Recovery Plan | | | | | | | | | | |
| *** See PC Services Recovery Plan | | | | | | | | | | |
| **** See Item Processing Recovery Plan | | | | | | | | | | |

Table 3 – Equipment Requirements

**GLBA Bank**
**Business Impact Assessment Report**

*Workaround Procedures*

Workaround procedures are contained in the bank's Disaster Management Plan, the ISD recovery plan, the Network recovery plan, and the Item Processing recovery plan. Please see earlier comments in Current State Assessment and later comments in Next Steps/Recommendations.

*Relationships and Dependencies*

The Dependencies worksheet shows the internal and external dependencies for each process and the inputs and outputs for each process.

*Recovery Space Requirements*

Alternate sites for recovery are shown in the Recovery 1 worksheet. Please see earlier comments about space requirements in Current State Assessment.

*Special Forms*

The requirement for special forms is shown in the Recovery 2 worksheet. When further BIAs are conducted, the bank will list specific special forms required by each business process. (Please see later comments in Next Steps/Recommendations.)

## Business Impact (Financial)

In many cases process owners could not estimate financial impacts if a process were unavailable to the bank. As stated earlier, Branch Processing was one of these processes and so a number was forced into the BIA Consolidated Table to push that process to the top of the criticality lists.

Where process owners have been able to assign financial impacts, the Impacts worksheet was sorted to show each process in order according to the financial impact its unavailability would have on the bank. (Note: Previously forced numbers have been left in the table.)

The business impacts (financial) are shown in Table 4 below:

**GLBA Bank**
**Business Impact Assessment Report**

| Process | Department | Owner | Criticality | | Impacts |
| | | | | | Financial |
| | | | Overall | Dept. | (month) |
|---|---|---|---|---|---|
| Branch Operations | Cashiers | | | 5 | 5 $1,000,000 |
| IS Services | ISD | | | 5 | 5 $900,000 |
| Item Processing | Cashiers | | | 5 | 5 $900,000 |
| Network | PC Services | | | 5 | 5 $900,000 |
| Mortgage Servicing | Mortgage | | | 4 | 5 $500,000 |
| Financial Statements | Accounting | | | 3 | 3 $300,000 |
| General Ledger | Accounting | | | 5 | 5 $300,000 |
| Mortgage Origination | Mortgage | | | 4 | 5 $50,000 |
| Corporate Banking | Corp. Banking | | | 3 | 5 $30,000 |
| Charge Card Issue | Charge Cards | | | 3 | 4 $15,000 |
| Payroll | Human Resources | | | 5 | 5 $10,000 |
| Payroll | Accounting | | | 5 | 5 $10,000 |
| Benefits | Human Resources | | | 4 | 4 $7,500 |
| Internet Banking | Cashiers | | | 5 | 5 $5,000 |
| Wire Transfer | Cashiers | | | 3 | 4 $5,000 |
| Accounts Payable | Accounting | | | 2 | 2 $0 |
| ATM Card Reissue | Cashiers | | | 1 | 2 $0 |
| Branch Support | Marketing | | | 2 | 5 $0 |
| Card Reissues | Charge Cards | | | 3 | 3 $0 |
| Credit Administration | Loan Administration | | | 2 | 5 $0 |
| Disputed Charges | Charge Cards | | | 3 | 3 $0 |
| Fedline | Cashiers | | | 3 | 4 $0 |
| Fixed Assets | Accounting | | | 1 | 1 $0 |
| Internal Communications | Marketing | | | 1 | 5 $0 |
| Loan Approval | Loan Services | | | 3 | 4 $0 |
| Loan Collection | Special Assets | | | 3 | 5 $0 |
| Loan Services | Loan Services | | | 3 | 5 $0 |
| Merchant Services | Charge Cards | | | 3 | 5 $0 |
| Recovery | Special Assets | | | 1 | 3 $0 |
| Recruitment | Human Resources | | | 3 | 3 $0 |
| Terminations | Charge Cards | | | 3 | 3 $0 |

**Table 4 – Business Impact (Financial)**

## Business Impacts (Non-Financial)

Impacts other than financial impacts are listed in the Impacts worksheet. To show the impacts to the bank in order of the process criticality, the processes were sorted in the following order: The first sort order was the criticality assigned to each process by the owner of the process. The second sort order was the impact on the bank's operating efficiency and the third sort order was the impact on the bank's reputation.

The business impacts (non-financial) are shown in Table 5 below:

**GLBA Bank**
**Business Impact Assessment Report**

| Process | Criticality<br>Overall | Int.<br>Customers | Ext.<br>Customers | Operating<br>Efficiency | Legal &<br>Reg. | Reputation | Morale |
|---|---|---|---|---|---|---|---|
| Branch Operations | 5 | 0 | 5 | 5 | 0 | 5 | 0 |
| General Ledger | 5 | 5 | 0 | 5 | 5 | 5 | 0 |
| Internet Banking | 5 | 0 | 4 | 5 | 0 | 5 | 0 |
| IS Services | 5 | 5 | 5 | 5 | 5 | 5 | 0 |
| Item Processing | 5 | 5 | 5 | 5 | 5 | 5 | 0 |
| Network | 5 | 5 | 5 | 5 | 5 | 5 | 0 |
| Payroll | 5 | 0 | 0 | 4 | 4 | 5 | 5 |
| Payroll | 5 | 0 | 0 | 4 | 4 | 5 | 5 |
| Mortgage Origination | 4 | 0 | 5 | 5 | 0 | 5 | 0 |
| Benefits | 4 | 4 | 0 | 4 | 4 | 3 | 4 |
| Mortgage Servicing | 4 | 0 | 5 | 3 | 5 | 0 | 0 |
| Loan Approval | 3 | 4 | 5 | 4 | 0 | 4 | 0 |
| Loan Services | 3 | 4 | 5 | 4 | 0 | 4 | 0 |
| Corporate Banking | 3 | 3 | 4 | 2 | 0 | 2 | 0 |
| Recruitment | 3 | 2 | 0 | 2 | 0 | 0 | 0 |
| Loan Collection | 3 | 1 | 1 | 1 | 0 | 1 | 0 |
| Financial Statements | 3 | 1 | 1 | 1 | 1 | 0 | 0 |
| Wire Transfer | 3 | 3 | 3 | 0 | 0 | 5 | 0 |
| Card Reissues | 3 | 0 | 4 | 0 | 0 | 3 | 0 |
| Charge Card Issue | 3 | 3 | 3 | 0 | 0 | 2 | 0 |
| Disputed Charges | 3 | 0 | 3 | 0 | 0 | 2 | 0 |
| Merchant Services | 3 | 3 | 3 | 0 | 0 | 2 | 0 |
| Terminations | 3 | 0 | 3 | 0 | 0 | 2 | 0 |
| Fedline | 3 | 1 | 1 | 0 | 2 | 0 | 0 |
| Accounts Payable | 2 | 3 | 3 | 1 | 1 | 1 | 0 |
| Branch Support | 2 | 1 | 0 | 1 | 1 | 1 | 0 |
| Credit Administration | 2 | 1 | 1 | 0 | 0 | 0 | 0 |
| Recovery | 1 | 0 | 0 | 1 | 0 | 1 | 0 |
| ATM Card Reissue | 1 | 0 | 1 | 0 | 0 | 0 | 0 |
| Fixed Assets | 1 | 1 | 0 | 0 | 0 | 0 | 0 |
| Internal Communications | 1 | 0 | 0 | 0 | 1 | 0 | 0 |

Table 5 – Non-Financial Impacts

**GLBA Bank**
**Business Impact Assessment Report**

## Continuity Approach

The bank has already put in place continuity plans for ISD and Item Processing and has tested both. Continuity plans for Network have been drafted and will be tested immediately following this BIA. As stated later in Next Steps/Recommendations, this report must be reviewed by the owners of these plans and the content of the report used to amend those plans where necessary. Of particular interest will be the technology resources required by each business process.

The Recovery 1 worksheet in the BIA Consolidated Table shows the computer systems and applications required by each process. This worksheet was sorted by order of criticality assigned to each process by the process owner.

Table 6 on the next page shows computer systems and applications required by each process.

**GLBA Bank**
**Business Impact Assessment Report**

| Process | Computer Applications | | | | | | | | |
|---|---|---|---|---|---|---|---|---|---|
| | Mainframe | | | Client/Server | LAN/WAN | | | Local | |
| Mortgage Servicing | ITI | | | | Morenet | Midanet | | MSOffice | |
| Benefits | | | | SOURCE | | | | MSOffice | |
| Payroll | | | | SOURCE | PSBOS32 | | | MSOffice | |
| Recruitment | | | | SOURCE | | | | MSOffice | |
| Accounts Payable | APS | | | | | | | | |
| Financial Statements | FMS | | | | | | | | |
| Fixed Assets | FAS | | | | | | | | |
| General Ledger | ITI | FMS | | | | | | | |
| Payroll | | | | SOURCE | | | | MSOffice | |
| Charge Card Issue | ITI | | | Total Systems | | | | | |
| Disputed Charges | | | | Vital Processing | | | | | |
| Merchant Services | ITI | | | Vital Processing | | | | | |
| Card Reissues | ITI | | | Total Systems | | | | | |
| Terminations | ITI | | | Total Systems | | | | | |
| Credit Administration | ITI | | | SOURCE | Impromptu | | | MSOffice | |
| ATM Card Reissue | ATM Reissue | | | | | | | Prime | |
| Branch Operations | ITI | | | | | | | MSOffice | |
| Fedline | ITI | | | | | | | Fedline | |
| Internet Banking | | | | Wizcenter | | | | | |
| Wire Transfer | | | | | | | | Fedline | |
| Branch Support | | | | | | | | MSOffice | Publisher |
| Internal Communications | | | | | | | | MSOffice | Publisher |
| Loan Approval | | | | | Credit Analysis | | | MSOffice | |
| Loan Services | ITI | | | | | | | MSOffice | |
| Mortgage Origination | | | | | Contour | Morenet | Websites | | |
| Loan Collection | ITI | Director | Charge Card | | PCLink | | | MSOffice | |
| Recovery | ITI | | | | PCLink | | | | |
| Corporate Banking | | | | | | | | MSOffice | |

Table 6 – Systems and Applications

**GLBA Bank**
**Business Impact Assessment Report**

As stated earlier in Current State Assessment, the bank's Disaster Management plans need to be reviewed. Please see later comments in Next Steps/Recommendations for further comment on continuity approach.

## Next Steps/Recommendations

4. This BIA report must be reviewed by the level of management immediately above the level that participated in the BIA interviews. That level of management must review the report to affirm the criticality and values assigned to each process and, where a question arises, the reviewer must discuss the question with the interviewee and — when appropriate, amend the entry. This action should be completed within one month of the release of this report.
5. The bank's Disaster Management Plan must be reviewed and, as part of that review, each department should undertake a Business Impact Analysis (BIA) led by the Vice President of Compliance. This second iteration of the BIA should examine each process at a lower level of detail and should form the basis for amendments to the bank's Disaster Management Plan. This action should commence as soon as possible after the release of this report.
6. The owners of the bank's ISD recovery plan, Item Processing recovery plan and Network recovery plan must review this report after the first recommendation in this section is completed. The criticality of each business process and the recovery sequence for business processes must be compared to relevant entries in these recovery plans and, where necessary, these recovery plans must be amended. We recommend this step should be started as soon as possible after the first recommendation is completed.

**GLBA Bank**
**Business Impact Assessment Report**

## Attachment 1 - BIA Consolidated Table

Please see accompanying Microsoft Excel file.

| Department | Owner | Criticality | | Impacts | | | | | | | | Maximum Tolerable Downtime (Business days) |
| --- | --- | --- | --- | --- | --- | --- | --- | --- | --- | --- | --- | --- |
| | | Overall | Dept. | Financial (month) | Int. Customers | Ext. Customers | Operating Efficiency | Legal & Reg. | Reputation | Morale | | |
| Cashiers | | 5 | 5 | $1,000,000 | 0 | 5 | 5 | 0 | 5 | 0 | | 0.5 |
| ISD | | 5 | 5 | $900,000 | 5 | 5 | 5 | 5 | 5 | 0 | | 0.5 |
| Cashiers | | 5 | 5 | $900,000 | 5 | 5 | 5 | 5 | 5 | 0 | | 0.5 |
| PC Services | | 5 | 5 | $900,000 | 5 | 5 | 5 | 5 | 5 | 0 | | 0.5 |
| Accounting | | 5 | 5 | $300,000 | 0 | 0 | 5 | 5 | 5 | 0 | | 0.5 |
| Human Resources | | 5 | 5 | $10,000 | 0 | 0 | 4 | 4 | 5 | 5 | | 5 |
| Accounting | | 5 | 5 | $10,000 | 0 | 0 | 5 | 4 | 5 | 5 | | 5 |
| Cashiers | | 5 | 5 | $5,000 | 0 | 4 | 5 | 0 | 5 | 0 | | 0.5 |
| Mortgage | | 4 | 5 | $500,000 | 0 | 5 | 5 | 5 | 0 | 0 | | 0.5 |
| Mortgage | | 4 | 5 | $50,000 | 0 | 5 | 4 | 0 | 5 | 0 | | 2 |
| Human Resources | | 4 | 4 | $7,500 | 4 | 0 | 1 | 4 | 3 | 4 | | 5 |
| Accounting | | 3 | 3 | $300,000 | 1 | 1 | 0 | 1 | 0 | 0 | | 20 |
| Charge Cards | | 3 | 4 | $15,000 | 3 | 3 | 0 | 0 | 2 | 0 | | 5 |
| Cashiers | | 3 | 4 | $5,000 | 3 | 3 | 0 | 0 | 5 | 0 | | 1 |
| Cashiers | | 3 | 4 | $0 | 1 | 1 | 4 | 2 | 0 | 0 | | 2 |
| Loan Services | | 3 | 5 | $0 | 4 | 5 | 4 | 0 | 4 | 0 | | 2 |
| Loan Services | | 3 | 4 | $0 | 4 | 5 | 0 | 0 | 4 | 0 | | 5 |
| Charge Cards | | 3 | 5 | $0 | 3 | 3 | 0 | 0 | 2 | 0 | | 5 |
| Charge Cards | | 3 | 3 | $0 | 0 | 3 | 0 | 0 | 2 | 0 | | 5 |
| Charge Cards | | 3 | 3 | $0 | 0 | 3 | 2 | 0 | 2 | 0 | | 10 |
| Human Resources | | 3 | 3 | $0 | 2 | 0 | 0 | 0 | 2 | 0 | | 10 |
| Charge Cards | | 3 | 3 | $0 | 0 | 4 | 1 | 0 | 3 | 0 | | 20 |
| Special Assets | | 3 | 5 | $0 | 1 | 1 | 1 | 0 | 1 | 0 | | 30 |
| Accounting | | 2 | 2 | $0 | 3 | 3 | 0 | 1 | 1 | 0 | | 10 |
| Marketing | | 2 | 5 | $0 | 1 | 0 | 0 | 1 | 1 | 0 | | 30 |
| Loan Administration | | 2 | 5 | $0 | 1 | 1 | 0 | 0 | 0 | 0 | | 30 |
| Cashiers | | 1 | 2 | $0 | 0 | 1 | 0 | 0 | 0 | 0 | | 1 |
| Accounting | | 1 | 1 | $0 | 1 | 0 | 0 | 0 | 0 | 0 | | 30 |
| Marketing | | 1 | 5 | $0 | 0 | 0 | 0 | 1 | 0 | 0 | | 30 |
| Special Assets | | 1 | 3 | $0 | 0 | 0 | 1 | 0 | 1 | 0 | | 30 |
| Corp. Banking | | 3 | 5 | $30,000 | 3 | 4 | 2 | 0 | 2 | 0 | | 30 |

**GLBA Bank**
**Business Impact Assessment Report**

## Attachment 2 – BIA Interview Summaries

**GLBA Bank**
**Business Impact Assessment Report**

| Business Process | Process Owner | Title |
|---|---|---|
| Mortgage Servicing | | Supervisor |
| **Department** | | **Process Frequency** |
| Mortgage | | Daily |

| Process Description |
|---|
| Contour produces a booking sheet which Servicing uses to input to ITI with offsetting monetary entries posted. Payments received by the bank are input to ITI. Servicing checks the daily transactions posted on ITI, performs all escrow disbursements, remits payments for monthly investor servicing, inputs ARM changes quarterly and does escrow analysis in Aug. each year. Other services performed are payoff processing, collections for commercial mortgage past-dues, loan modifications and forced placed insurance services. |

| Critical Time Periods |
|---|
| ☐ daily ☐ end of week **X** month-end   **X** quarter-end   **X** year-end   ☐ other<br>Month-end – management reports, quarterly – call reports for OCC, end of year – 1098 statement mailing. |

| Peak Processing Periods |
|---|
| Feb. & Aug. – Real property taxes, Quarterly – ARM changes, Aug./Sep. escrow analysis, Dec./Jan. year-end |

| Maximum Tolerable Downtime |
|---|
| Less than one business day. |

| Impacts (0 = No Impact, 5 = Greatest Impact) | |
|---|---|
| *Financial Impact* | $500,000 per month |
| *Internal Customers* | 0 – No identifiable impact |
| *External Customers* | 5 – After one day |
| *Bank Operation Efficiency* | 5 – After one week |
| *Legal and Regulatory* | 3 – Failure to submit call reports, etc. |
| *Industry Reputation* | 5 – After two days |
| *Employee Morale* | 0 – No identifiable impact |

| Dependencies | | | |
|---|---|---|---|
| *Interdepartmental* | *Department* | *Inputs* | *Outputs* |
| | Wire Xfer | Approved loans | Reports – see earlier |
| | Acctg. | Future disbursements (new notes, escrow, etc.) | |
| | ISD | Daily system reports | Wiring instructions (inv pmts) |
| | PC services | Participation note bookings / wired pmts | |
| | Branches | Loan pmts (manual/auto) | |

**GLBA Bank**
**Business Impact Assessment Report**

| External | Company | Inputs | Outputs |
|---|---|---|---|
| | 3rd-party vendors | Real Prop Tax – CD upload to ITI | Annual certifications to investors |
| | | Use of Mornet & Midanet to perform Inv reporting/servicing | Investor servicing / remit (modem/Internet, etc.) |
| | | Wired funds from participant | Wired funds to participant |
| | | Payments, P/O proceeds, etc. | |

| Computer Applications | | | |
|---|---|---|---|
| Mainframe | Client/Server | LAN/WAN | Local |
| ITI | | Morenet (dial) | MSOffice |
| | | Midanet (dial) | |
| | | | |
| | | | |

| Alternates | |
|---|---|
| Loss of Facility | See disaster management plan |
| Loss of IT Systems | See ISD recovery plan |
| Alternate Sites | Ualena Street |

| Recovery Resource Requirements | | | | | |
|---|---|---|---|---|---|
| Personnel | 4 | Modems | 1 | Hardcopy Files | Y |
| Telephones | 4 | Printers | 1 | Microfilm | N |
| Networked PCs | 4 | Photocopiers | 1 | Special Forms | Y |
| Standalone PCs | 0 | Fax Machines | 1 | Other (Below) | |

| Overall Criticality (0 = Least Critical, 5 = Most Critical) | |
|---|---|
| Within This Department Only | 5 |
| Criticality to Overall Bank Operations | 4 |

**GLBA Bank**
**Business Impact Assessment Report**

| Business Process | Process Owner | Title |
|---|---|---|
| IS Services | | Sen. Vice President |
| **Department** | | **Process Frequency** |
| ISD | | Daily |

| Process Description |
|---|
| Provision of IS services to bank. |
| **Critical Time Periods** |
| **X** daily ☐ end of week ☐ month-end ☐ quarter-end ☐ year-end ☐ other<br>As needed. |
| **Peak Processing Periods** |
| Weekly. |

| Maximum Tolerable Downtime |
|---|
| Less than one day. |

| Impacts (0 = No Impact, 5 = Greatest Impact) | |
|---|---|
| *Financial Impact* | No quantifiable impact |
| *Internal Customers* | 5 – Loss of IS service |
| *External Customers* | 5 – Loss of bank services |
| *Bank Operation Efficiency* | 5 – Loss of IS service |
| *Legal and Regulatory* | 5 – Unable to comply |
| *Industry Reputation* | 5 – Immediate – loss of bank services |
| *Employee Morale* | 5 – Unable to process payroll and benefits |

| Dependencies | | | |
|---|---|---|---|
| *Interdepartmental* | *Department* | *Inputs* | *Outputs* |
| | All retail depts. | All | All |
| | | | |
| | | | |
| | | | |
| *External* | *Company* | *Inputs* | *Outputs* |
| | Vendors | | |
| | | | |
| | | | |
| | | | |

**GLBA Bank**
**Business Impact Assessment Report**

| Computer Applications | | | |
|---|---|---|---|
| *Mainframe* | *Client/Server* | *LAN/WAN* | *Local* |
| All | | | |
| | | | |
| | | | |
| | | | |

| Alternates | |
|---|---|
| *Loss of Facility* | See ISD recovery plan |
| *Loss of IT Systems* | See ISD recovery plan |
| *Alternate Sites* | Sunguard Arizona |

| Recovery Resource Requirements (See ISD Recovery Plan) | | | | | |
|---|---|---|---|---|---|
| Personnel | | Modems | | Hardcopy Files | |
| Telephones | | Printers | | Microfilm | |
| Networked PCs | | Photocopiers | | Special Forms | |
| Standalone PCs | | Fax Machines | | Other (Below) | |
| | | | | | |

| Overall Criticality (0 = Least Critical, 5 = Most Critical) | |
|---|---|
| *Within This Department Only* | 5 |
| *Criticality to Overall Bank Operations* | 5 |

**GLBA Bank**
**Business Impact Assessment Report**

| Business Process | Process Owner | Title |
|---|---|---|
| Benefits | | Vice President & Director |
| **Department** | | **Process Frequency** |
| Human Resources | | Daily, monthly, annually |

| Process Description |
|---|
| Collect elective decisions. Enroll employees in insurance plans. Pay insurance. Enter changes. |
| **Critical Time Periods** |
| ☐ daily ☐ end of week **X** month-end ☐ quarter-end **X** year-end ☐ other<br>Monthly, pay insurance bills. Annually, open enrollment. |
| **Peak Processing Periods** |
| August – open enrollment. |

| Maximum Tolerable Downtime |
|---|
| 5 days before month-end to enter changes. |

| Impacts (0 = No Impact, 5 = Greatest Impact) | |
|---|---|
| *Financial Impact* | $25 or $1 per employee per day. If > 30 days, close business |
| *Internal Customers* | 4 – For employees one week after failure to pay |
| *External Customers* | 0 – No identifiable impact |
| *Bank Operation Efficiency* | 4 – One week after failure to pay |
| *Legal And Regulatory* | 4 – See Financial Impact |
| *Industry Reputation* | 3 – One month after failure to pay |
| *Employee Morale* | 4 – One week after failure to pay |

| Dependencies | | | |
|---|---|---|---|
| *Interdepartmental* | *Department* | *Inputs* | *Outputs* |
| | All depts. | Enrollments | HMSA & Kaiser payments |
| | | Changes | |
| | | | |
| | | | |
| *External* | *Company* | *Inputs* | *Outputs* |
| | HMSA | | |
| | Kaiser | | |
| | | | |
| | | | |

**GLBA Bank**
**Business Impact Assessment Report**

| Computer Applications | | | |
|---|---|---|---|
| *Mainframe* | *Client/Server* | *LAN/WAN* | *Local* |
| | SOURCE | | MSOffice |
| | | | |
| | | | |
| | | | |

| Alternates | |
|---|---|
| *Loss of Facility* | See disaster management plan |
| *Loss of IT Systems* | See disaster management plan |
| *Alternate Sites* | Proof dept. |

| Recovery Resource Requirements | | | | | |
|---|---|---|---|---|---|
| *Personnel* | 1 | *Modems* | 0 | *Hardcopy Files* | Y |
| *Telephones* | 1 | *Printers* | 1 | *Microfilm* | N |
| *Networked PCs* | 1 | *Photocopiers* | 0 | *Special Forms* | Y |
| *Standalone PCs* | 0 | *Fax Machines* | 0 | *Other (Below)* | |
| | | | | | |

| Overall Criticality (0 = Least Critical, 5 = Most Critical) | |
|---|---|
| *Within This Department Only* | 4 |
| *Criticality to Overall Bank Operations* | 4 |

**GLBA Bank**
**Business Impact Assessment Report**

| Business Process | Process Owner | Title |
|---|---|---|
| Payroll | | Vice President & Director |
| **Department** | | **Process Frequency** |
| Human Resources | | Semi-monthly |

| Process Description |
|---|
| Timesheets and other payroll input are entered to SOURCE and batch transmitted. Ceridean processes and messengers deposit advices and checks to HR. HR sends these out by interoffice pouch to different departments. |

| Critical Time Periods |
|---|
| ☐ daily ☐ end of week ☐ month-end ☐ quarter-end ☐ year-end **X** other |
| Cutoff is the 8th and 22nd of month, transmit to Ceridean is the 12th and 3 days before month-end. |

| Peak Processing Periods |
|---|
| None. |

| Maximum Tolerable Downtime |
|---|
| 2 days up to cutoff dates above. |

| Impacts (0 = No Impact, 5 = Greatest Impact) | |
|---|---|
| Financial Impact | $100 to $10,000 for failure to pay + unpaid payroll + 6% p.a. |
| Internal Customers | 0 – No identifiable impact |
| External Customers | 0 – No identifiable impact |
| Bank Operation Efficiency | 4 – Within five business days |
| Legal and Regulatory | 4 – Seven days after payroll date |
| Industry Reputation | 5 – Three days after payroll date |
| Employee Morale | 5 – Immediately on failure to pay |

| Dependencies | | | |
|---|---|---|---|
| Interdepartmental | Department | Inputs | Outputs |
| | All depts. | Timesheets, etc. | Deposit advice |
| | Accounting | Transaction report | Checks |
| | | Deduction changes | |
| | | | |
| External | Company | Inputs | Outputs |
| | Ceridean | | |
| | | | |
| | | | |
| | | | |

**GLBA Bank**
**Business Impact Assessment Report**

| Computer Applications | | | |
|---|---|---|---|
| *Mainframe* | *Client/Server* | *LAN/WAN* | *Local* |
| | SOURCE | PSBOS32 | MSOffice |
| | | | |
| | | | |
| | | | |

| Alternates | |
|---|---|
| *Loss of Facility* | See disaster management plan |
| *Loss of IT Systems* | See disaster management plan |
| *Alternate Sites* | Proof dept. |

| Recovery Resource Requirements | | | | | |
|---|---|---|---|---|---|
| *Personnel* | 1 | *Modems* | 0 | *Hardcopy Files* | Y |
| *Telephones* | 1 | *Printers* | 1 | *Microfilm* | N |
| *Networked PCs* | 1 | *Photocopiers* | 0 | *Special Forms* | N |
| *Standalone PCs* | 0 | *Fax Machines* | 0 | *Other (Below)* | |
| | | | | | |

| Overall Criticality (0 = Least Critical, 5 = Most Critical) | |
|---|---|
| *Within This Department Only* | 5 |
| *Criticality to Overall Bank Operations* | 5 |

**GLBA Bank**
**Business Impact Assessment Report**

| Business Process | Process Owner | Title |
|---|---|---|
| Recruitment | | Vice President & Director |
| **Department** | | **Process Frequency** |
| Human Resources | | Daily |

| Process Description |
|---|
| Hiring manager submits request. Request is posted internally and then externally. HR screens résumés. Create interview list. Screen interview and test employees. Create interview shortlist. Manager interviews and hire is made. Half-day orientation. Review documentation of disciplinary process. Administration of annual performance review. In case of termination, manager has to discuss with HR first. Prepare termination documentation. Contact employee to discuss termination. Contact other departments to terminate access rights, etc. |

| Critical Time Periods |
|---|
| ☐ daily ☐ end of week ☐ month-end ☐ quarter-end ☐ year-end ☐ other None. |

| Peak Processing Periods |
|---|
| None. |

| Maximum Tolerable Downtime |
|---|
| Two weeks to support departmental targets. |

| Impacts (0 = No Impact, 5 = Greatest Impact) | |
|---|---|
| *Financial Impact* | No identifiable impact |
| *Internal Customers* | 2 – After one month (departmental hiring/term.would halt) |
| *External Customers* | 0 – No identifiable impact |
| *Bank Operation Efficiency* | 2 – After one month (departmental hiring/term.would halt) |
| *Legal and Regulatory* | 0 – No identifiable impact |
| *Industry Reputation* | 0 – No identifiable impact |
| *Employee Morale* | 0 – No identifiable impact |

| Dependencies | | | |
|---|---|---|---|
| *Interdepartmental* | *Department* | *Inputs* | *Outputs* |
| | All depts. | Hiring requests | Performance review forms |
| | | Performance reviews | Employee hiring forms |
| | | Notice of unsat. perf. | |
| | | | |
| *External* | *Company* | *Inputs* | *Outputs* |
| | | | |
| | | | |
| | | | |
| | | | |

**GLBA Bank**
**Business Impact Assessment Report**

| Computer Applications | | | |
|---|---|---|---|
| *Mainframe* | *Client/Server* | *LAN/WAN* | *Local* |
| | SOURCE | | MSOffice |
| | | | |
| | | | |
| | | | |

| Alternates | |
|---|---|
| *Loss of Facility* | See disaster management plan |
| *Loss of IT Systems* | See disaster management plan |
| *Alternate Sites* | Proof dept. |

| Recovery Resource Requirements | | | | | |
|---|---|---|---|---|---|
| *Personnel* | 1 | *Modems* | 0 | *Hardcopy Files* | Y |
| *Telephones* | 1 | *Printers* | 1 | *Microfilm* | N |
| *Networked PCs* | 1 | *Photocopiers* | 1 | *Special Forms* | N |
| *Standalone PCs* | 0 | *Fax Machines* | 1 | *Other (Below)* | |

| Overall Criticality (0 = Least Critical, 5 = Most Critical) | |
|---|---|
| *Within This Department Only* | 3 |
| *Criticality to Overall Bank Operations* | 3 |

**GLBA Bank**
**Business Impact Assessment Report**

| Business Process | Process Owner | Title |
|---|---|---|
| Accounts Payable | | Assistant Vice President |
| **Department** | | **Process Frequency** |
| Accounting | | Daily |

| Process Description |
|---|
| Receive invoices. Log invoices. Send invoices for approval. Receive invoices and check extensions and totals. Send all invoices to senior management for approval. Input invoices on APS (Accounts Payable System). Print checks. Assemble checks for signature. Receive checks and mail out. |

| Critical Time Periods |
|---|
| ☐ daily ☐ end of week ☐ month-end ☐ quarter-end ☐ year-end **X** other Middle of each month. |

| Peak Processing Periods |
|---|
| Year-end to clear books. |

| Maximum Tolerable Downtime |
|---|
| Up to middle of month. |

| Impacts (0 = No Impact, 5 = Greatest Impact) | |
|---|---|
| *Financial Impact* | No quantifiable impact |
| *Internal Customers* | 3 – Mgmnt. expense reimbursement after middle of month |
| *External Customers* | 3 – After middle of month |
| *Bank Operation Efficiency* | 1 – Impacted after two months |
| *Legal and Regulatory* | 1 – Non-payment of bills |
| *Industry Reputation* | 1 – After 1 month |
| *Employee Morale* | 0 – No identifiable impact |

| Dependencies | | | |
|---|---|---|---|
| *Interdepartmental* | *Department* | *Inputs* | *Outputs* |
| | All depts. | Invoices | Checks |
| | | | |
| | | | |
| | | | |
| *External* | *Company* | *Inputs* | *Outputs* |
| | All suppliers | Invoices | Checks |
| | | | |
| | | | |
| | | | |

**GLBA Bank**
**Business Impact Assessment Report**

| Computer Applications | | | |
|---|---|---|---|
| *Mainframe* | *Client/Server* | *LAN/WAN* | *Local* |
| APS | | | |
| | | | |
| | | | |
| | | | |

| Alternates | |
|---|---|
| *Loss of Facility* | See disaster management plan |
| *Loss of IT Systems* | See ISD recovery plan |
| *Alternate Sites* | Dillingham |

| Recovery Resource Requirements | | | | | |
|---|---|---|---|---|---|
| *Personnel* | 1 | *Modems* | 0 | *Hardcopy Files* | Y |
| *Telephones* | 1 | *Printers* | 1 | *Microfilm* | N |
| *Networked PCs* | 1 | *Photocopiers* | 0 | *Special Forms* | Y |
| *Standalone PCs* | 0 | *Fax Machines* | 0 | *Other (Below)* | |
| | | | | | |

| Overall Criticality (0 = Least Critical, 5 = Most Critical) | |
|---|---|
| *Within This Department Only* | 2 |
| *Criticality to Overall Bank Operations* | 2 |

**GLBA Bank**
**Business Impact Assessment Report**

| Business Process | Process Owner | Title |
|---|---|---|
| Financial Statements | | Assistant Vice President |
| **Department** | | **Process Frequency** |
| Accounting | | Daily and monthly (monthly is P&L) |

| Process Description |
|---|
| Close General Ledger. Produce financial statement. Review financial statement. Enter adjustments to General Ledger. Distribute financial statements to branches, cost centers, and management |
| **Critical Time Periods** |
| ☐ daily ☐ end of week **X** month-end **X** quarter-end ☐ year-end ☐ other Quarterly regulatory reports for OCC and FDIC, year-end closing. |
| **Peak Processing Periods** |
| End of each quarter, (March, June, September, and December) for report production. |

| Maximum Tolerable Downtime |
|---|
| One month. |

| Impacts (0 = No Impact, 5 = Greatest Impact) | |
|---|---|
| *Financial Impact* | Regulatory fines: If quarterly reports are not produced, $10,000 per day each day after due date. |
| *Internal Customers* | 1 – Management is impacted after one month. |
| *External Customers* | 1 – Federal regulators impacted after one quarter. |
| *Bank Operation Efficiency* | 1 – Impacted after one month. |
| *Legal and Regulatory* | 1 – As for external customers. |
| *Industry Reputation* | 0 – No identifiable impact. |
| *Employee Morale* | 0 – No identifiable impact. |

| Dependencies | | | |
|---|---|---|---|
| *Interdepartmental* | *Department* | *Inputs* | *Outputs* |
| | ISD | General ledger entries | Financial statements |
| | | | |
| | | | |
| | | | |
| *External* | *Company* | *Inputs* | *Outputs* |
| | | | |
| | | | |
| | | | |
| | | | |

**GLBA Bank**
**Business Impact Assessment Report**

| Computer Applications | | | |
|---|---|---|---|
| *Mainframe* | *Client/Server* | *LAN/WAN* | *Local* |
| FMS | | | |
| | | | |
| | | | |
| | | | |

| Alternates | |
|---|---|
| *Loss of Facility* | See disaster management plan |
| *Loss of IT Systems* | See ISD recovery plan |
| *Alternate Sites* | Dillingham |

| Recovery Resource Requirements | | | | | |
|---|---|---|---|---|---|
| *Personnel* | 1 | *Modems* | 0 | *Hardcopy Files* | Y |
| *Telephones* | 0 | *Printers* | 1 | *Microfilm* | N |
| *Networked PCs* | 1 | *Photocopiers* | 1 | *Special Forms* | N |
| *Standalone PCs* | 0 | *Fax Machines* | 0 | *Other (Below)* | |

| Overall Criticality (0 = Least Critical, 5 = Most Critical) | |
|---|---|
| *Within This Department Only* | 3 |
| *Criticality to Overall Bank Operations* | 3 |

**GLBA Bank**
**Business Impact Assessment Report**

| Business Process | Process Owner | Title |
|---|---|---|
| Fixed Assets | | Assistant Vice President |
| **Department** | | **Process Frequency** |
| Accounting | | Monthly |

| Process Description |
|---|
| If APS pays an invoice of greater than $1,000, input the asset information into the FAS (Fixed Asset System) on the mainframe. |
| **Critical Time Periods** |
| ☐ daily ☐ end of week **X** month-end ☐ quarter-end ☐ year-end ☐ other |

| Peak Processing Periods |
|---|
| June and December. Running special reports for audit. |

| Maximum Tolerable Downtime |
|---|
| Not critical. |

| Impacts (0 = No Impact, 5 = Greatest Impact) | |
|---|---|
| *Financial Impact* | No identifiable impact |
| *Internal Customers* | 1 – At month-end fixed asset report may not be run |
| *External Customers* | 0 – No identifiable impact |
| *Bank Operation Efficiency* | 0 – No identifiable impact |
| *Legal and Regulatory* | 0 – No identifiable impact |
| *Industry Reputation* | 0 – No identifiable impact |
| *Employee Morale* | 0 – No identifiable impact |

| Dependencies | | | |
|---|---|---|---|
| *Interdepartmental* | *Department* | *Inputs* | *Outputs* |
| | | | |
| | | | |
| | | | |
| | | | |
| *External* | *Company* | *Inputs* | *Outputs* |
| | | | |
| | | | |
| | | | |
| | | | |

**GLBA Bank**
**Business Impact Assessment Report**

| Computer Applications | | | |
|---|---|---|---|
| *Mainframe* | *Client/Server* | *LAN/WAN* | *Local* |
| FAS | | | |
| | | | |
| | | | |
| | | | |

| Alternates | |
|---|---|
| *Loss of Facility* | Not in the disaster management plan |
| *Loss of IT Systems* | See ISD recovery plan |
| *Alternate Sites* | None specified |

| Recovery Resource Requirements | | | | | |
|---|---|---|---|---|---|
| *Personnel* | 1 | *Modems* | 0 | *Hardcopy Files* | Y |
| *Telephones* | 0 | *Printers* | 1 | *Microfilm* | N |
| *Networked PCs* | 1 | *Photocopiers* | 0 | *Special Forms* | N |
| *Standalone PCs* | 0 | *Fax Machines* | 0 | *Other (Below)* | |
| | | | | | |

| Overall Criticality (0 = Least Critical, 5 = Most Critical) | |
|---|---|
| *Within This Department Only* | 1 |
| *Criticality to Overall Bank Operations* | 1 |

**GLBA Bank**
**Business Impact Assessment Report**

| Business Process | Process Owner | Title |
|---|---|---|
| General Ledger | | Assistant Vice President |
| **Department** | | **Process Frequency** |
| Accounting | | Daily and weekly (Weekly is Fedline) |

| Process Description |
|---|
| All departments input general ledger entries. Accounting balances the general ledger inputs. Accounting receives daily reports from ISD (FMS General Ledger system) and reviews reports. Accounting makes correcting entries. Accounting sends out general ledger reports to all departments. |

| Critical Time Periods |
|---|
| ☐ daily **X** end of week **X** month-end **X** quarter-end **X** year-end ☐ other Produce Fedline reports weekly, profit and loss statement monthly, quarterly regulatory reports for OCC and FDIC, year-end closing. |

| Peak Processing Periods |
|---|
| End of each quarter, (March, June, September, and December) for report production. |

| Maximum Tolerable Downtime |
|---|
| Less than one day: General ledger is used to sell excess funds daily. |

| Impacts (0 = No Impact, 5 = Greatest Impact) | |
|---|---|
| *Financial Impact* | Regulatory fines: If quarterly reports are not produced, $10,000 per day each day after due date. |
| *Internal Customers* | 5 – All departments are impacted after one day. |
| *External Customers* | 0 – No identifiable impact. |
| *Bank Operation Efficiency* | 5 – Impacted after one day. |
| *Legal and Regulatory* | 5 – Fedline reports impacted after one week. |
| *Industry Reputation* | 5 – Inability to conduct wire transfer after three days. |
| *Employee Morale* | 0 – No identifiable impact. |

| Dependencies | | | |
|---|---|---|---|
| *Interdepartmental* | *Department* | *Inputs* | *Outputs* |
| | All | General ledger entries | Balance reports |
| | | | Fedline |
| | | | OCC & FDIC reports |
| | | | Monthly & annual statements |
| *External* | *Company* | *Inputs* | *Outputs* |
| | | | |
| | | | |
| | | | |
| | | | |

**GLBA Bank**
**Business Impact Assessment Report**

| Computer Applications | | | |
|---|---|---|---|
| *Mainframe* | *Client/Server* | *LAN/WAN* | *Local* |
| ITI | | | |
| FMS | | | |
| | | | |
| | | | |

| Alternates | |
|---|---|
| *Loss of Facility* | See disaster management plan |
| *Loss of IT Systems* | See ISD recovery plan |
| *Alternate Sites* | Dillingham |

| Recovery Resource Requirements | | | | | |
|---|---|---|---|---|---|
| *Personnel* | 5 | *Modems* | 0 | *Hardcopy Files* | Y |
| *Telephones* | 2 | *Printers* | 1 | *Microfilm* | Y |
| *Networked PCs* | 3 | *Photocopiers* | 0 | *Special Forms* | N |
| *Standalone PCs* | 0 | *Fax Machines* | 1 | *Other (Below)* | |
| | | | | | |

| Overall Criticality (0 = Least Critical, 5 = Most Critical) | |
|---|---|
| *Within This Department Only* | 5 |
| *Criticality to Overall Bank Operations* | 5 |

**GLBA Bank**
**Business Impact Assessment Report**

| Business Process | Process Owner | Title |
|---|---|---|
| Payroll | | Assistant Vice President |
| Department | | Process Frequency |
| Accounting | | Daily |

| Process Description |
|---|
| HR sends hours and exceptions Payroll to input on SOURCE. Payroll receives prints & balances transaction report. HR reviews report. Signal okay for Payroll to transmit to Ceridian. Ceridian prints deposit acknowledgments and check statements. HR & Payroll check Ceridian's edit report. HR distributes. |
| **Critical Time Periods** |
| ☐ daily ☐ end of week ☐ month-end  X quarter-end  X year-end  **X** other 15th and last day of each month. |
| **Peak Processing Periods** |
| Year-end. |

| Maximum Tolerable Downtime |
|---|
| 2 days before cutoff dates of the 8th and the 22nd for Ceridian. |

| Impacts (0 = No Impact, 5 = Greatest Impact) | |
|---|---|
| *Financial Impact* | $100 to $10,000 for failure to pay + unpaid payroll + 6% p.a. |
| *Internal Customers* | 0 – No identifiable impact |
| *External Customers* | 0 – No identifiable impact |
| *Bank Operation Efficiency* | 4 – Within five business days |
| *Legal and Regulatory* | 4 – Seven days after payroll date |
| *Industry Reputation* | 5 – Three days after payroll date |
| *Employee Morale* | 5 – Immediately on failure to pay |

| Dependencies | | | |
|---|---|---|---|
| *Interdepartmental* | *Department* | *Inputs* | *Outputs* |
| | All depts. | Timesheets, etc. | Deposit advice |
| | Accounting | Transaction report | Checks |
| | | Deduction changes | |
| | | | |
| *External* | *Company* | *Inputs* | *Outputs* |
| | Ceridian | | |
| | | | |
| | | | |
| | | | |

**GLBA Bank**
**Business Impact Assessment Report**

| Computer Applications | | | |
|---|---|---|---|
| *Mainframe* | *Client/Server* | *LAN/WAN* | *Local* |
| | SOURCE | | MSOffice |
| | | | |
| | | | |
| | | | |

| Alternates | |
|---|---|
| *Loss of Facility* | See disaster management plan |
| *Loss of IT Systems* | See ISD recovery plan |
| *Alternate Sites* | Dillingham |

| Recovery Resource Requirements | | | | | |
|---|---|---|---|---|---|
| *Personnel* | 1 | *Modems* | 0 | *Hardcopy Files* | Y |
| *Telephones* | 1 | *Printers* | 1 | *Microfilm* | N |
| *Networked PCs* | 1 | *Photocopiers* | 0 | *Special Forms* | N |
| *Standalone PCs* | 0 | *Fax Machines* | 0 | *Other (Below)* | |

| Overall Criticality (0 = Least Critical, 5 = Most Critical) | |
|---|---|
| *Within This Department Only* | 5 |
| *Criticality to Overall Bank Operations* | 5 |

**GLBA Bank**
**Business Impact Assessment Report**

| Business Process | Process Owner | Title |
|---|---|---|
| Charge Card Issue | | Asst. Vice President |
| **Department** | | **Process Frequency** |
| Charge Card | | Twice weekly |

| Process Description |
|---|
| Customer application. Credit check. (If the application is by mail, does credit check. If customer is at branch, loan officer does credit check.) Approved application goes to Charge Cards who set up the account file and order a card from Total Systems. Total Systems set up their cardholder file and transmit it to Charge Card who inputs it to the card printer. The card is then mailed to the cardholder. |

| Critical Time Periods |
|---|
| ☐ daily  ☐ end of week  ☐ month-end   ☐ quarter-end   ☐ year-end      ☐ other<br>No critical time periods. |

| Peak Processing Periods |
|---|
| No peak processing periods. |

| Maximum Tolerable Downtime |
|---|
| 5 business days. |

| Impacts (0 = No Impact, 5 = Greatest Impact) | |
|---|---|
| *Financial Impact* | $12,000 to $15,000 per month |
| *Internal Customers* | 3 – For branches after one week |
| *External Customers* | 3 – For cardholders after one week |
| *Bank Operation Efficiency* | 0 – No identifiable impact |
| *Legal and Regulatory* | 0 – No identifiable impact |
| *Industry Reputation* | 2 – After one week |
| *Employee Morale* | 0 – No identifiable impact |

| Dependencies | | | |
|---|---|---|---|
| *Interdepartmental* | *Department* | *Inputs* | *Outputs* |
| | Branches | Approved applications | Charge cards |
| | ISD | Credit reports | Creation reports |
| | | | Monthly new acct. report |
| | | | Daily transaction log |
| *External* | *Company* | *Inputs* | *Outputs* |
| | Total Systems | | |
| | Metanvante | | |
| | Credit Bureau | | |
| | | | |

**GLBA Bank**
**Business Impact Assessment Report**

| Computer Applications | | | |
|---|---|---|---|
| *Mainframe* | *Client/Server* | *LAN/WAN* | *Local* |
| ITI | Total Systems | | |
| | | | |
| | | | |
| | | | |

| Alternates | |
|---|---|
| *Loss of Facility* | See disaster management plan |
| *Loss of IT Systems* | Total Systems' recovery plan |
| *Alternate Sites* | Operations center – Ualena Street |

| Recovery Resource Requirements | | | | | |
|---|---|---|---|---|---|
| *Personnel* | 1 | *Modems* | 0 | *Hardcopy Files* | Y |
| *Telephones* | 0 | *Printers* | 1 | *Microfilm* | Y |
| *Networked PCs* | 1 | *Photocopiers* | 0 | *Special Forms* | N |
| *Standalone PCs* | 0 | *Fax Machines* | 0 | *Other (Below)* | |
| | | | | | |

| Overall Criticality (0 = Least Critical, 5 = Most Critical) | |
|---|---|
| *Within This Department Only* | 4 |
| *Criticality to Overall Bank Operations* | 3 |

## GLBA Bank
### Business Impact Assessment Report

| Business Process | Process Owner | Title |
|---|---|---|
| Dispute Resolution | | Asst. Vice President |
| **Department** | | **Process Frequency** |
| Charge Card | | As needed |

| Process Description |
|---|
| Customer disputes a charge. Charge Cards gather the transaction information. Customer writes a letter with dispute details. Charge Cards orders a copy of the sales slip from the merchant's bank. Charge Cards evaluates and either resolves with the customer or credits the customer and charges the merchant's bank for the amount of the credit. |

| Critical Time Periods |
|---|
| ☐ daily  ☐ end of week  ☐ month-end   ☐ quarter-end   ☐ year-end      ☐ other |
| No critical time periods. |

| Peak Processing Periods |
|---|
| No peak processing periods. |

| Maximum Tolerable Downtime |
|---|
| 10 business days. |

| Impacts (0 = No Impact, 5 = Greatest Impact) | |
|---|---|
| *Financial Impact* | No identifiable impact |
| *Internal Customers* | 0 – No identifiable impact |
| *External Customers* | 3 – For customers after one week |
| *Bank Operation Efficiency* | 0 – No identifiable impact |
| *Legal and Regulatory* | 0 – No identifiable impact |
| *Industry Reputation* | 2 – After one week |
| *Employee Morale* | 0 – No identifiable impact |

| Dependencies | | | |
|---|---|---|---|
| *Interdepartmental* | *Department* | *Inputs* | *Outputs* |
| | | Disputed charges | Credits to customer account |
| | | Sales slips | Charges to merchants acct. |
| | | | |
| | | | |
| *External* | *Company* | *Inputs* | *Outputs* |
| | Total Systems | | |
| | Merchants banks | | |
| | | | |
| | | | |

**GLBA Bank**
**Business Impact Assessment Report**

| Computer Applications | | | |
|---|---|---|---|
| *Mainframe* | *Client/Server* | *LAN/WAN* | *Local* |
| | Vital Processing | | |
| | | | |
| | | | |
| | | | |

| Alternates | |
|---|---|
| *Loss of Facility* | See disaster management plan |
| *Loss of IT Systems* | Vital Processing's recovery plan |
| *Alternate Sites* | Operations center – Ualena Street |

| Recovery Resource Requirements | | | | | |
|---|---|---|---|---|---|
| *Personnel* | 1 | *Modems* | 0 | *Hardcopy Files* | Y |
| *Telephones* | 1 | *Printers* | 1 | *Microfilm* | Y |
| *Networked PCs* | 1 | *Photocopiers* | 0 | *Special Forms* | N |
| *Standalone PCs* | 0 | *Fax Machines* | 0 | *Other (Below)* | |
| | | | | | |

| Overall Criticality (0 = Least Critical, 5 = Most Critical) | |
|---|---|
| *Within This Department Only* | 3 |
| *Criticality to Overall Bank Operations* | 3 |

**GLBA Bank**
**Business Impact Assessment Report**

| Business Process | Process Owner | Title |
|---|---|---|
| Merchant Services | | Asst. Vice President |
| **Department** | | **Process Frequency** |
| Charge Card | | As needed |

| Process Description |
|---|
| When an application is approved and underwritten, set up the merchant, program the terminal and train the merchant. |
| **Critical Time Periods** |
| ☐ daily ☐ end of week ☐ month-end ☐ quarter-end ☐ year-end ☐ other<br>No critical time periods. |
| **Peak Processing Periods** |
| Period leading up to Christmas. |

| Maximum Tolerable Downtime |
|---|
| 5 business days. |

| Impacts (0 = No Impact, 5 = Greatest Impact) | |
|---|---|
| *Financial Impact* | No identifiable impact |
| *Internal Customers* | 3 – For branches after one week |
| *External Customers* | 3 – For business customers after one week |
| *Bank Operation Efficiency* | 0 – No identifiable impact |
| *Legal and Regulatory* | 0 – No identifiable impact |
| *Industry Reputation* | 2 – After one week |
| *Employee Morale* | 0 – No identifiable impact |

| Dependencies | | | |
|---|---|---|---|
| *Interdepartmental* | *Department* | *Inputs* | *Outputs* |
| | Branches | Approved applications | Daily transaction log |
| | | Credit reports | Monthly new acct. report |
| | | | |
| | | | |
| *External* | *Company* | *Inputs* | *Outputs* |
| | Vital Processing | | |
| | Credit Bureau | | |
| | | | |
| | | | |

**GLBA Bank**
**Business Impact Assessment Report**

| Computer Applications | | | |
|---|---|---|---|
| *Mainframe* | *Client/Server* | *LAN/WAN* | *Local* |
| ITI | Vital Processing | | |
| | | | |
| | | | |
| | | | |

| Alternates | |
|---|---|
| *Loss of Facility* | See disaster management plan |
| *Loss of IT Systems* | Vital Processing's recovery plan |
| *Alternate Sites* | Operations center – Ualena Street |

| Recovery Resource Requirements | | | | | |
|---|---|---|---|---|---|
| *Personnel* | 1 | *Modems* | 0 | *Hardcopy Files* | Y |
| *Telephones* | 1 | *Printers* | 1 | *Microfilm* | Y |
| *Networked PCs* | 1 | *Photocopiers* | 0 | *Special Forms* | N |
| *Standalone PCs* | 0 | *Fax Machines* | 0 | *Other (Below)* | |
| | | | | | |
| | | | | | |
| | | | | | |

| Overall Criticality (0 = Least Critical, 5 = Most Critical) | |
|---|---|
| *Within This Department Only* | 5 |
| *Criticality to Overall Bank Operations* | 3 |

**GLBA Bank**
**Business Impact Assessment Report**

| Business Process | Process Owner | Title |
|---|---|---|
| Card Reissues | | Asst. Vice President |
| **Department** | | **Process Frequency** |
| Charge Card | | Monthly |

| Process Description |
|---|
| Charge Cards receives a pre-issue report from Total Systems and reviews flagged accounts. Where necessary, changes flags. Total Systems modifies files to reflect changed flags and reissues cards. |

| Critical Time Periods |
|---|
| ☐ daily ☐ end of week ☐ month-end ☐ quarter-end ☐ year-end **X** other |
| By the 10th of the month between the pre-issue report being generated and the card being reissued. |

| Peak Processing Periods |
|---|
| No peak processing periods. |

| Maximum Tolerable Downtime |
|---|
| One month. |

| Impacts (0 = No Impact, 5 = Greatest Impact) | |
|---|---|
| *Financial Impact* | No identifiable impact |
| *Internal Customers* | 0 – No identifiable impact |
| *External Customers* | 4 – For customers after one month |
| *Bank Operation Efficiency* | 0 – No identifiable impact |
| *Legal and Regulatory* | 0 – No identifiable impact |
| *Industry Reputation* | 3 – After one month |
| *Employee Morale* | 0 – No identifiable impact |

| Dependencies | | | |
|---|---|---|---|
| *Interdepartmental* | *Department* | *Inputs* | *Outputs* |
| | | Pre-issue report | Renewed cards |
| | | | |
| | | | |
| | | | |
| *External* | *Company* | *Inputs* | *Outputs* |
| | Total Systems | | |
| | | | |
| | | | |
| | | | |

**GLBA Bank**
**Business Impact Assessment Report**

| Computer Applications | | | |
|---|---|---|---|
| *Mainframe* | *Client/Server* | *LAN/WAN* | *Local* |
| ITI | Total Systems | | |
| | | | |
| | | | |
| | | | |

| Alternates | |
|---|---|
| *Loss of Facility* | See disaster management plan |
| *Loss of IT Systems* | Total Systems' recovery plan |
| *Alternate Sites* | Operations center – Ualena Street |

| Recovery Resource Requirements | | | | | |
|---|---|---|---|---|---|
| *Personnel* | 1 | *Modems* | 0 | *Hardcopy Files* | Y |
| *Telephones* | 1 | *Printers* | 1 | *Microfilm* | Y |
| *Networked PCs* | 1 | *Photocopiers* | 0 | *Special Forms* | N |
| *Standalone PCs* | 0 | *Fax Machines* | 0 | *Other (Below)* | |

| Overall Criticality (0 = Least Critical, 5 = Most Critical) | |
|---|---|
| *Within This Department Only* | 3 |
| *Criticality to Overall Bank Operations* | 3 |

**GLBA Bank**
**Business Impact Assessment Report**

| Business Process | Process Owner | Title |
|---|---|---|
| Terminations | | Asst. Vice President |
| **Department** | | **Process Frequency** |
| Charge Card | | As needed |

| Process Description |
|---|
| Special Assets or Charge Cards views the collection report and makes a decision to terminate charge privileges. Charge Cards sends a notice to the customer and performs file maintenance to suspend charge privileges. |

| Critical Time Periods |
|---|
| ☐ daily ☐ end of week ☐ month-end ☐ quarter-end ☐ year-end ☐ other<br>No critical time periods. |

| Peak Processing Periods |
|---|
| No peak processing periods. |

| Maximum Tolerable Downtime |
|---|
| 5 business days. |

| Impacts (0 = No Impact, 5 = Greatest Impact) | |
|---|---|
| *Financial Impact* | No identifiable impact |
| *Internal Customers* | 0 – No identifiable impact |
| *External Customers* | 3 – For customers after one week |
| *Bank Operation Efficiency* | 0 – No identifiable impact |
| *Legal and Regulatory* | 0 – No identifiable impact |
| *Industry Reputation* | 2 – After one week |
| *Employee Morale* | 0 – No identifiable impact |

| Dependencies | | | |
|---|---|---|---|
| *Interdepartmental* | *Department* | *Inputs* | *Outputs* |
| | Special Assets | Collections report | Customer notices |
| | | | File maintenance |
| | | | |
| | | | |
| *External* | *Company* | *Inputs* | *Outputs* |
| | Total Systems | | |
| | | | |
| | | | |
| | | | |

**GLBA Bank**
**Business Impact Assessment Report**

| Computer Applications | | | |
|---|---|---|---|
| *Mainframe* | *Client/Server* | *LAN/WAN* | *Local* |
| ITI | Total Systems | | |
| | | | |
| | | | |
| | | | |

| Alternates | |
|---|---|
| *Loss of Facility* | See disaster management plan |
| *Loss of IT Systems* | ISD recovery plan, Total Systems' recovery plan |
| *Alternate Sites* | Operations center – Ualena Street |

| Recovery Resource Requirements | | | | | |
|---|---|---|---|---|---|
| *Personnel* | 1 | *Modems* | 0 | *Hardcopy Files* | Y |
| *Telephones* | 1 | *Printers* | 1 | *Microfilm* | Y |
| *Networked PCs* | 1 | *Photocopiers* | 0 | *Special Forms* | N |
| *Standalone PCs* | 0 | *Fax Machines* | 0 | *Other (Below)* | |

| Overall Criticality (0 = Least Critical, 5 = Most Critical) | |
|---|---|
| *Within This Department Only* | 3 |
| *Criticality to Overall Bank Operations* | 3 |

**GLBA Bank**
**Business Impact Assessment Report**

| Business Process | Process Owner | Title |
|---|---|---|
| Credit Administration | | Vice President |
| **Department** | | **Process Frequency** |
| Loan Administration | | Weekly |

| Process Description |
|---|
| Support for senior loan administrator. Send out loan policies and procedures. Maintain loan manuals for changes in regulations. |
| **Critical Time Periods** |
| ☐ daily **X** end of week **X** month-end   **X** quarter-end   **X** year-end      ☐ other<br>Weekly – loan committee folders. Friday – Management, Tuesday – Discount. Monthly – Action Plan Committee. Quarterly – FDIC call report. Year-end – annual notices. |
| **Peak Processing Periods** |
| At end of April and October when external audit comes in. |

| Maximum Tolerable Downtime |
|---|
| Not applicable. |

| Impacts (0 = No Impact, 5 = Greatest Impact) | |
|---|---|
| *Financial Impact* | No identifiable impact |
| *Internal Customers* | 1 – After one week – unable to respond to credit inquiries |
| *External Customers* | 1 – As for Internal Customers |
| *Bank Operation Efficiency* | 0 – No identifiable impact |
| *Legal and Regulatory* | 0 – No identifiable impact |
| *Industry Reputation* | 0 – No identifiable impact |
| *Employee Morale* | 0 – No identifiable impact |

| Dependencies | | | |
|---|---|---|---|
| *Interdepartmental* | *Department* | *Inputs* | *Outputs* |
| | Loan officers | Delinquency reports | Loan folders |
| | | | |
| | | | |
| | | | |
| *External* | *Company* | *Inputs* | *Outputs* |
| | | | |
| | | | |
| | | | |
| | | | |

**GLBA Bank**
**Business Impact Assessment Report**

| Computer Applications | | | |
|---|---|---|---|
| *Mainframe* | *Client/Server* | *LAN/WAN* | *Local* |
| ITI | SOURCE | Impromptu | MSOffice |
| | | | |
| | | | |
| | | | |

| Alternates | |
|---|---|
| *Loss of Facility* | None |
| *Loss of IT Systems* | None |
| *Alternate Sites* | Dillingham |

| Recovery Resource Requirements | | | | | |
|---|---|---|---|---|---|
| *Personnel* | 3 | *Modems* | 0 | *Hardcopy Files* | Y |
| *Telephones* | 1 | *Printers* | 1 | *Microfilm* | N |
| *Networked PCs* | 2 | *Photocopiers* | 1 | *Special Forms* | N |
| *Standalone PCs* | 0 | *Fax Machines* | 1 | *Other (Below)* | |
| | | | | | |

| Overall Criticality (0 = Least Critical, 5 = Most Critical) | |
|---|---|
| *Within This Department Only* | 5 |
| *Criticality to Overall Bank Operations* | 2 |

**GLBA Bank**
**Business Impact Assessment Report**

| Business Process | Process Owner | Title |
|---|---|---|
| ATM Card Issue | | Sen. Vice President |
| **Department** | | **Process Frequency** |
| Cashiers | | Every two months |

| Process Description |
|---|
| Branch issues a temporary ATM card. Every two months Cashiers receives a report from Prime and the ATM Reissue program, reviews the customers' files and then ISD prints and issues cards. |

| Critical Time Periods |
|---|
| ☐ daily ☐ end of week ☐ month-end ☐ quarter-end ☐ year-end ☐other<br>No critical time periods. |

| Peak Processing Periods |
|---|
| No peak processing periods. |

| Maximum Tolerable Downtime |
|---|
| 1 business day at the point of renewal. |

| Impacts (0 = No Impact, 5 = Greatest Impact) | |
|---|---|
| *Financial Impact* | No identifiable impact |
| *Internal Customers* | 0 – No identifiable impact |
| *External Customers* | 1 – Inconvenience for customers getting another temp. card |
| *Bank Operation Efficiency* | 0 – No identifiable impact |
| *Legal and Regulatory* | 0 – No identifiable impact |
| *Industry Reputation* | 0 – No identifiable impact |
| *Employee Morale* | 0 – No identifiable impact |

| Dependencies | | | |
|---|---|---|---|
| *Interdepartmental* | *Department* | *Inputs* | *Outputs* |
| | ISD | Reissue report | ATM Cards |
| | Charge Cards | | |
| | | | |
| | | | |
| *External* | *Company* | *Inputs* | *Outputs* |
| | Bank of Brotherhood | (Supports CAPS terminals for PIN selection) | |
| | | | |
| | | | |
| | | | |

**GLBA Bank**
**Business Impact Assessment Report**

| Computer Applications | | | |
|---|---|---|---|
| *Mainframe* | *Client/Server* | *LAN/WAN* | *Local* |
| ATM Reissue | | | Prime |
| | | | |
| | | | |
| | | | |

| Alternates | |
|---|---|
| *Loss of Facility* | None specified |
| *Loss of IT Systems* | ISD recovery plan |
| *Alternate Sites* | Ualena Street |

| Recovery Resource Requirements | | | | | |
|---|---|---|---|---|---|
| *Personnel* | 1 | *Modems* | 0 | *Hardcopy Files* | N |
| *Telephones* | 0 | *Printers* | 1 | *Microfilm* | N |
| *Networked PCs* | 1 | *Photocopiers* | 0 | *Special Forms* | N |
| *Standalone PCs* | 0 | *Fax Machines* | 0 | *Other (Below)* | |
| | | | | | |

| Overall Criticality (0 = Least Critical, 5 = Most Critical) | |
|---|---|
| *Within This Department Only* | 2 |
| *Criticality to Overall Bank Operations* | 1 |

**GLBA Bank**
**Business Impact Assessment Report**

| Business Process | Process Owner | Title |
|---|---|---|
| Bank Operations | | Sen. Vice President |
| Department | | Process Frequency |
| Cashiers | | Daily |

| Process Description |
|---|
| Paying and receiving funds, updating ITI, teller daily balances |
| **Critical Time Periods** |
| ☐ daily ☐ end of week **X** month-end ☐ quarter-end ☐ year-end ☐other |
| Cashier's report showing suspense items, tellers' overages and underages, etc. |
| **Peak Processing Periods** |
| No peak processing periods. |

| Maximum Tolerable Downtime |
|---|
| Less than one business day. |

| Impacts (0 = No Impact, 5 = Greatest Impact) | |
|---|---|
| *Financial Impact* | No identifiable impact |
| *Internal Customers* | 0 – No identifiable impact |
| *External Customers* | 5 – Customers unable to access funds or bank services |
| *Bank Operation Efficiency* | 5 – Immediate |
| *Legal and Regulatory* | 0 – No identifiable impact |
| *Industry Reputation* | 5 – Immediate |
| *Employee Morale* | 0 – No identifiable impact |

| Dependencies | | | |
|---|---|---|---|
| *Interdepartmental* | *Department* | *Inputs* | *Outputs* |
| | All depts. | Customer transactions | File updates |
| | | | All bank retail services |
| | | | |
| | | | |
| *External* | *Company* | *Inputs* | *Outputs* |
| | 3rd-party services | | |
| | | | |
| | | | |
| | | | |

**GLBA Bank**
**Business Impact Assessment Report**

| Computer Applications | | | |
|---|---|---|---|
| *Mainframe* | *Client/Server* | *LAN/WAN* | *Local* |
| ITI | | | MSOffice |
| | | | |
| | | | |
| | | | |

| Alternates | |
|---|---|
| *Loss of Facility* | None specified |
| *Loss of IT Systems* | ISD recovery plan |
| *Alternate Sites* | Alternate branch, depending on the event |

| Recovery Resource Requirements | | | | | |
|---|---|---|---|---|---|
| *Personnel* | 6 | *Modems* | 1 | *Hardcopy Files* | Y |
| *Telephones* | 3 | *Printers* | 2 | *Microfilm* | Y |
| *Networked PCs* | 5 | *Photocopiers* | 1 | *Special Forms* | Y |
| *Standalone PCs* | 0 | *Fax Machines* | 1 | *Other (Below)* | |
| Entries are average per branch | | | | | |

| Overall Criticality (0 = Least Critical, 5 = Most Critical) | |
|---|---|
| *Within This Department Only* | 5 |
| *Criticality to Overall Bank Operations* | 5 |

**GLBA Bank**
**Business Impact Assessment Report**

| Business Process | Process Owner | Title |
|---|---|---|
| Fedline | | Sen. Vice President |
| **Department** | | **Process Frequency** |
| Cashiers | | Daily |

| Process Description |
|---|
| Savings bonds are ordered, tax deposits and payments, ACH |

| Critical Time Periods |
|---|
| ☐ daily ☐ end of week ☐ month-end ☐ quarter-end ☐ year-end ☐other |
| No critical time periods |

| Peak Processing Periods |
|---|
| No peak processing periods. |

| Maximum Tolerable Downtime |
|---|
| 2 business days. |

| Impacts (0 = No Impact, 5 = Greatest Impact) | |
|---|---|
| Financial Impact | No identifiable impact |
| Internal Customers | 1 – Branches |
| External Customers | 1 – Customers unable to order savings bonds |
| Bank Operation Efficiency | 0 – No identifiable impact |
| Legal and Regulatory | 2 – Tax payments cannot be made |
| Industry Reputation | 0 – No identifiable impact |
| Employee Morale | 0 – No identifiable impact |

| Dependencies | | | |
|---|---|---|---|
| Interdepartmental | Department | Inputs | Outputs |
| | ISD | Tax payments | Tax payments |
| | Branches | ACH inputs | ACH outputs |
| | | | |
| | | | |
| External | Company | Inputs | Outputs |
| | Fedline | | |
| | | | |
| | | | |
| | | | |

**GLBA Bank**
**Business Impact Assessment Report**

| Computer Applications | | | |
|---|---|---|---|
| *Mainframe* | *Client/Server* | *LAN/WAN* | *Local* |
| ITI | | | Fedline (modem) |
| | | | |
| | | | |
| | | | |

| Alternates | |
|---|---|
| *Loss of Facility* | None specified |
| *Loss of IT Systems* | ISD recovery plan, Fedphone |
| *Alternate Sites* | Ualena Street |

| Recovery Resource Requirements | | | | | |
|---|---|---|---|---|---|
| *Personnel* | 2 | *Modems* | 1 | *Hardcopy Files* | Y |
| *Telephones* | 0 | *Printers* | 1 | *Microfilm* | N |
| *Networked PCs* | 1 | *Photocopiers* | 0 | *Special Forms* | N |
| *Standalone PCs* | 0 | *Fax Machines* | 1 | *Other (Below)* | |
| | | | | | |

| Overall Criticality (0 = Least Critical, 5 = Most Critical) | |
|---|---|
| *Within This Department Only* | 4 |
| *Criticality to Overall Bank Operations* | 3 |

**GLBA Bank**
**Business Impact Assessment Report**

| Business Process | Process Owner | Title |
|---|---|---|
| Internet Banking | | Sen. Vice President |
| **Department** | | **Process Frequency** |
| Cashiers | | Daily |

| Process Description |
|---|
| Customers can pay bills, transfer funds between accounts, check balances, pay taxes, stop payments, wire transfer, order cash, and order checks. |
| **Critical Time Periods** |
| □ daily □ end of week **X** month-end □ quarter-end □ year-end □other |
| End of month for service charge assessment. |
| **Peak Processing Periods** |
| No peak processing periods. |

| Maximum Tolerable Downtime |
|---|
| Less than one business day. |

| Impacts (0 = No Impact, 5 = Greatest Impact) | |
|---|---|
| *Financial Impact* | $5,000 in service fees |
| *Internal Customers* | 0 – No identifiable impact |
| *External Customers* | 4 – Customers unable to use Internet banking |
| *Bank Operation Efficiency* | 5 – Immediate |
| *Legal and Regulatory* | 0 – No identifiable impact |
| *Industry Reputation* | 5 – Immediate |
| *Employee Morale* | 0 – No identifiable impact |

| Dependencies | | | |
|---|---|---|---|
| *Interdepartmental* | *Department* | *Inputs* | *Outputs* |
| | ISD | Customer requests | Transactions and orders |
| | | | |
| | | | |
| | | | |
| *External* | *Company* | *Inputs* | *Outputs* |
| | | | |
| | | | |
| | | | |
| | | | |

**GLBA Bank**
**Business Impact Assessment Report**

| Computer Applications | | | |
|---|---|---|---|
| *Mainframe* | *Client/Server* | *LAN/WAN* | *Local* |
| | | Wizcenter | |
| | | | |
| | | | |
| | | | |

| Alternates | |
|---|---|
| *Loss of Facility* | None specified |
| *Loss of IT Systems* | ISD recovery plan |
| *Alternate Sites* | Ualena Street |

| Recovery Resource Requirements | | | | | |
|---|---|---|---|---|---|
| *Personnel* | 1 | *Modems* | 0 | *Hardcopy Files* | Y |
| *Telephones* | 0 | *Printers* | 1 | *Microfilm* | N |
| *Networked PCs* | 1 | *Photocopiers* | 0 | *Special Forms* | N |
| *Standalone PCs* | 0 | *Fax Machines* | 1 | *Other (Below)* | |

| Overall Criticality (0 = Least Critical, 5 = Most Critical) | |
|---|---|
| *Within This Department Only* | 5 |
| *Criticality to Overall Bank Operations* | 5 |

**GLBA Bank**
**Business Impact Assessment Report**

| Business Process | Process Owner | Title |
|---|---|---|
| Item Processing | | Sen. Vice President |
| **Department** | | **Process Frequency** |
| Cashiers | | Daily |

| Process Description |
|---|
| Provision of Item Processing services to bank |

| Critical Time Periods |
|---|
| **X** daily ☐ end of week ☐ month-end ☐ quarter-end ☐ year-end ☐ other As needed. |

| Peak Processing Periods |
|---|
| Weekly. |

| Maximum Tolerable Downtime |
|---|
| Less than one day. |

| Impacts (0 = No Impact, 5 = Greatest Impact) ||
|---|---|
| *Financial Impact* | No quantifiable impact |
| *Internal Customers* | 5 – Loss of IS service |
| *External Customers* | 5 – Loss of bank services |
| *Bank Operation Efficiency* | 5 – Loss of IS service |
| *Legal and Regulatory* | 5 – Unable to comply |
| *Industry Reputation* | 5 – Immediate – loss of bank services |
| *Employee Morale* | 5 – Unable to process payroll and benefits |

| Dependencies ||||
|---|---|---|---|
| *Interdepartmental* | *Department* | *Inputs* | *Outputs* |
| | All retail depts. | All | All |
| | | | |
| | | | |
| | | | |
| *External* | *Company* | *Inputs* | *Outputs* |
| | Vendors | | |
| | | | |
| | | | |
| | | | |

**GLBA Bank**
**Business Impact Assessment Report**

| Computer Applications | | | |
|---|---|---|---|
| *Mainframe* | *Client/Server* | *LAN/WAN* | *Local* |
| All | | | |
| | | | |
| | | | |
| | | | |

| Alternates | |
|---|---|
| *Loss of Facility* | See Item Processing recovery plan |
| *Loss of IT Systems* | See Item Processing recovery plan |
| *Alternate Sites* | See Item Processing recovery plan |

| Recovery Resource Requirements (See Item Processing Recovery Plan) | | | | | |
|---|---|---|---|---|---|
| *Personnel* | | *Modems* | | *Hardcopy Files* | |
| *Telephones* | | *Printers* | | *Microfilm* | |
| *Networked PCs* | | *Photocopiers* | | *Special Forms* | |
| *Standalone PCs* | | *Fax Machines* | | *Other (Below)* | |
| | | | | | |

| Overall Criticality (0 = Least Critical, 5 = Most Critical) | |
|---|---|
| *Within This Department Only* | 5 |
| *Criticality to Overall Bank Operations* | 5 |

**GLBA Bank**
**Business Impact Assessment Report**

| Business Process | Process Owner | Title |
|---|---|---|
| Wire Transfer | | Sen. Vice President |
| **Department** | | **Process Frequency** |
| Cashiers | | Daily |

| Process Description |
|---|
| Branch takes a customer request. Branch calls and faxes. Cashiers verifies the test key. Domestic transfers are prepared and sent on Fedline. Branch prepares the entry to charge the customer and sends it to Cashiers. (For foreign wires, Cashiers uses 3rd-party services.) |

| Critical Time Periods |
|---|
| ☐ daily ☐ end of week ☐ month-end ☐ quarter-end ☐ year-end ☐other<br>No critical time periods. |

| Peak Processing Periods |
|---|
| No peak processing periods. |

| Maximum Tolerable Downtime |
|---|
| 1 business day. |

| Impacts (0 = No Impact, 5 = Greatest Impact) | |
|---|---|
| *Financial Impact* | $5,000 per month |
| *Internal Customers* | 3 – Branches |
| *External Customers* | 3 – Customers |
| *Bank Operation Efficiency* | 0 – No identifiable impact |
| *Legal and Regulatory* | 0 – No identifiable impact |
| *Industry Reputation* | 5 – After 3 days |
| *Employee Morale* | 0 – No identifiable impact |

| Dependencies | | | |
|---|---|---|---|
| *Interdepartmental* | *Department* | *Inputs* | *Outputs* |
| | Branches | Wire transfer requests | Wire transfers |
| | Acctg. | Federal reserve balances | |
| | | | |
| | | | |
| *External* | *Company* | *Inputs* | *Outputs* |
| | Fedline | | |
| | 3rd-party vendors | | |
| | | | |
| | | | |

**GLBA Bank**
**Business Impact Assessment Report**

| Computer Applications | | | |
|---|---|---|---|
| *Mainframe* | *Client/Server* | *LAN/WAN* | *Local* |
| | | | Fedline (modem) |
| | | | |
| | | | |
| | | | |

| Alternates | |
|---|---|
| *Loss of Facility* | Backup Fedline terminal or Fedphone |
| *Loss of IT Systems* | Fedphone |
| *Alternate Sites* | Ualena Street |

| Recovery Resource Requirements | | | | | |
|---|---|---|---|---|---|
| *Personnel* | 2 | *Modems* | 0 | *Hardcopy Files* | Y |
| *Telephones* | 1 | *Printers* | 1 | *Microfilm* | N |
| *Networked PCs* | 2 | *Photocopiers* | 0 | *Special Forms* | N |
| *Standalone PCs* | 0 | *Fax Machines* | 1 | *Other (Below)* | |
| | | | | | |

| Overall Criticality (0 = Least Critical, 5 = Most Critical) | |
|---|---|
| *Within This Department Only* | 4 |
| *Criticality to Overall Bank Operations* | 3 |

**GLBA Bank**
**Business Impact Assessment Report**

| Business Process | Process Owner | Title |
|---|---|---|
| Branch Support | | Assist. Vice President |
| Department | | Process Frequency |
| Marketing | | As needed |

| Process Description |
|---|
| Department heads and compliance approves new material. Cashiers gives updates on regulatory-related material. Marketing maintains and creates brochures, disclosures, lobby signs, envelope stuffers, etc. Marketing goes through internal printing and the bank's advertising agency. |
| **Critical Time Periods** |
| ☐ daily ☐ end of week ☐ month-end ☐ quarter-end ☐ year-end  **X** other |
| Produce account totals by branch for branch managers by the 3rd Thursday of each month. |
| **Peak Processing Periods** |
| Varies – to handle special projects. |

| Maximum Tolerable Downtime |
|---|
| 30 days to get disclosure updates to branches. |

| Impacts (0 = No Impact, 5 = Greatest Impact) | |
|---|---|
| *Financial Impact* | No identifiable impact |
| *Internal Customers* | 1 – 30 days when disclosure notices run out |
| *External Customers* | 0 – No identifiable impact |
| *Bank Operation Efficiency* | 1 – 30 days when disclosure notices run out |
| *Legal and Regulatory* | 1 – Disclosures and signs quarterly for OCC & FDIC |
| *Industry Reputation* | 1 – 30 days when disclosure notices run out |
| *Employee Morale* | 0 – No identifiable impact |

| Dependencies | | | |
|---|---|---|---|
| *Interdepartmental* | *Department* | *Inputs* | *Outputs* |
| | Sen. Mgmnt. | New product information | Brochures |
| | Printing | New regulations | Signs |
| | Compliance | | Disclosure notices |
| | Cashiers | | Other marketing material |
| *External* | *Company* | *Inputs* | *Outputs* |
| | Ad. Agency | | |
| | | | |
| | | | |
| | | | |

## GLBA Bank
## Business Impact Assessment Report

| Computer Applications | | | |
|---|---|---|---|
| *Mainframe* | *Client/Server* | *LAN/WAN* | *Local* |
| | | | MSOffice |
| | | | Publisher |
| | | | |
| | | | |

| Alternates | |
|---|---|
| *Loss of Facility* | See disaster management plan |
| *Loss of IT Systems* | See disaster management plan |
| *Alternate Sites* | Operations Center Ualena Street |

| Recovery Resource Requirements | | | | | |
|---|---|---|---|---|---|
| *Personnel* | 1 | *Modems* | 0 | *Hardcopy Files* | Y |
| *Telephones* | 1 | *Printers* | 1 | *Microfilm* | N |
| *Networked PCs* | 1 | *Photocopiers* | 1 | *Special Forms* | N |
| *Standalone PCs* | 0 | *Fax Machines* | 0 | *Other (Below)* | |
| | | | | | |

| Overall Criticality (0 = Least Critical, 5 = Most Critical) | |
|---|---|
| *Within This Department Only* | 5 |
| *Criticality to Overall Bank Operations* | 2 |

**GLBA Bank**
**Business Impact Assessment Report**

| Business Process | Process Owner | Title |
| --- | --- | --- |
| Internal Communications | | Assist. Vice President |
| **Department** | | **Process Frequency** |
| Marketing | | As needed |

| Process Description | | |
| --- | --- | --- |
| Marketing generates newsletters, special projects materials, incentive program materials, etc. | | |
| **Critical Time Periods** | | |
| ☐ daily ☐ end of week ☐ month-end ☐ quarter-end ☐ year-end **X** other | | |
| As needed. | | |
| **Peak Processing Periods** | | |
| No peak processing periods. | | |

| Maximum Tolerable Downtime |
| --- |
| Not critical. |

| Impacts (0 = No Impact, 5 = Greatest Impact) | |
| --- | --- |
| *Financial Impact* | No identifiable impact |
| *Internal Customers* | 0 – No identifiable impact |
| *External Customers* | 0 – No identifiable impact |
| *Bank Operation Efficiency* | 0 – No identifiable impact |
| *Legal and Regulatory* | 1 – Changes in regulations – 30 days |
| *Industry Reputation* | 0 – No identifiable impact |
| *Employee Morale* | 0 – No identifiable impact |

| Dependencies | | | |
| --- | --- | --- | --- |
| *Interdepartmental* | *Department* | *Inputs* | *Outputs* |
| | Cashiers | | Newsletters |
| | Compliance | | Special projects material |
| | Internet Support | | Incentive program material, etc. |
| | | | Other marketing material |
| *External* | *Company* | *Inputs* | *Outputs* |
| | | | |
| | | | |
| | | | |
| | | | |

## GLBA Bank
## Business Impact Assessment Report

| Computer Applications | | | |
|---|---|---|---|
| *Mainframe* | *Client/Server* | *LAN/WAN* | *Local* |
| | | | MSOffice |
| | | | Publisher |
| | | | |
| | | | |

| Alternates | |
|---|---|
| *Loss of Facility* | Not covered by disaster management plan |
| *Loss of IT Systems* | Not covered by disaster management plan |
| *Alternate Sites* | Operations Center Ualena Street |

| Recovery Resource Requirements | | | | | |
|---|---|---|---|---|---|
| *Personnel* | 1 | *Modems* | 0 | *Hardcopy Files* | Y |
| *Telephones* | 1 | *Printers* | 1 | *Microfilm* | N |
| *Networked PCs* | 1 | *Photocopiers* | 1 | *Special Forms* | N |
| *Standalone PCs* | 0 | *Fax Machines* | 0 | *Other (Below)* | |

| Overall Criticality (0 = Least Critical, 5 = Most Critical) | |
|---|---|
| *Within This Department Only* | 5 |
| *Criticality to Overall Bank Operations* | 1 |

**GLBA Bank**
**Business Impact Assessment Report**

| Business Process | Process Owner | Title |
|---|---|---|
| Loan Approval | | Vice President |
| **Department** | | **Process Frequency** |
| Loan Services | | Daily |

| Process Description |
|---|
| |

| Critical Time Periods |
|---|
| ☐ daily **X** end of week ☐ month-end ☐ quarter-end ☐ year-end ☐ other<br>For management loan committee approvals – has to be in on that afternoon  Management Loan Committee approvals must be submitted to the Credit Dept. by Tuesday evening for presentation on Friday mornings. |
| **Peak Processing Periods** |
| None. |

| Maximum Tolerable Downtime |
|---|
| Five business days – customers waiting for approval. |

| Impacts (0 = No Impact, 5 = Greatest Impact) | |
|---|---|
| *Financial Impact* | No identifiable impact |
| *Internal Customers* | 4 – After one week – unable approve loans |
| *External Customers* | 5 – After one week – unable to approve loans |
| *Bank Operation Efficiency* | 4 – After one week – unable to approve loans |
| *Legal and Regulatory* | 0 – No identifiable impact |
| *Industry Reputation* | 4 – After one week – unable approve loans |
| *Employee Morale* | 0 – No identifiable impact |

| Dependencies | | | |
|---|---|---|---|
| *Interdepartmental* | *Department* | *Inputs* | *Outputs* |
| | Loan Admin. | Name & SS# | Credit score |
| | Loan Services | All approved loan info. | Loan record |
| | | Promissory note | Daily maintenance |
| | | Loan approval sheet | |
| *External* | *Company* | *Inputs* | *Outputs* |
| | Credit scoring | | |
| | | | |
| | | | |
| | | | |

**GLBA Bank**
**Business Impact Assessment Report**

| Computer Applications | | | |
|---|---|---|---|
| *Mainframe* | *Client/Server* | *LAN/WAN* | *Local* |
| | | Credit Analysis | MSOffice |
| | | | |
| | | | |
| | | | |

| Alternates | |
|---|---|
| *Loss of Facility* | See disaster management plans |
| *Loss of IT Systems* | See disaster management plans |
| *Alternate Sites* | Not known |

| Recovery Resource Requirements | | | | | |
|---|---|---|---|---|---|
| *Personnel* | 16 | *Modems* | 0 | *Hardcopy Files* | Y |
| *Telephones* | 16 | *Printers* | 3 | *Microfilm* | Y |
| *Networked PCs* | 13 | *Photocopiers* | 1 | *Special Forms* | N |
| *Standalone PCs* | 0 | *Fax Machines* | 1 | *Other (Below)* | |
| | | | | | |

| Overall Criticality (0 = Least Critical, 5 = Most Critical) | |
|---|---|
| *Within This Department Only* | 4 |
| *Criticality to Overall Bank Operations* | 3 |

**GLBA Bank**
**Business Impact Assessment Report**

| Business Process | Process Owner | Title |
|---|---|---|
| Loan Services | | Vice President |
| **Department** | | **Process Frequency** |
| Loan Services | | Daily |

| Process Description |
|---|
| Enter approved loans. Prepare loan documents. Once loan documents are signed by the borrower, D disburse non-commercial, consumer loans. Indicate approval for commercial loans |

| Critical Time Periods |
|---|
| **X** daily ☐ end of week ☐ month-end ☐ quarter-end ☐ year-end ☐ other<br>New loans or changes must be in force  boarded within 24 hours. |

| Peak Processing Periods |
|---|
| At March, June, September, and December for portfolio update. |

| Maximum Tolerable Downtime |
|---|
| Two business days. |

| Impacts (0 = No Impact, 5 = Greatest Impact) | |
|---|---|
| *Financial Impact* | No identifiable impact |
| *Internal Customers* | 4 – After one week – unable issue approved loans |
| *External Customers* | 5 – Immediately – unable to issue approved loans |
| *Bank Operation Efficiency* | 4 – Immediately – unable to issue approved loans |
| *Legal and Regulatory* | 0 – No identifiable impact. |
| *Industry Reputation* | 4 – After one week – unable issue approved loans |
| *Employee Morale* | 0 – No identifiable impact |

| Dependencies | | | |
|---|---|---|---|
| *Interdepartmental* | *Department* | *Inputs* | *Outputs* |
| | All depts. Loan Services Department | Monetary fields of loan | File maint. |
| | Special Assets Loan Document Review Dept. | Loan document audit | Insurance follow-up to assure that all signed loan documents and collateral are as required. |
| | Corp. Banking | | Customer inquiries & requests. |

**GLBA Bank**
**Business Impact Assessment Report**

| Dependencies | | | |
|---|---|---|---|
| *Interdepartmental* | *Department* | *Inputs* | *Outputs* |
| | Credit Dept. Loan Services Department | | Coupon payment books, billings, insurance follow-up, reports, inquiries (internal & external) |
| *External* | *Company* | *Inputs* | *Outputs* |
| | Tracking insurance | Borrower information | Credit Dept Loan Services Dept., extracts |
| | Mortgage release | Loan terms | |
| | | | |
| | | | |

| Computer Applications | | | |
|---|---|---|---|
| *Mainframe* | *Client/Server* | *LAN/WAN* | *Local* |
| ITI | | | MSOffice |
| | | | |
| | | | |
| | | | |

| Alternates | |
|---|---|
| *Loss of Facility* | See disaster management plans |
| *Loss of IT Systems* | See disaster management plans |
| *Alternate Sites* | Not known |

| Recovery Resource Requirements | | | | | |
|---|---|---|---|---|---|
| *Personnel* | 6 | *Modems* | 0 | *Hardcopy Files* | Y |
| *Telephones* | 3 | *Printers* | 2 | *Microfilm* | N |
| *Networked PCs* | 6 | *Photocopiers* | 1 | *Special Forms* | N |
| *Standalone PCs* | 0 | *Fax Machines* | 1 | *Other (Below)* | |

| Overall Criticality (0 = Least Critical, 5 = Most Critical) | |
|---|---|
| *Within This Department Only* | 5 |
| *Criticality to Overall Bank Operations* | 3 |

**GLBA Bank**
**Business Impact Assessment Report**

| Business Process | Process Owner | Title |
|---|---|---|
| Mortgage Origination | | Assistant Vice President |
| **Department** | | **Process Frequency** |
| Mortgage | | As need |

| Process Description |
|---|
| Buyer may go to branch but will be referred to. An application packet is sent to the customer. The customer comes in to review the application **with the loan officer. If the loan request conforms to a bank program, the application is accepted and data inputted** to **the loan origination software, which will up-load** the automated underwriting **investor program (AU). AU** generates a findings report **detailing the necessary documentation needed for final loan approval and sale to the investor. The** Mortgage **processor** orders the appraisal, flood details, title search, etc. Mortgage sends a letter to the buyer. If the buyer accepts the terms, Mortgage **will lock in the rate with the investor,** orders **loan** documents from the attorney's office **(Note and Mortgage)** and schedules a closing. After closing, documents are recorded with the Bureau of Conveyance and the loan is boarded on ITI. |

| Critical Time Periods |
|---|
| ☐ daily ☐ end of week ☐ month-end ☐ quarter-end ☐ year-end **X** other |
| 3 days after an application is made to get the federal disclosure done. If buyer wants to lock rate, 30 days to deliver loan to investor. **Credit decision within 30 days of a completed application.** |

| Peak Processing Periods |
|---|
| Summer months are busy. |

| Maximum Tolerable Downtime |
|---|
| 2 business days. |

| Impacts (0 = No Impact, 5 = Greatest Impact) | |
|---|---|
| *Financial Impact* | $50,000 per month |
| *Internal Customers* | 0 – No identifiable impact |
| *External Customers* | 5 – After two days |
| *Bank Operation Efficiency* | 5 – After one week |
| *Legal and Regulatory* | 0 – No identifiable impact |
| *Industry Reputation* | 5 – After 2 days |
| *Employee Morale* | 0 – No identifiable impact |

| Dependencies | | | |
|---|---|---|---|
| *Interdepartmental* | *Department* | *Inputs* | *Outputs* |
| | Branches | Loan applications | Loan files |
| | ISD | Findings report | Loan |
| | Appraisals | Appraisal report | |
| | Acctg. | Title, flood det., etc. | |
| *External* | *Company* | *Inputs* | *Outputs* |

**GLBA Bank**
**Business Impact Assessment Report**

|  | Attorney |  |  |
|--|----------|--|--|
|  | Secondary lenders |  |  |
|  | Escrow, title co., etc. |  |  |
|  |  |  |  |

| Computer Applications | | | |
|-----------------------|--|--|--|
| *Mainframe* | *Client/Server* | *LAN/WAN* | *Local* |
| ITI |  | Contour |  |
|  |  | **Mornet** |  |
|  |  | 3rd-party Websites |  |
|  |  |  |  |

| Alternates | |
|------------|--|
| *Loss of Facility* | See disaster management plan |
| *Loss of IT Systems* | See ISD recovery plan (Contour not included) |
| *Alternate Sites* | Ualena Street |

| Recovery Resource Requirements | | | | | |
|-------------------------------|--|--|--|--|--|
| *Personnel* | 4 | *Modems* | 1 | *Hardcopy Files* | Y |
| *Telephones* | 3 | *Printers* | 1 | *Microfilm* | N |
| *Networked PCs* | 3 | *Photocopiers* | 1 | *Special Forms* | Y |
| *Standalone PCs* | 0 | *Fax Machines* | 1 | *Other (Below)* |  |
|  |  |  |  |  |  |

| Overall Criticality (0 = Least Critical, 5 = Most Critical) | |
|-----------------------------------------------------------|--|
| *Within This Department Only* | 5 |
| *Criticality to Overall Bank Operations* | 4 |

**GLBA Bank**
**Business Impact Assessment Report**

| Business Process | Process Owner | Title |
|---|---|---|
| Loan Collection | | Vice President |
| **Department** | | **Process Frequency** |
| Special Assets | | Daily |

| Process Description |
|---|
| Action Plan Committee transfers a loan to Special Assets (or a branch notifies SA or SA reviews the delinquency report). SA gets the loan files, reviews them and discusses them with the loan officer to decide strategy. If it is a legal matter, engage an attorney. If the loan can be worked out then interview borrower and set up a plan. Modify the loan record. |
| **Critical Time Periods** |
| ☐ daily ☐ end of week **X** month-end **X** quarter-end **X** year-end ☐ other Depends on the loan. Try to get workout be end of month. |
| **Peak Processing Periods** |
| Busier toward the end of year trying to clean up the portfolio. |

| Maximum Tolerable Downtime |
|---|
| Up to one month – or by the time the next delinquency report comes. |

| Impacts (0 = No Impact, 5 = Greatest Impact) | |
|---|---|
| Financial Impact | No quantifiable impact |
| Internal Customers | 1 – Loan portfolio impacted after a month |
| External Customers | 1 – As for internal customers |
| Bank Operation Efficiency | 1 – Collected amounts decrease after one month |
| Legal and Regulatory | 0 – No identifiable impact |
| Industry Reputation | 1 – After more than 1 month |
| Employee Morale | 0 – No identifiable impact |

| Dependencies | | | |
|---|---|---|---|
| Interdepartmental | Department | Inputs | Outputs |
| | Action Committee. | Delinquency reports | Loan workouts |
| | Loan Officers | | Action plans |
| | ISD | | Delinquency report updates |
| | | | |
| External | Company | Inputs | Outputs |
| | Attorneys | | |
| | Collection agencies | | |
| | Credit bureau | | |

**GLBA Bank**
**Business Impact Assessment Report**

| Computer Applications | | | |
|---|---|---|---|
| *Mainframe* | *Client/Server* | *LAN/WAN* | *Local* |
| ITI | | PC Link | MSOffice |
| Director | | | |
| Charge Card | | | |
| | | | |

| Alternates | |
|---|---|
| *Loss of Facility* | See disaster management plan |
| *Loss of IT Systems* | Work from last delinquency report |
| *Alternate Sites* | Dillingham |

| Recovery Resource Requirements | | | | | |
|---|---|---|---|---|---|
| *Personnel* | 3 | *Modems* | 0 | *Hardcopy Files* | Y |
| *Telephones* | 3 | *Printers* | 1 | *Microfilm* | N |
| *Networked PCs* | 3 | *Photocopiers* | 1 | *Special Forms* | N |
| *Standalone PCs* | 0 | *Fax Machines* | 1 | *Other (Below)* | |
| | | | | | |

| Overall Criticality (0 = Least Critical, 5 = Most Critical) | |
|---|---|
| *Within This Department Only* | 5 |
| *Criticality to Overall Bank Operations* | 3 |

**GLBA Bank**
**Business Impact Assessment Report**

| Business Process | Process Owner | Title |
|---|---|---|
| Recovery | | Vice President |
| **Department** | | **Process Frequency** |
| Special Assets | | Daily |

| Process Description |
|---|
| Lending unit generates a charge off request. Request is approved. Loan servicing modifies the loan status on the system. Special assets takes responsibility. Recovery process (calls, letters, litigation, etc.). Cash goes to Loan Servicing. |
| **Critical Time Periods** |
| ☐ daily  ☐ end of week  ☐ month-end  ☐ quarter-end  ☐ year-end  ☐ other As needed. |
| **Peak Processing Periods** |
| None. |

| Maximum Tolerable Downtime |
|---|
| Not applicable. |

| Impacts (0 = No Impact, 5 = Greatest Impact) | |
|---|---|
| Financial Impact | No quantifiable impact |
| Internal Customers | 0 – No identifiable impact |
| External Customers | 0 – No identifiable impact |
| Bank Operation Efficiency | 1 – Recoveries go down after one month |
| Legal and Regulatory | 0 – No identifiable impact |
| Industry Reputation | 1 – After more than 1 month |
| Employee Morale | 0 – No identifiable impact |

| Dependencies | | | |
|---|---|---|---|
| Interdepartmental | Department | Inputs | Outputs |
| | Action Committee | Delinquency reports | |
| | Loan Officers | | |
| | | | |
| | | | |
| External | Company | Inputs | Outputs |
| | Attorneys | | |
| | Collection agencies | | |
| | Credit Bureau | | |
| | | | |

**GLBA Bank**
**Business Impact Assessment Report**

| Computer Applications | | | |
|---|---|---|---|
| *Mainframe* | *Client/Server* | *LAN/WAN* | *Local* |
| ITI | | | |
| | | | |
| | | PC Link | |
| | | | |

| Alternates | |
|---|---|
| *Loss of Facility* | See disaster management plan |
| *Loss of IT Systems* | |
| *Alternate Sites* | Dillingham |

| Recovery Resource Requirements | | | | | |
|---|---|---|---|---|---|
| *Personnel* | 1 | *Modems* | 0 | *Hardcopy Files* | Y |
| *Telephones* | 1 | *Printers* | 1 | *Microfilm* | N |
| *Networked PCs* | 1 | *Photocopiers* | 1 | *Special Forms* | Y |
| *Standalone PCs* | 0 | *Fax Machines* | 1 | *Other (Below)* | |

| Overall Criticality (0 = Least Critical, 5 = Most Critical) | |
|---|---|
| *Within This Department Only* | 3 |
| *Criticality to Overall Bank Operations* | 1 |

**GLBA Bank**
**Business Impact Assessment Report**

| Business Process | Process Owner | Title |
|---|---|---|
| Provision of Network | | PC Services Manager |
| **Department** | | **Process Frequency** |
| PC Services | | Daily |

| Process Description |
|---|
| Provision of network services to bank |
| **Critical Time Periods** |
| **X** daily ☐ end of week ☐ month-end ☐ quarter-end ☐ year-end ☐ other As needed. |
| **Peak Processing Periods** |
| Daily. |

| Maximum Tolerable Downtime |
|---|
| Less than one day. |

| Impacts (0 = No Impact, 5 = Greatest Impact) | |
|---|---|
| *Financial Impact* | No quantifiable impact |
| *Internal Customers* | 5 – Loss of IS service |
| *External Customers* | 5 – Loss of bank services |
| *Bank Operation Efficiency* | 5 – Loss of IS service |
| *Legal and Regulatory* | 5 – Unable to comply |
| *Industry Reputation* | 5 – Immediate loss of bank services |
| *Employee Morale* | 5 – Unable to process payroll and benefits |

| Dependencies | | | |
|---|---|---|---|
| *Interdepartmental* | *Department* | *Inputs* | *Outputs* |
| | All depts. | All | All |
| | | | |
| | | | |
| *External* | *Company* | *Inputs* | *Outputs* |
| | Vendors | | |
| | | | |
| | | | |
| | | | |

**GLBA Bank**
**Business Impact Assessment Report**

| Computer Applications | | | |
|---|---|---|---|
| *Mainframe* | *Client/Server* | *LAN/WAN* | *Local* |
| All | | | |
| | | | |
| | | | |
| | | | |

| Alternates | |
|---|---|
| *Loss of Facility* | See PC Services recovery plan |
| *Loss of IT Systems* | See PC Services recovery plan |
| *Alternate Sites* | Ualena Street |

| Recovery Resource Requirements (See PC Services Recovery Plan) | | | | | |
|---|---|---|---|---|---|
| *Personnel* | | *Modems* | | *Hardcopy Files* | |
| *Telephones* | | *Printers* | | *Microfilm* | |
| *Networked PCs* | | *Photocopiers* | | *Special Forms* | |
| *Standalone PCs* | | *Fax Machines* | | *Other (Below)* | |
| | | | | | |

| Overall Criticality (0 = Least Critical, 5 = Most Critical) | |
|---|---|
| *Within This Department Only* | 5 |
| *Criticality to Overall Bank Operations* | 5 |

# Sample Risk Assessment Management Summary Report

## Customer Information Held and Processed at GLBA Bank, October 21, 2008

## Attendees

### Assessment Team

| | |
|---|---|
| Gilbert Godfried | Nicole Kidmann |
| Katherine Turner | Lloyd Nolan |
| Bill Aikman | Liane Bronco |
| Leonard Elmore | Gerry Lee |
| Myra Osmond | Melvinia Nattia |
| Mike Illich | Ryan Harris |
| Wayne Fontes | MaryJane Ashman |
| Linda Wright | |

### Facilitator

Thomas R. Peltier, Peltier and Associates

### Scribes

Lisa Bryson and Julie Peltier, Peltier and Associates

## Risk Assessment Scope Summary

On October 23, 2008, the GLBA Bank (GLBA) risk assessment team and Peltier and Associates met to review the scope of a risk assessment to be conducted on Nonpublic Personal Customer Information held and/or processed at GLBA. The team discussed the most recent Office of the Comptroller of the Currency (OCC) examination of GLBA. The team also reviewed the December 21, 2003, Visioneering, Inc. (VI) information system audit; the Gross Technology Partners (GTP) November 18, 2003 Penetration Test and Network Vulnerability Assessment report; and the GLBA Internal Audit report of November 30, 2003. The findings of these reviews, assessments, and audits were used to develop a risk assessment scope statement.

On October 24, 2008, GLBA Bank (GLBA) staff at the 45 North Main Avenue, Buzzover, UT, conducted the risk assessment. The intent of this process was to identify threats that could signify risk to the integrity, confidentiality, and availability of Nonpublic Personal Customer Information being held and/or processed by GLBA.

Fifteen (15) GLBA employees participated in the process. These employees represented a variety of users with a broad range of expertise and knowledge of GLBA operations and business processes. The various Bank areas represented helped support a multidisciplinary and knowledge based approach to the risk assessment process. These employees were asked to participate within a candid, reflective atmosphere so that a thorough and clear representation of GLBA's potential business risks to customer information could be developed.

## Assessment Methodology Used

The Facilitated Risk Analysis and Assessment Process (FRAAP) was created by Peltier and Associates in 1993. The FRAAP was received within the information security industry through its inclusion as a course in the 1995 Computer Security Institute's calendar of classes. The FRAAP was further promoted in the industry upon publication of the book *Information Security Risk Analysis* by Auerbach Publications. The General Accounting Office (GAO) reviewed the FRAAP in 1998 and issued the Government Accounting Office May 1998 Executive Guide for Information Security Management (GAO/AIMD 98-68). This executive guide supplemented the Office of Management and Budget's revision of Circular A-130, Appendix III recommending qualitative risk analysis for government agencies.

The FRAAP process is consistent with the National Institute of Standards and Technology October 2001 Special Publication *Risk Management Guide of Information Technology Systems* and the FFIEC December 2002 *Information Security Risk Assessment*.

A senior facilitator led the process, assisted by GLBA Information Security personnel. Participants were asked to identify risks to the availability, confidentiality, and integrity of Customer Information held and/or processed by GLBA Bank.

All risks were reviewed and consolidated to eliminate redundancy. All risks were then examined to determine whether an existing control or safeguard was in place at GLBA. Typically, the examination of existing controls is conducted after the risk level has been established. Due to time constraints, these steps were transposed to affect a more streamlined, accelerated risk assessment process.

Participants were asked to rate each risk in terms of probability of occurrence (high, medium, and low) and then business impact (high, medium, low). The GLBA risk assessment team, with assistance from Peltier and Associates, examined the controls identified to determine whether existing controls were adequate. Low criticality items are not included in final counts summarized in the assessment findings below, as they are normally deferred to a "Monitor" status in final recommendations

## Assessment Findings and Action Plan

The risk assessment process identified one hundred and thirteen (113) potential risks in the areas of confidentiality, integrity, and availability. Approximately sixty percent of the risks identified were classified by the team as moderate to low level of risk. Of the remaining risks, six (6) were categorized as Priority A (requiring immediate correction), and fifty-four (54) Priority B (corrective action should be taken). The open number of priority risks has been significantly reduced through diligent efforts undertaken by the GLBA team.

The threat scenario categories with the highest rated risk levels are as follows:

| Risk Level | Number of Similar Threats | Description of Threat Scenario |
|:---:|:---:|---|
| A | 4 | Physical intrusion |
| A | 2 | Power failure |
| B | 10 | Information handling and classification |
| B | 4 | Password weakness or sharing |
| B | 4 | People masquerading as customers |
| B | 3 | Firewall concerns |
| B | 2 | Computer viruses |
| B | 2 | Workstations left unattended |
| B | 2 | Employee training |
| B | 27 | Individual threats identified |

The risk assessment identified five key areas of concern:

1. Restricted physical access areas should be considered throughout GLBA. *Action plan:* A physical security risk assessment will be conducted to determine whether there is a need to create restricted access areas and/or increase physical access controls.
2. Power failure could cause corruption of information or prevent access to the system. *Action plan:* Network UPS may not be adequate for a power outage out of regular business hours. Install a backup domain controller at Ualena Street and connect it to the Ualena Street UPS.
3. Information classification scheme is incomplete. *Action plan:* GLBA has created a draft Information Classification Policy that addresses five categories: public, internal use, restricted, confidential, and classified. The new policy requirements are to be disseminated to the GLBA staff and will become part of the new employee orientation and the annual employee awareness program.
4. Concern that the weakness of passwords for some information systems user accounts could allow compromise of the password and permit unauthorized access to GLBA systems and information. *Action plan:* The GLBA Passwords Policy is to be modified to require strong passwords. GLBA ISD will investigate software solutions to enforce a strong password requirement.
5. Someone could impersonate a customer to corrupt or access bank records or accounts. *Action plan:* Concern to be addressed in GLBA employee awareness program and new employee orientation.

## Full Findings Documentation

The completed risk assessment worksheets have been turned over to the GLBA Information Security Officer and are available through his office.

## Conclusion

The results of this risk assessment exercise proved to be fairly comprehensive in the breadth of the threat scenarios considered. The breadth of consideration can be directly attributed to the collaborative approach to the risk assessment process embraced by the GLBA participants. The results of this assessment should provide a solid foundation upon which to build and enhance future risk assessment efforts as GLBA moves forward to ensure that assessments are completed whenever changes to any relevant factors, such as new products, business processes, or new technologies occur.

**Pre-FRAAP Meeting Checklist**

| Issue | Remarks |
|---|---|
| **Prior to the meeting** | |
| 1. *Date of pre-FRAAP meeting:* Record when and where the meeting is scheduled. | |
| 2. *Project executive sponsor or owner:* Identify the owner or sponsor who has executive responsibility for the project. | |
| 3. *Project leader:* Identify the individual who is the primary point of contact for the project or asset under review. | |
| 4. *Pre-FRAAP meeting objective:* Identify what you hope to gain from the meeting — typically, the seven deliverables will be discussed. | |
| 5. *Project overview:* Prepare a project overview for presentation to the pre-FRAAP members during the meeting. | |
| Your understanding of the project scope | |
| The FRAAP methodology | |
| Milestones | |
| Pre-screening methodology | |
| 6. *Assumptions:* Identify assumptions used in developing the approach to performing the FRAAP project. | |
| 7. *Pre-screening results:* Record the results of the pre-screening process. | |
| **During the meeting** | |
| 8. *Business strategy, goals, and objectives:* Identify what the owner's objectives are and how they relate to larger company objectives. | |
| 9. *Project scope:* Define specifically the scope of the project and document it during the meeting so that all participating will know and agree. | |
| Applications/systems | |
| Business processes | |
| Business functions | |
| People and organizations | |
| Locations/facilities | |

*continued*

## Pre-FRAAP Meeting Checklist (continued)

| Issue | Remarks |
|---|---|
| **During the meeting (continued)** | |
| 10. *Time dependencies:* Identify time limitations and considerations the client may have. | |
| 11. *Risks/constraints:* Identify risks and constraints that could affect the successful conclusion of the project. | |
| 12. *Budget:* Identify any open budget/funding issues. | |
| 13. *FRAAP participants:* Identify by name and position the individuals whose participation in the FRAAP session is required. | |
| 14. *Administrative requirements:* Identify facility and equipment needs to perform the FRAAP session. | |
| 15. *Documentation:* Identify what documentation is required to prepare for the FRAAP session (provide the client the FRAAP document checklist). | |

| Issue | Remarks |
|---|---|
| **Prior to the meeting** | |
| 1. *Date of pre-FRAAP meeting:* Record when and where the meeting is scheduled. | |
| 2. *Project executive sponsor or owner:* Identify the owner or sponsor who has executive responsibility for the project. | |
| 3. *Project leader:* Identify the individual who is the primary point of contact for the project or asset under review. | |
| 4. *Pre-FRAAP meeting objective:* Identify what you hope to gain from the meeting — typically, the seven deliverables will be discussed. | |
| 5. *Project overview:* Prepare a project overview for presentation to the pre-FRAAP members during the meeting. | |
| Your understanding of the project scope | |
| The FRAAP methodology | |
| Milestones | |
| Pre-screening methodology | |
| 6. *Assumptions:* Identify assumptions used in developing the approach to performing the FRAAP project. | |

## Pre-FRAAP Meeting Checklist (continued)

| *Issue* | *Remarks* |
|---|---|
| **Prior the meeting (continued)** | |
| 7. *Pre-screening results:* Record the results of the pre-screening process. | |
| **During the meeting** | |
| 8. *Business strategy, goals, and objectives:* Identify what the owner's objectives are and how they relate to larger company objectives. | |
| 9. *Project scope:* Define specifically the scope of the project and document it during the meeting so that all participating will know and agree. | |
| Applications/systems | |
| Business processes | – |
| Business functions | |
| People and organizations | |
| Locations/facilities | |
| 10. *Time dependencies:* Identify time limitations and considerations the client may have. | |
| 11. *Risks/constraints:* Identify risks and constraints that could affect the successful conclusion of the project. | |
| 12. *Budget:* Identify any open budget/funding issues. | |
| 13. *FRAAP participants:* Identify by name and position the individuals whose participation in the FRAAP session is required. | |
| 14. *Administrative requirements:* Identify facility and equipment needs to perform the FRAAP session. | |
| 15. *Documentation:* Identify what documentation is required to prepare for the FRAAP session (provide the client the FRAAP document checklist). | |

# *Appendix J*

# Project Scope Statement

## Introduction

For any project to be successful, one must establish the boundaries for that specific project. Describe in detail which process is to be managed, precisely what resources are required, and what deliverables will constitute being finished. For any project to be successful, the development of the project scope statement must be as thorough as possible. It will be difficult to complete a project if all of the team members do not have the same vision of what is to be accomplished.

Typically, the team lead, the customer or owner, and a facilitator meet to complete the project scope statement during the initial phase of project planning. The key here is to establish the boundaries of what is to be accomplished. Most failed projects come to grief because the scope of the project is poorly defined to begin with or because the scope is not managed well and is allowed to "creep" until the project goes out of control. If you are going to manage any project, then the purpose of the project must be captured in the contents of the scope statement. All of the elements that go into writing a successful scope statement should be used to define the asset, and we will examine those elements shortly.

As with any project, the deliverable from the asset definition step is to reach agreement with the owner on what the assessment is to review and all relevant parameters. The objective here is to put in writing a risk assessment statement of opportunity that consists of two elements: project statement and specifications.

## Project Statement

For the project statement, identify the desired outcome. For example:

> The team will identify potential threats to the asset under review and will prioritize those threats by assessing the probability of the threat occurring and the impact to the asset if the threat happened. Using the prioritized list of risks, the team will identify possible controls, countermeasures, and/or safeguards that can reduce the risk exposure to an acceptable level.

This will become the risk assessment scope statement and provides the focus for the specifications.

## Specifications

Take enough time during the scope statement development to discuss and clarify the parameters of the project. Although these parameters will vary from project to project, the following items should be considered each time:

- *Purpose:* Fully understand the purpose of the project. What is the need driving the project? If the purpose is to correct a problem, identify the cause of the problem. The bulk of the supporting information should be found in the documentation generated from the project impact analysis (PIA) or risk analysis that was completed in the analysis phase of the system development life cycle (SDLC). A PIA has been performed that has decided that the project is to move forward. Review the results of this process to understand better the project's purpose. (More details on the PIA and risk analysis processes can be found in Chapter 2.)
- *Customer:* Your customer is the person or unit that has the need that this project is meant to fill. Determine who the real customer is and note other stakeholders. Typically, the stakeholders will become members of the project team. They will be assigned various tasks throughout the SDLC.
- *Deliverables:* These are specific things that are to be delivered to the customer. This is the statement that defines when a project is complete. For example, in a risk assessment the deliverables typically are (1) threats have been identified, (2) risk levels have been established, and (3) possible controls have been identified.
- *Resources:* Here the team wants to identify which of the following resources will be required to accomplish the project:
  - *Money:* Typically, we don't have "money," but we will need budget for the project.

- *Personnel:* This is where the identification of stakeholders comes into play. We also need to identify the infrastructure support requirements for the project.
- *Equipment:* Here is where the need for hardware, software, firmware, or anything else will be identified.
- *Supplies:* The team involved in the project may need to be housed together and the materials they need to support the project need to be identified.
- *Services:* As with equipment, there may be a need for services from other groups or third-party providers.

■ *Constraints:* Identify those activities that could impact the deliverables of the project. Consider such things as:

- *Laws:* It is very important that any project be developed with an understanding of the legal and regulatory climate currently impacting the organization. One of the team members should be from legal and regulatory affairs.
- *Policies:* Every organization should have a basic set of policies that discuss the expected conduct of the employees, business units, and organization. All new projects should have completed the PIA process. During the PIA, the team specifically addresses policy compliance.
- *Procedures:* Basic operating procedures ensure that the organization is able to function in a consistent manner. Even the development process must follow the development methodology procedures; included in this review is adherence to the change management procedures.

■ *Resource limitations:* Another key constraint is the impact of resources being unavailable. This includes hardware, software, firmware, and wetware. An example of a constraint that impacted a risk assessment project I was working on turned out to be an added-on front-end authenticator. The application was developed to be used by third parties that accessed the resources through the Internet. To provide some level of security, the team had developed a front-end authentication program. This program had never gone through the change management process and had not been subject to the development methodology requirements. Therefore, the results of the application risk assessment were skewed pending a risk assessment of the authenticator program.

■ *Assumptions:* Identify those things that the project team believes to be true or complete. Assumptions are ways to document what the team believes is the current operating environment. The following are examples of assumptions:

- An infrastructure risk assessment has been completed and that industry-accepted standards of control have been implemented.
- The project has gone through the PIA and has been registered as a formal project with an active budget code.

The work of the PIA process also addresses the viability of the vendor supplying the service or product. Without this due diligence process, vendor viability could be either a constraint or an assumption.

- *Criteria:* Agree specifically on how the customer will evaluate the success of the project. What are the customer's criteria to determine that the deliverables were presented on time? Within budget? With quality?

    Criteria should be relevant and valid measures of how well the project accomplishes its stated purpose. You may need to help the customer clarify their true needs to assure that the criteria to be used are valid indicators of project success.

## Well-Defined Standards and Metrics

Criteria should be relevant and valid measures of how well the project accomplishes its stated purpose. You may need to help the customer clarify their true needs to assure that the criteria to be used are valid and measurable indicators of project success.

The most difficult will be the quality issue. When creating a new program, we look to the requirements gathered in the analysis and design phases of the SDLC. If these key indicators are met and the application or system is developed according to the development methodology and was subject to the requirements of the change management process, then there is a good chance the quality issue will be satisfied.

For a project such as risk assessment, the quality issue is often resolved by the use of industry-accepted standards of control. An organization would select industry-accepted standards such as the following:

| International Standard | Formal Title |
| --- | --- |
| CobiT® | Control Objectives for Information and related Technology |
| ISO 27002 | Code of Practice for Information Security Management |
| ITIL | Information Technology Infrastructure Library |
| NIST 800-53 | Recommended Security Controls for Federal Information Systems |

Once the appropriate industry standard has been selected, the organization will have to identify the laws and regulations that are relevant for it. Once this list is created, the organization performs a gap analysis to determine their current compliance level.* The results of the GAP analysis will be a compliance program that will provide the risk assessment process with a level of expected quality.

---

* See, for example, Whiting, R. (2002). "Analysis Gap." *Information Week* (April 22, 2002). Available at http://www.informationweek.com/story/IWK20020418S0007.

| International Standard | Formal Title |
|---|---|
| CobiT | Control Objective for Information and Related Technology |
| ISO 27002 | Code of Practice for Information Security Management |
| ITIL | Information Technology Infrastructure Library |
| NIST 800–53 | Recommended Security Controls for Federal Information Systems |

**Figure J.1    Industry-accepted information security standards. Resources: CobiT® (http://www.isaca.org/Template.cfm?Section=COBIT6&Template=/ TaggedPage/TaggedPageDisplay.cfm&TPLID=55&ContentID=7981); ISO 27002 (renamed from ISO 17799 as of July 2007) (http://www.standardsdirect.org/ iso17799.htm); ITIL (http://www.itil-officialsite.com/home/home.asp); and NIST SP 800-53 (http://csrc.nist.gov/publications/nistpubs/800-53/SP800-53.pdf).**

## Summary

When Christopher Columbus headed off in 1492, he didn't know where he was going. When he got there, he didn't know where he was, and when he got home he didn't know where he had been. Although this project plan may work for fifteenth-century explorers, it is a bad model for twenty-first-century business and industry.

To run a successful project the boundaries of what is to be accomplished must be identified and agreed upon. This process must be documented and approved by the interested parties. An effective project scope statement provides for a solid road map to success.

# *Appendix K*

# Why Risk Assessments Fail

A risk assessment is the backbone of any effective information security program. It is impossible to know where to implement controls until the risks, threats, concerns, and issues have been identified. This process can only be completed if the risk assessment process is treated as any other properly run project. This appendix examines some of the key areas that cause risk assessment processes to fail.

## Scope Creep

Every successful project begins with a definition of what is to be accomplished. For risk assessment, this involves describing what is to be examined. This could be a physical environment such as a data center, a specific system such as a VAX cluster supporting research and development, a processing entity such as the corporate WAN or a subsection of the network such as the payroll administration LAN, or a specific application such as accounts payable.

In creating a statement of work or a scope statement, it is customary to begin with identifying the sponsor. This is normally the owner of the application, system, data, or process. The owner is typically described as the management person responsible for the protection of the asset in question. In most organizations, the sponsor is not an information systems (IS) person.

To limit the possibility of scope creep, it is necessary to establish the boundaries of what is to be examined. An application that uses the corporate network to pass data is within the scope of a normal risk assessment. However, conducting a corporate analysis of the security of the Internet may be counterproductive. Keep the focus on those processes that the organization can effect change.

The scope statement should address the overall objectives of the analysis. For information security, these objectives are normally the impact of threats on the integrity, confidentiality, and availability of information being processed by specific applications or systems. Consider the types of information security challenges facing your organization, and use this to define the objectives.

## Ineffective Project Team

Many information security professionals attempt to conduct the risk assessment either alone or just with other members of the security group. To be effective, the risk assessment process must have representatives from the following areas:

- Functional owners
- System users
- Systems analysts
- Applications programming
- Database administration
- Auditing (if appropriate)
- Physical security
- Communications networks
- Legal (if necessary)
- Processing operations management
- Systems programming (operating systems)

The key members of this team are the owner and the users. Make certain that there is representation from every business unit affected by the new application or system. This will assist in the acceptance of the final results or the analysis. By ensuring proper representation, the agreed-upon controls will come from the owners and users and not as an edict from security or audit.

## Stating Concerns as How They Impact Security

When conducting a risk assessment, it is necessary to state the concerns as to how they impact the business objectives or the mission of the organization and not as how they impact security objectives. Proper controls are implemented because there is a strong business need, not so that the business unit will be in compliance with security requirements. Keep the business of the organization foremost in the discussions during the risk assessment process.

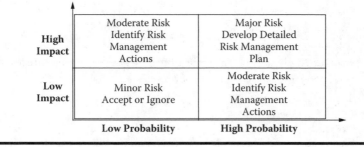

**Figure K.1   Possible ranking process.**

## Every Threat Is a Major Concern

Establish a method to prioritize the identified risks into categories of minor, moderate, or major. No organization has sufficient resources to control every identified risk. An effective risk assessment gains support when it attempts to ensure that limited corporate resources are spent where they will do the most good. A possible ranking process might be as simple as the one shown in figure K.1.

## Conclusion

Risk assessment is a necessary and cost-effective part of an effective information security program. It will support management in fulfilling its mandate to exercise their fiduciary duty to protect the assets and resources of the enterprise. By understanding how a risk assessment can fail, the security professional can take appropriate steps to ensure success.

# Appendix L

# Gap Analysis Examples

## Overview

There are three different examples of a gap analysis for you in this section. The first examines a specific company and maps its security program to ISO 17799. The highest severity issues are identified with five stars (*****) so that management can quickly grasp which issues need to be addressed first. This is done by first identifying which components exist in the security program based on the questions asked. After the issue is identified, a recommendation for compliance is made. Many times we examine the policy or procedures to determine whether they meet minimum security standards.

The review of the policies and procedures allows the reviewer to determine whether the documents need to be updated as indicated with the use of four stars (****). This particular organization also needed to identify issues where no policy or procedure was currently available. Note that the gray shading identified those areas outside the scope of the analysis.

The second example of a gap analysis uses a special set of security requirements for a utility company. Here the reviewer examines the requirements. The next item established is whether the company has a corresponding control, policy, or procedure. Once that is determined, the reviewer develops a recommendation.

The third gap analysis maps the new ISO 27002 to a regulation that the company must comply with. Here they used Payment Card Industry Data Security Standard (PCI DSS) and then identified the existing company policies and procedures. I like the third example best because it identifies more than one requirement and maps the organization's current program to those requirements.

## Gap Analysis Using ISO 17799

| Findings Key | |
|:---:|:---|
| ***** | Immediate action required |
| **** | Needs updating |
| *** | No corporation direction currently available |
| Gray | Outside the scope |

### *Answer the Following Questions*

## 3 SECURITY POLICY

*Note:* ISO17799 Sections 1 and 2 are non-action items and are not included in this checklist.

| 3.1 | Information Security Policy | Management direction and support for information security must be clearly established. | | |
|-----|----------------------------|---------------------------------------------------------------------------------------|-----|---|
| 3.1.1 | Information Security Policy Document Development | Has an information security policy document been developed? | Yes | IT Security Policies: Acceptable Use Policy<br>IT Policies: Forward, Scope, and Introduction (3.1.1) |
| 3.1.2 | Information Security Policy Document Publication | Has an information security policy document been published? | Yes | March 15, 2005<br>March 21, 2005 |

| 4 ORGANIZATIONAL SECURITY | | |
|---|---|---|
| 4.1 Information Security Infrastructure | A management framework must be established to initiate and control the implementation of information security within the organization. | |
| 4.1.1 Management Information Security Forum | Has a forum been established to oversee and represent information security? | Yes | IT Policies: Information Security Roles and Responsibilities Policy (9.1) |
| 4.1.2 Information Security Coordination | Has a process been established to coordinate implementation of information security measures? | Yes | IT Policies: Information Security Roles and Responsibilities Policy |
| 4.1.3 Allocation of Information Security Responsibilities | Are responsibilities for accomplishment of information security requirements clearly defined? | Yes | IT Policies: Information Security Roles and Responsibilities Policy |
| 4.1.4 Authorization Process for Information Processing Facilities | Has a management approval process been established to authorize new IT facilities from both a business and technical standpoint? | Y ___ N ___ | Out of scope of assessment |
| 4.1.5 Specialist Information Security Advice | Has a capability been established that provides specialized information security advice? | Yes | IT Policies: Information Security Roles and Responsibilities Policy (8.1.2) |
| 4.1.6 Cooperation between Organizations | Is there a liaison with external information security personnel and organizations including industry and/or government security specialists; law enforcement authorities; IT service providers; telecommunications authorities? | Yes | CISO is a member of ISSA and a CISSP and attends the CSI conferences |

| 4.1.7 | Independent Review of Information Security | Has an independent review of information security practices been conducted to ensure feasibility, effectiveness, and compliance with written policies? | Yes | IT Policies: Information Security Roles and Responsibilities Policy (6.1) |
|---|---|---|---|---|
| 4.2 | Security of Third-Party Access | The organizational IT facilities and information assets that control the access of non-organizational third parties must be kept secure. | | |
| 4.2.1 | Identification of Risks from Third-Party Access | Have third-party connection risks been analyzed? | Yes | IT Policies: Contractors, Vendors, Consultants and Third-Parties Policy (5.1.2) |
| | Combating Risks from Third-Party Connections | Have specific security measures been identified to combat third-party connection risks? | Yes | IT Policies: Contractors, Vendors, Consultants and Third-Parties Policy (5.1.2) |
| 4.2.2 | Security Conditions in Third-Party Contracts | Are security requirements included in formal third-party contracts? | Yes | IT Policies: Contractors, Vendors, Consultants and Third-Parties Policy (4.1.3) |
| 4.3 | Outsourcing | The security of information should be maintained even when the responsibility for the processing has been outsourced to another organization. | | |
| 4.3.1 | Security Requirements in Outsourcing Contracts | Have the security requirements of the information owners been addressed in a contract between the owners and the outsource organization? | Yes | IT Policies: Contractors, Vendors, Consultants and Third-Parties Policy (4.1.2) |

| 5 ASSET CLASSIFICATION & CONTROL | | | |
|---|---|---|---|
| 5.1 Accounting for Assets | All information assets should be accounted for and have a nominated owner assigned. | | |
| 5.1.1 Inventory of Assets ***** | Have all information assets been identified? | No | Should be completed annually |
| ***** | Has an inventory of all important information assets been created and maintained? | No | Should be completed annually |
| 5.1.2 Ownership of Assets | Has a nominated owner been assigned to all information assets and services? | Yes | IT Policies: Information Security Roles and Responsibilities Policy (5.1.1) |
| 5.2 Information Classification | Information assets should be classified to indicate the need, priorities and expected degree of protection required when handling these assets. | | |
| 5.2.1 Classification Guidelines | Have policies, procedures, standards, and practices been implemented to classify information assets in terms of their value, sensitivity, and criticality to the organization? | No | However, the Employee Handbook does address protecting and handling confidential and proprietary information (pages 12–13) |
| 5.2.2 Information Labeling and Handling | Has an appropriate set of standards and procedures been implemented to address the labeling and handling of information assets based on the classification categories established by the organization? | No | However, the Employee Handbook does address protecting and handling confidential and proprietary information (pages 12–13) |

| 6 PERSONNEL SECURITY | | | |
|---|---|---|---|
| 6.1 Security in Job Definitions and Resourcing | Security should be addressed at the recruitment stage, included in job descriptions and contracts, and monitored during an individual's employment. | | |
| 6.1.1 Security in Job Descriptions | Are security responsibilities included in employee job descriptions? | Yes | Included as part of the "Confidential Information and Intellectual Property Agreement" form |
| 6.1.2 Personnel Screening and Policy | Are employment applications screened for jobs that require access to sensitive information? | Yes | Background Check — Release & Authorization Form |
| 6.1.3 Confidentiality Agreement | Are non-disclosure agreements required? | Yes | IT Policies: Contractors, Vendors, Consultants and Third-Parties Policy |
| 6.1.4 Terms and Conditions of Employment | Do the terms and conditions of employment include the employee's responsibility for information security, including duration after employment and consequences of failure to fulfill these terms? | Yes | Included as part of the "Confidential Information and Intellectual Property Agreement" form |
| 6.2 User Training | Users should be trained in security procedures and the correct use of IT facilities. | | |
| 6.2.1 Information Security Education and Training | Before they are granted access to IT facilities, are users trained in information security policies and procedures, security requirements, business controls, and correct use of IT facilities? | Yes | IT Policies: Foreword, Scope and Introduction<br>However, no formal awareness sessions were discovered. |
| 6.3 Responding to Security Incidents and Malfunctions | Incidents affecting security should be reported through management channels as quickly as possible. | | |

| 6.3.1 Reporting of Security Incidents ***** | Do formal reporting and incident response procedures exist to identify action to be taken on receipt of an incident report? | No | Headquarters issued procedures and standards required |
| 6.3.2 Reporting of Security Weaknesses | Are users required to note and report all observed or suspected security weaknesses in or threats to systems or services? | Yes | IT Policies: Information Security Roles and Responsibilities (3.1.1) |
| 6.3.3 Reporting of Software Malfunctions ***** | Are users required to note and report to IT support any software that does not function correctly? | No | Headquarters issued procedures and standards required |
| 6.3.4 Learning from Incidents ***** | Are mechanisms in place to monitor the types, volumes, and costs of incidents and malfunctions? | No | A formal de-briefing process should be implemented |
| 6.3.5 Disciplinary Process | Does a formal disciplinary process exist for dealing with employees who violate security policies and procedures? | Yes | Employee Handbook pages 24–25 |

| 7 PHYSICAL & ENVIRONMENTAL SECURITY | | |
|---|---|---|
| 7.1 Secure Areas | IT facilities supporting critical or sensitive business activities belong in secure areas. | |
| 7.1.1 Physical Security Perimeter | Does physical security protection exist, based on defined perimeters through strategically located barriers throughout the organization? | Yes | IT Security Policies: Acceptable Use Policy (16) |
| 7.1.2 Physical Entry Controls | Are entry controls employed over secure areas to ensure only authorized personnel can gain access? | Yes | IT Security Policies: Acceptable Use Policy (16) |
| 7.1.3 Securing Offices, Rooms, and Facilities       *** | Is physical security for data centers and computer rooms commensurate with threats? | Y ___  N ___ | No corporate direction currently available |
| 7.1.4 Working in Secure Areas       *** | Are additional controls used for personnel or third parties working in the secure area? | Y ___  N ___ | No corporate direction currently available |
| 7.1.5 Isolated Delivery and Loading Areas       *** | Are the computer room/data center delivery and loading areas isolated to prevent unauthorized access? | Y ___  N ___ | No corporate direction currently available |
| 7.2 Equipment Security | Equipment must be physically protected from security threats and environmental hazards. | |
| 7.2.1 Equipment Location and Protection       *** | Is equipment located to reduce risks of environmental hazards and unauthorized access? | Y ___  N ___ | No corporate direction currently available |

| | | | |
|---|---|---|---|
| 7.2.2 Power Supplies *** | Is electronic equipment protected from power failures and other electrical anomalies? | Y___ N___ | No corporate direction currently available |
| 7.2.3 Cabling Security *** | Is power and telecommunications cabling protected from interception or damage? | Y___ N___ | No corporate direction currently available |
| 7.2.4 Equipment Maintenance *** | Have procedures been established to correctly maintain IT equipment to ensure its continued availability and integrity? | Y___ N___ | No corporate direction currently available |
| 7.2.5 Security of Equipment Off-Premises | Is equipment used off-site, regardless of ownership, provided the same degree of protection afforded on-site IT equipment? | Yes | IT Security Policies: Acceptable Use Policy (19) |
| 7.3 General Controls | Information and information processing facilities should be protected from disclosure to, modification of, or theft by, unauthorized persons, and controls should be in place to minimize loss or damage. | | |
| 7.3.1 Clear Desk and Clear Screen Policy **** | Has a clear desk/clear screen policy for sensitive material been adopted to reduce risks of unauthorized access, loss, or damage outside normal working hours? | No | However, the Employee Handbook does address a Desk Inspection Policy (pages 16–17) |
| 7.3.2 Removal of Property **** | Are personnel required to have documented management authorization to take equipment, data, or software off-site? | No | However, the Employee Handbook does address Computer Equipment (page 14) addresses unauthorized software |

| 8 | COMPUTER AND NETWORK MANAGEMENT | | |
|---|---|---|---|
| 8.1 | Operational Procedures and Responsibilities | Responsibilities and procedures must be established for the management and operation of all computers and networks. | |
| 8.1.1 | Documented Operating Procedures <br> *** | Are operating procedures clearly documented for all operational computer systems to ensure their correct, secure operation? | Y___ <br> N___ | No corporate direction currently available |
| 8.1.2 | Operational Change Control | Is there a process for controlling changes to IT facilities and systems to ensure satisfactory control of all changes to equipment, software, or procedures? | Yes | IT Security Policies: Acceptable Use Policy (4.2) |
| 8.1.3 | Incident Management Procedures <br> *** | Are incident management responsibilities and procedures in place to ensure a quick, effective, orderly response to security incidents? | Y___ <br> N___ | No corporate direction currently available |
| 8.1.4 | Segregation of Duties | Are sensitive duties or areas of responsibility kept separate to reduce opportunities for unauthorized modification or misuse of data or services? | Yes | IT Security Policies: Acceptable Use Policy (6.1) |
| 8.1.5 | Separation of Development and Operational Facilities <br> *** | Are development and operational facilities segregated to reduce the risk of accidental changes or unauthorized access to operational software and business data? | Y___ <br> N___ | No corporate direction currently available |

| 8.2 | System Planning and Acceptance | Advance planning and preparation can ensure the availability of adequate capacity and resources. | | |
|---|---|---|---|---|
| 8.2.1 | Capacity Planning ∗∗∗ | Are capacity requirements monitored, and future requirements projected, to reduce the risk of system overload? | Y ___ N ___ | No corporate direction currently available |
| 8.2.2 | System Acceptance ∗∗∗ | Has acceptance criteria for new systems been established, and have suitable tests been performed prior to acceptance? | Y ___ N ___ | No corporate direction currently available |
| 8.3 | Protection from Malicious Software | Applying precautions to prevent and detect the introduction of malicious software can safeguard the integrity of software and data. | | |
| 8.3.1 | Controls against Malicious Software | Have virus detection and prevention measures and user awareness procedures been implemented? | Yes | IT Policies: Anti-Virus Policy |
| 8.4 | Housekeeping | Routine procedures should be established for making backup copies of data, logging events and faults, and where appropriate, monitoring the equipment environment. | | |
| 8.4.1 | Information Backup ∗∗∗ | Has a process been established for making regular backup copies of essential business data and software to ensure that it can be recovered following a computer disaster or media failure? | Y ___ N ___ | No corporate direction currently available |
| 8.4.2 | Operator Logs ∗∗∗ | Are computer operators required to maintain a log of all work performed? | Y ___ N ___ | No corporate direction currently available |

| | | | |
|---|---|---|---|
| 8.4.3 Fault Logging<br>*** | Do procedures exist for logging faults reported by users regarding problems with computer or communications systems? | Y __<br>N __ | No corporate direction currently available |
| 8.5 Network Management | The security of computer networks that may span organizational boundaries must be managed to safeguard information and to protect the supporting infrastructure. | | |
| 8.5.1 Network Controls | Do appropriate controls ensure the security of data in networks, and the protection of connected services from unauthorized access? | Yes | IT Policies: Network Connectivity Policy (4) |
| 8.6 Media Handling and Security | Computer media should be controlled and physically protected to prevent damage to assets and interruptions to business activities. | | |
| 8.6.1 Management of Removable Computer Media<br>**** | Do procedures exist for the management of removable computer media such as tapes, disks, cassettes, and printed reports? | Y __<br>N __ | No corporate direction currently available |
| 8.6.2 Disposal of Media | Is a process in place to ensure that computer media is disposed of securely and safely when no longer required? | Yes | IT Security Policies: Acceptable Use Policy (18) |
| 8.6.3 Information Handling Procedures<br>***** | Do procedures exist for handling sensitive data to protect such data from unauthorized disclosure or misuse? | No | However, the Employee Handbook does address handling of Confidential and Proprietary Information (pages 12–13) |
| 8.6.4 Security of System Documentation<br>*** | Is system documentation protected from unauthorized access? | Y __<br>N __ | No corporate direction currently available |

| 8.7 | Exchanges of Information and Software | Exchanges of data and software between organizations should be controlled to prevent loss, modification, or misuse of data. | | |
|---|---|---|---|---|
| 8.7.1 | Information and Software Exchange Agreements *** | Do formal agreements exist, including software escrow agreements when appropriate, for exchanging data and software (whether electronically or manually) between organizations? | Y___ N___ | No corporate direction currently available |
| 8.7.2 | Security of Media in Transit *** | Are controls applied to safeguard computer media being transported between sites to minimize its vulnerability to unauthorized access, misuse, or corruption during transportation? | Y___ N___ | No corporate direction currently available |
| 8.7.3 | Electronic Commerce Security *** | Are security controls applied where necessary to protect electronic commerce (electronic data interchange, electronic mail, and online transactions across a public network such as the Internet) against unauthorized interception or modification? | Y___ N___ | No corporate direction currently available |
| 8.7.4 | Security of Electronic Mail | Are controls applied where necessary to reduce the business and security risks associated with electronic mail to include interception, modification, and errors? | Yes | IT Security Policies: Acceptable Use Policy (9) |

| 8.7.5 | Security of Electronic Office Systems | Do clear policies and guidelines exist to control business and security risks associated with electronic office systems? | Yes | IT Security Policies: Acceptable Use Policy (9, 10, 19) |
| 8.7.6 | Publicly Available Systems | Is there a formal authorization process before information is made publicly available? | Yes | Employee Handbook: Confidential and Proprietary Information (12–13) |
| 8.7.7 | Other Forms of Information Exchange | Are procedures and controls in place to protect the exchange of information through the use of voice, facsimile, and video communications facilities? | Yes | IT Security Policies: Acceptable Use Policy (12) |

| 9 SYSTEM ACCESS CONTROL | | | |
|---|---|---|---|
| 9.1 | Business Requirement for System Access | Policies for information dissemination and entitlement should control access to computer services and data on the basis of business requirements. | |
| 9.1.1 | Access Control Policy | Are business requirements defined and documented for access control? | Yes | IT Security Policy: Acceptable Use Policy (6.1) |
| 9.2 | User Access Management | Formal procedures are needed to control allocation of access rights to IT services. | | |
| 9.2.1 | User Registration | Is there a formal user registration and deregistration procedure for access to all multi-use IT services? | Yes | IT Policies: Password Authentication and Authorization Policy |
| 9.2.2 | Privilege Management | Are there restrictions and controls over the use of any feature or facility of a multi-user IT system that enables a user to override system or application controls? | Yes | IT Policies: Password Authentication and Authorization Policy (4.3) |
| 9.2.3 | User Password Management | Has a formal password management process been established to control passwords? | Yes | IT Policies: Password Authentication and Authorization Policy |
| 9.2.4 | Review of User Access Rights | Does a formal process exist for periodic review of users' access rights? | Yes | IT Policies: Password Authentication and Authorization Policy (9.1) |
| 9.3 | User Responsibilities | Users should be made aware of their responsibilities for maintaining effective access controls, particularly regarding the use of passwords and security of user equipment. | | |
| 9.3.1 | Password Use | Have users been taught good security practices in the selection and use of passwords? | Yes | IT Policies: Password Authentication and Authorization Policy |

| | | | |
|---|---|---|---|
| 9.3.2 Unattended User Equipment | Are all users and contractors made aware of the security requirements and procedures for protecting unattended equipment? | Yes | Confidential Information and Intellectual Property Form |
| | Are all users and contractors made aware of their responsibilities for implementing such protection? | Yes | Confidential Information and Intellectual Property Form |
| 9.4 Network Access Control | Connections to network services should be controlled to ensure that connected users or computer services do not compromise the security of any other networked services. | | |
| 9.4.1 Policy on Use of Network Services | Does a process exist to ensure that network and computer services that can be accessed by an individual user or from a particular terminal are consistent with business access control policy? | Yes | IT Policies: Network Connectivity Policy (7) |
| 9.4.2 Enforced Path *** | Have controls been incorporated that restrict the route between a user terminal and the computer services that its user is authorized to access? | Y __ N __ | No corporate direction currently available |
| 9.4.3 User Authentication for External Connections | Are connections by remote users via public or non-organization networks authenticated to prevent unauthorized access to business applications? | Yes | IT Policies: Network Connectivity Policy (6) |

| | | | |
|---|---|---|---|
| 9.4.4 Node Authentication | Are connections by remote computer systems authenticated to prevent unauthorized access to a business application? | Yes | IT Policies: Network Connectivity Policy (6.1.2) |
| 9.4.5 Remote Diagnostic Port Protection | Does a process exist to control access to diagnostic ports designed for remote use by maintenance engineers? | Yes | IT Policies: Remote Vendor Support Connection Policy |
| 9.4.6 Network Segregation *** | Have large networks been divided into separate domains to mitigate the risk of unauthorized access to existing computer systems that use the network? | Y ___ N ___ | No corporate direction currently available |
| 9.4.7 Network Connection Control *** | Have controls been incorporated to restrict the connection capability of users, in support of access policy requirements of business applications that extend across organizational boundaries? | Y ___ N ___ | No corporate direction currently available |
| 9.4.8 Network Routing Control *** | Have routing controls been incorporated over shared networks across organizational boundaries to ensure that computer connections and information flows conform to the access policy of business units? | Y ___ N ___ | No corporate direction currently available |

| | | | |
|---|---|---|---|
| 9.4.9 Security in Network Services *** | Have network providers clearly described the security attributes of all services used, and established the security implications for the confidentiality, integrity, and availability of business applications? | Y __ N __ | No corporate direction currently available |
| 9.5 Operating System Access Control | Access to computers should be strictly limited through the use of: ■ Automatic terminal identification ■ Terminal logon procedures ■ Userids ■ Password management ■ A duress alarm ■ Terminal time-out ■ Limited connection time | | |
| 9.5.1 Automatic Terminal Identification *** | Is automatic terminal identification employed to authenticate connections to specific locations? | Y __ N __ | No corporate direction currently available |
| 9.5.2 Terminal Logon Procedures | Have procedures been designed for logging into a computer system to minimize the opportunity for unauthorized access? | Y __ N __ | |
| 9.5.3 User Identification and Authentication | Do all users have a unique identifier (userid) for their personal and sole use, to ensure that their activities can be traced to them? | Yes | IT Policies: Password Authentication and Authorization Policy (5) |

| | | Yes | IT Policies: Password Authentication and Authorization Policy |
|---|---|---|---|
| 9.5.4 Password Management System | Is an effective password management system employed to authenticate users? | | |
| 9.5.5 Use of System Utilities \*\*\* | Are the system utility programs that could be used to override system and application controls strictly controlled and their use restricted? | Y ___ N ___ | No corporate direction currently available |
| 9.5.6 Duress Alarm to Safeguard Users \*\*\* | Based on an assessment of risk, is a duress alarm provided for users who might be the target of coercion? | Y ___ N ___ | No corporate direction currently available |
| | Are responsibilities defined for responding to duress alarms? | Y ___ N ___ | No corporate direction currently available |
| 9.5.7 Terminal Time-Out \*\*\* | Are terminals in high-risk locations set to time out when inactive to prevent access by unauthorized persons? | Y ___ N ___ | No corporate direction currently available |
| 9.5.8 Limitation of Connection Time \*\*\* | Has a limit been set on the period during which terminals may be connected to sensitive application systems? | Y ___ N ___ | No corporate direction currently available |
| 9.6 Application Access Control | Logical access controls should be enacted to protect application systems and data from unauthorized access. | | |
| 9.6.1 Information Access Restriction \*\*\* | Is access to applications system data and functions restricted in accordance with defined access policy and based on individual requirements? | Y ___ N ___ | No corporate direction currently available |

| | | | |
|---|---|---|---|
| 9.6.2 Isolation of Sensitive Systems *** | According to identified risks, do sensitive application systems operate in an isolated processing environment? | Y ___ N ___ | No corporate direction currently available |
| 9.7 Monitoring System Access and Use | Systems should be monitored to ensure conformity with access policy and standards, to detect unauthorized activities, and to determine the effectiveness of security measures adopted. | | |
| 9.7.1 Event Logging *** | Have audit trails that record exceptions and other security-relevant events been produced and maintained to assist in future investigations and in access control monitoring? | Y ___ N ___ | No corporate direction currently available |
| 9.7.2 Monitoring System Use *** | Have procedures been established for monitoring system use to ensure that users are only performing processes that have been explicitly authorized? | Y ___ N ___ | No corporate direction currently available |
| 9.7.3 Clock Synchronization *** | To ensure the accuracy of audit logs, have computer or communications device clocks been set to an agreed upon standard? | Y ___ N ___ | No corporate direction currently available |
| 9.8 Mobile Commuting and Telecommuting | When using mobile computing and telecommuting, the organization should examine the risks and apply appropriate protection to the equipment or site. | | |

| 9.8.1 Mobile Commuting | Has a formal policy been developed that addresses the risks of working with mobile computing facilities, including requirements for physical protection, access controls, cryptographic techniques, backup, and virus protection? | Yes | IT Acceptable Use Policy Section 19 |
| 9.8.2 Telecommuting | Have policies and procedures been developed to control telecommuting, encompassing existing facilities, the proposed telecommuting environment, communications security requirements, and the threat of unauthorized access to equipment or the network? | Yes | IT Acceptable Use Policy Section 19 |

| 10 SYSTEMS DEVELOPMENT & MAINTENANCE | | | |
|---|---|---|---|
| 10.1 | Security Requirements of Systems | To ensure that security is built into IT systems, security requirements should be identified, justified, agreed to, and documented as part of the requirements definition stage of all IT system development projects. | |
| 10.1.1 | Security Requirements Analysis and Specification  *** | Is an analysis of security requirements part of the requirements analysis stage of each development project? | Y ___ N ___ | No corporate direction currently available |
| 10.2 | Security in Application Systems | Security controls that conform to commonly accepted industry standards of good security practice should be designed into applications systems to prevent loss, modification, or misuse of user data. | |
| 10.2.1 | Input Data Validation  *** | Is data that is input into applications systems validated to ensure that it is correct and appropriate? | Y ___ N ___ | No corporate direction currently available |
| 10.2.2 | Control of Internal Processing  *** | Have validation checks been incorporated into systems to detect corruption caused by processing errors or through deliberate acts? | Y ___ N ___ | No corporate direction currently available |
| 10.2.3 | Message Authentication  *** | Has message authentication been considered for applications that involve the transmission of sensitive data? | Y ___ N ___ | No corporate direction currently available |
| 10.2.4 | Output Data Validation  *** | Is data that is output from applications systems validated to ensure that it is correct and appropriate? | Y ___ N ___ | No corporate direction currently available |

| | | | |
|---|---|---|---|
| 10.3 | Cryptographic Controls | To protect the confidentiality, authenticity, or integrity of information, cryptographic systems and techniques should be used for complete protection of information that is considered at risk. | |
| 10.3.1 | Policy on the Use of Cryptographic Controls *** | Has management developed a policy on the use of cryptographic controls, including management of encryption keys, and effective implementation? | Y ___ N ___ | No corporate direction currently available |
| 10.3.2 | Encryption *** | Is data encryption used to protect highly sensitive data during transmission or in storage? | Y ___ N ___ | No corporate direction currently available |
| 10.3.3 | Digital Signatures *** | Are digital signatures in use to protect the authenticity and integrity of electronic documents? | Y ___ N ___ | No corporate direction currently available |
| 10.3.4 | Non-Repudiation Services *** | Are non-repudiation services in place where disputes might arise based on the use of encryption or digital signatures? | Y ___ N ___ | No corporate direction currently available |
| 10.3.5 | Key Management *** | Is a management system in place to support the organization's use of cryptographic techniques, including secret key techniques and public key techniques? | Y ___ N ___ | No corporate direction currently available |
| 10.4 | Security of System Files | To ensure that IT projects and support activities are conducted in a secure manner, the responsibility for controlling access to application system files should be assigned to and carried out by the owning user function or development group. | |

| | | | |
|---|---|---|---|
| 10.4.1 | Control of Operational Software | Is strict control exercised over the implementation of software on operational systems? | Y —— N —— | No corporate direction currently available |
| 10.4.2 | Protection of System Test Data | Is all application system test data protected and controlled? | Y —— N —— | No corporate direction currently available |
| 10.4.3 | Access Control to Program Source Library | To reduce the potential for corruption of computer programs, is access to program source libraries strictly controlled? | Y —— N —— | No corporate direction currently available |
| 10.5 | Security in Development and Support Environments | Project and support environments must be strictly controlled to maintain the security of application system software and data. | | |
| 10.5.1 | Change Control Procedures | Have formal change control procedures been implemented? | Yes | IT Policies: IT Infrastructure Change and Problem Management Policy |
| 10.5.2 | Technical Review of Operating System Changes | Are application systems reviewed when changes to the operating systems occur? | Yes | IT Policies: IT Infrastructure Change and Problem Management Policy |
| 10.5.3 | Restrictions on Changes to Software Packages | Are modifications to vendor-supplied software discouraged, and when such modifications are necessary, are they strictly controlled? | Y —— N —— | No corporate direction currently available |

| 10.5.4 | Covert Channels and Trojan Code | To avoid covert channels or Trojan codes, does the organization:<br>■ Buy programs only from a reputable source.<br>■ Buy programs in source code that is verifiable.<br>■ Use only evaluated products.<br>■ Inspect all source code before operational use.<br>■ Control access to, and modification of, installed code.<br>■ Use trusted staff to work on key systems. | Y ___<br>N ___ | No corporate direction currently available |
| --- | --- | --- | --- | --- |
| 10.5.5 | Outsourced Software Development | When software development is outsourced, have details been arranged to protect the project from intellectual property to pre-installation testing? | Y ___<br>N ___ | No corporate direction currently available |

| 11 | BUSINESS CONTINUITY MANAGEMENT | | |
|---|---|---|---|
| 11.1 | Aspects of Business Continuity Planning | Business continuity plans should be available to counteract interruptions to business activities. | |
| 11.1.1 | Business Continuity Management Process | Is there a managed process for developing/maintaining business continuity plans across the organization? | Y ___ <br> N ___ | Outside the scope of this assessment |
| 11.1.2 | Business Continuity and Impact Analysis | Has a strategy been developed to determine the overall approach to business continuity, and endorsed by management? | Y ___ <br> N ___ | Outside the scope of this assessment |
| 11.1.3 | Writing and Implementing Continuity Plans | Has the business continuity planning process encompassed identification and agreement of all responsibilities and emergency procedures? | Y ___ <br> N ___ | Outside the scope of this assessment |
| 11.1.4 | Business Continuity Planning Framework | Is a single business continuity plan framework maintained to ensure that all levels of the plan are consistent? | Y ___ <br> N ___ | Outside the scope of this assessment |
| 11.1.5 | Testing, Maintaining, and Re-Assessing Business Continuity Plans | Are business continuity plans tested regularly to ensure that they are current and effective? | Y ___ <br> N ___ | Outside the scope of this assessment |

| 12 | COMPLIANCE | | |
|---|---|---|---|
| 12.1 | Compliance with Legal Requirements | All relevant requirements for each IT system should be identified and documented. | |
| 12.1.1 | Identification of Applicable Legislation | Are all relevant statutory, regulatory, and contractual requirements specifically defined and documented for each information system? | Y ___<br>N ___ | Outside the scope of this assessment |
| 12.1.2 | Intellectual Property Rights | Is there compliance with legal restrictions on the use of copyright material ensuring that only software developed by the organization, or licensed or provided by the developer to the organization, is used? | Y ___<br>N ___ | Outside the scope of this assessment |
| 12.1.3 | Safeguarding of Organizational Records | Are important organizational records securely maintained to meet statutory requirements, as well as to support essential business activities? | Y ___<br>N ___ | Outside the scope of this assessment |
| 12.1.4 | Data Protection and Privacy of Personal Information | Do applications that process personal data on individuals comply with applicable data protection legislation? | Y ___<br>N ___ | Outside the scope of this assessment |
| 12.1.5 | Prevention of Misuse of IP Facilities | Are IT facilities to be used only for business purposes? | Y ___<br>N ___ | Outside the scope of this assessment |

| | | | |
|---|---|---|---|
| 12.1.6 | Regulation of Cryptographic Controls | Has legal advice been sought on the organization's compliance with national and international laws on cryptographic controls? | Y __ N __ | Outside the scope of this assessment |
| 12.1.7 | Collection of Evidence | When an action against a person involves the law, have the rules for evidence been followed for admissibility, quality, and completeness? | Y __ N __ | Outside the scope of this assessment |
| 12.2 | Reviews of Security Policy and Technical Compliance | To ensure compliance of IT systems with organizational security policies and standards, compliance reviews should be conducted regularly. | | |
| 12.2.1 | Compliance with Security Policy | Are all areas within the organization considered for regular review to ensure compliance with security policies and standards? | Y | Yes, part of the SOX 404 Compliance testing completed annually. |
| 12.2.2 | Technical Compliance Checking | Are IT facilities regularly checked for compliance with security implementation standards? | Y | IT facility security is reviewed annually as part of SOX 404 compliance testing |
| 12.3 | System Audit Considerations | There should be controls over operational systems and audit tools during system audits to minimize interference to and from the system audit process, and to protect the integrity and prevent the misuse of audit tools. | | |
| 12.3.1 | System Audit Controls | Are audits and activities involving checks on operational systems carefully planned and arranged? | Y | Completed as part of the SOX 404 Compliance testing annually. |
| 12.3.2 | Protection of System Audit Tools | Is access to system audit tools controlled? | Y | Not sure. (sorry!) I'll have to check the SOX documentation and get back to you. |

## Gap Analysis Using Utility-Specific Standards

| NERC CIP-002-1 CRITICAL CYBER ASSET IDENTIFICATION | | | |
|---|---|---|---|
| R 1 | Critical Asset Identification Method | Management is required to implement a standard risk-based methodology to identify and document Critical Assets (CA). | |
| R 1.1 | Critical Impact Methodology | Are procedures in place that support a TDF-wide CA assessment process? | Y | IT Risk Management has created a draft policy on Business Continuity Planning. A portion of the draft policy requires that TDF Management perform a Business Impact Analysis (BIA) using a risk-based assessment process. |
| R 1.2 | CA Assessment Process | Does the CA Assessment Process (CAAP) include provisions for the following: | | |
| R 1.2.1 | Control Centers | Control centers and backup control centers performing the functions of the entities listed in the Applicability section of this standard. | Y ___ N ___ | A BIA was performed by IT BCP a few years ago using a risk-based assessment process very similar to those used at NIST and other industry specialists. |
| R 1.2.2 | Bulk Electric System | Transmission substations that support the reliable operation of the Bulk Electric System. | Y ___ N ___ | RECOMMENDATION — review, edit and approve the proposed BCP Policy and move it into ESM: 09.003.001. |
| R 1.2.3 | Bulk Electric System | Generation resources that support the reliable operation of the Bulk Electric System. | Y ___ N ___ | |
| R 1.2.4 | Critical System Restoration | Systems and facilities critical to system restoration, including blackstart generators and substations in the electrical path of transmission lines used for initial system restoration. | Y ___ N ___ | Review the documentation created by IT BCP (Critical Applications Disaster Recovery Strategy) and review, edit and publish as a supporting ITS standard. |

| R 1.2.5 | Automatic Load Shedding | Systems and facilities critical to automatic load shedding under a common control system capable of shedding 300 MW or more. | Y __ N __ |
| --- | --- | --- | --- |
| R 1.2.6 | Bulk Electric System | Special Protection Systems that support the reliable operation of the Bulk Electric System. | Y __ N __ |
| R 1.2.7 | Bulk Electric System | Any additional assets that support the reliable operation of the BES. | Y __ N __ |

| NERC CIP-002-1  Critical Cyber Asset Identification | | | |
|---|---|---|---|
| R 2 | Information Security Infrastructure | | |
| | TDF management shall document a list of all Critical Assets. | | |
| | Has a documented list of all TDF CA been developed? | Y __ N __ | See above |
| | Has the list of TDF CA been reviewed and approved by senior TDF management? | Y __ N __ | |
| | Is the list of TDF CA reviewed and recertified by senior TDF management at least annually? | Y __ N __ | |

| NERC CIP-002-1 Critical Cyber Asset Identification | | | |
|---|---|---|---|
| R 3 | Identification of Supporting Critical Cyber Assets | Once the TDF CA are identified and approved, a process to identify all supporting assets must be implemented. | |
| | | Are procedures in place to identify and document all Critical Cyber Assets (hardware, software, data, documentation, etc.) that support TDF CA? | Y ___<br>N ___ | See above |
| | | Does senior TDF management review and recertify this list on at least an annual basis? | Y ___<br>N ___ | |
| | | Are procedures in place to review and recertify exceptions at least on an annual basis? | Y ___<br>N ___ | |
| R 3 | Additional Characteristics | Does the identification process take into account the following characteristics: | | ITS-207 Standards for Remote Access<br>ITS-217 Standards for Virtual Private Networks (VPN) |
| R 3.1 | | Does the Cyber Asset use a routable protocol to communicate outside the Electronic Security Perimeter? | Y ___<br>N ___ | ITS-207 should be edited to incorporate additional R3 requirements |
| R 3.2 | | Does the Cyber Asset use a routable protocol to communicate within the Electronic Security Perimeter? | Y ___<br>N ___ | |
| R 3.3 | | Does the Cyber Asset use remote access? | Y | |

| NERC CIP-002-1 Critical Cyber Asset Identification | | | |
|---|---|---|---|
| R 4 | Annual Approval | Senior TDF management must annually review and recertify the list of Critical Assets and supporting Critical Cyber Assets. | |
| | | Are procedures in place to have senior TDF management review and recertify the TDF CA documentation? | Y ___ <br> N ___ | This is identified in the Draft BCP policy; supporting procedures need to be created. |
| | | Are procedures in place to have senior TDF management review and recertify the list of supporting Critical Cyber Assets? | Y ___ <br> N ___ | |

| NERC CIP-003-1 Cyber Security Policy | | | |
|---|---|---|---|
| R 1 | Cyber Security Policy | Management direction and support for cyber security must be clearly established. | |
| R 1.1 | Cyber Security Policy Contents | Has a cyber security policy document been developed? | Y \_\_\_ N\_\_\_ | Cyber Security Policy (Status: DRAFT) |
| | | Does the policy include provisions for emergency situations? | Y \_\_\_ N\_\_\_ | Cyber Security Policy (Status: DRAFT) |
| R 1.2 | Policy Availability | Has an information security policy document been published and available to those responsible for Critical Cyber Assets? | | ESM: 04.001.001 ISTA Information Management — Policy needs to be updated |
| R 1.3 | Annual Review | Are controls in place to ensure that senior management reviews and approves the cyber security policy at least annually? | Y \_\_\_ N\_\_\_ | Cyber Security Policy (Status: DRAFT) |

### NERC CIP-003-1 Cyber Security Leadership

| | | | |
|---|---|---|---|
| R 2 | Information Security Infrastructure | A management framework must be established to initiate and control the implementation of cyber security within the TDF. | |
| R 2.1 | Responsible Entity Identified | Has a senior manager been identified to oversee and represent cyber security interests? | Y __ <br> N __ |
| R 2.2 | Changes to Management | Are controls in place to document within 30 days changes in senior management? | Y <br> ITP-02-02 Information Security — Applications and Data Security — update required |
| R 2.3 | Exception Authorization | Are procedures in place to formally review and authorize exceptions to the cyber security policy? | Y __ <br> N __ <br> Cyber Security Policy (Status: DRAFT) |

| NERC CIP-003-1 Cyber Security Exceptions | | |
|---|---|---|
| R 3 | Exceptions | Instances where the Responsible Entity cannot conform to its cyber security policy must be documented as exceptions and authorized by the senior manager or delegate(s). | |
| R 3.1 | Documenting Exceptions | Are procedures in place to ensure that all approved exceptions are documented within 30 days? | Y ___ N ___ | Cyber Security Policy (Status: DRAFT) – supporting procedures must be developed |
| R 3.2 | Business Case Requirements | Do procedures include business reason why exception was approved? | Y ___ N ___ | Cyber Security Policy (Status: DRAFT) – supporting procedures must be developed |
| R 3.3 | Ongoing Approval | Are procedures in place to review and recertify authorized exceptions at least on an annual basis? | Y ___ N ___ | Cyber Security Policy (Status: DRAFT) – supporting procedures must be developed |

| NERC CIP-003-1 Cyber Security Information Protection | | | |
|---|---|---|---|
| R 4 | Information Protection | The Responsible Entity shall implement and document a program to identify, classify, and protect information associated with Critical Cyber Assets. | |
| R 4.1 | Information Protection Controls | Are procedures and standards in place to ensure that Critical Cyber Asset information is protected and in compliance with Standard CIP-002? | Y ___ N ___ | ESM: 04.001.001 Information Management — needs to be updated to include CIP |
| | | Do these procedures include control requirements for network topology or similar diagrams, floor plans of computing centers that contain Critical Cyber Assets, equipment layouts of Critical Cyber Assets, disaster recovery plans, incident response plans, and security configuration information? | Y ___ N ___ | Need to develop supporting procedures |
| R 4.2 | Information Classification | Are controls in place to classify and protect information based on information sensitivity? | Y | ITS-109 Standards for IT Information Classification ESM: 04.001.001 Information Management |
| R 4.3 | Annual Assessment | Are procedures in place to annually assess adherence to its Critical Cyber Asset? | | ITS-111 Procedures for Security Non-Compliance — needs updating |
| | | Are controls in place to implement an action plan to remediate deficiencies identified during annual assessment? | | ITS-111 Procedures for Security Non-Compliance — needs updating |

## NERC CIP-003-1 Cyber Security Access Control

| ID | Name | Question | Y/N | Reference/Notes |
|---|---|---|---|---|
| R 5 | Access Control | The Responsible Entity shall document and implement a program for managing access to protected Critical Cyber Asset information. | | |
| R 5.1 | Information Owner | Are procedures in place to designate TDF personnel who are responsible for authorizing access to Critical Cyber Assets? | Y | ITS-104 Standards for System Access |
| | | Are controls in place to grant access based on business need? | Y | ITS-104 Standards for System Access |
| R 5.1.1 | Owner Information | Are procedures in place to record the name, title, business phone number of the information owner? | Y __ N __ | ESM: 04.001.001 Information Management<br>ESM: 04.002.001 Records Retention<br>Designation of owner needs to be established in TDF documentation |
| R 5.1.2 | Verification | Are procedures in place to annually review and reconcile the list of information owners? | Y __ N __ | ESM: 04.001.001 Information Management<br>ESM: 04.002.001 Records Retention<br>Requires updating |
| R 5.2 | Review Access Privileges | Are procedures in place to annually review all access privileges and reconcile any discrepancies? | Y | ITS-104 Standards for System Access |
| R 5.3 | Document Assessment Process | Are procedures in place to document all findings in the annually access privilege review assessment? | Y | ITS-104 Standards for System Access |

| NERC CIP-003-1 Change Control and Configuration Management | | | |
|---|---|---|---|
| R 6 | Change Control and Configuration Management | Responsibilities and procedures must be established for the tracking and approval for all changes to the production environment. | |
| R 6.1 | Change Control | Are procedures in place for controlling changes to CCA facilities and systems to ensure satisfactory control of all changes to equipment, software or procedures? | Y | ITP-02-02 Information Security — Applications and Data Security |
| | | Are procedures in place to ensure that all operating systems, software, and hardware are at the correct production level? | Y ___ N ___ | CMP-002 System Configuration Management Policy OMPI-RLP-001 Release Management Requires procedures |

**NERC CIP-004-1 Personnel and Training**

| R 1 | Awareness | An ongoing security awareness program must be implemented. | | |
|---|---|---|---|---|
| | | Has a cyber security awareness program been implemented? | Y ___ N ___ | This task is being performed on an "informal" formal basis. TDF needs to document the process. RECOMMENDATION – Add a policy to ESM: 09 to address Security Awareness and Training issues. |
| | | Are employees required to attend the awareness sessions on an ongoing basis? | Y ___ N ___ | |
| | | Does the awareness program use a variety of methods to reinforce the message? | Y ___ N ___ | |
| | | Does TDF management actively support the security awareness program? | Y ___ N ___ | |

| NERC CIP-004-1 Personnel and Training | | | | |
|---|---|---|---|---|
| R2 | Cyber Security Training | An annual cyber security training program must be implemented. | | |
| | | Has a program to train personnel with access to Critical Cyber Assets on security measures been implemented? | Y __ N __ | This task is being performed on an "informal" formal basis. TDF needs to document the process. RECOMMENDATION — Add a policy to ESM: 09 to address Security Awareness and Training issues. |
| | | Has a program to train personnel with unescorted access to Critical Cyber Assets on security measures been implemented? | Y __ N __ | |
| | | Are procedures in place to ensure the security training is conducted at least annually? | Y __ N __ | |
| R 2.1 | Third-Party Training | Are procedures and contracts in place to ensure that all third parties with access to Critical Cyber Assets are properly trained on all security requirements? | Y | ITS-104 Standards for System Access |
| R 2.2 | Third-Party Training Requirements | Does the third-party training cover at a minimum the following: | Y | |
| R 2.2.1 | | The proper use of Critical Cyber Assets | Y | ESM: 04.005.001 Protection of TDF's Critical Energy Infrastructure Information |
| R 2.2.2 | | Physical and electronic access controls | Y __ N __ | ESM: 04.005.001 Protection of TDF's Critical Energy Infrastructure Information ESM: 09.006.001 Physical Security — requires updating |

| R 2.2.3 | | Proper handling of Critical Cyber Assets | Y | ESM: 04.005.001 Protection of TDF's Critical Energy Infrastructure Information<br>ITS-108 Standards for Data Integrity |
| R 2.2.4 | | Cyber Security Incident action plans | Y | ITS-102 Standards for Security Incidents |
| R 2.3 | Training Documentation | Are procedures in place to record all training session dates and attendees? | Y __<br>N __ | This task is being performed on an "informal" formal basis. TDF needs to document the process.<br>RECOMMENDATION — Add a policy to ESM: 09 to address Security Awareness and Training issues. |

| NERC CIP-004-1 Personnel and Training | | | |
|---|---|---|---|
| R 3 | Background Checking | TDF management shall implement a program to perform background investigations on all personnel with access to Critical Cyber Assets. | |
| R 3.1 | Minimum Requirements | Do the background checks include at a minimum a verification of the Social Security Number and seven (7)-year criminal check? | Y —<br>N — | TDF #201 General Employment ISO 17799:2005 has expanded the requirements under the section of Human Resources. TDF should look to this set on international standards for direction. |
| R 3.2 | Update Requirements | Are procedures in place to update personnel background information on a seven (7)-year cycle? | Y —<br>N — | |
| R 3.3 | Documentation | Are the results of all background checks documented and reviewed appropriate TDF management? | Y —<br>N — | |

| NERC CIP-004-1 Personnel and Training | | | |
|---|---|---|---|
| R 4 | Access | Access to Critical Cyber Assets will be granted on a business need and all access permissions will be recorded. | |
| R 4.1 | Access Control Lists | Are procedures in place to grant personnel access based on business need? | Y | ITS-104 Standards for System Access |
| | | Are procedures in place to update changes to access control lists within seven (7) calendar days? | Y | ITS-104 Standards for System Access |
| R 4.2 | Revoke Access | Are controls in place to revoke access to Critical Cyber Assets within 24 hours for terminated personnel? | Y | ITS-104 Standards for System Access |
| | | Are controls in place to revoke access to Critical Cyber Assets within seven (7) calendar days for personnel who no longer have a business need for access? | Y | ITS-104 Standards for System Access |

| NERC CIP-005-1 Electronic Security Perimeter(s) | | | |
|---|---|---|---|
| R 1 | Electronic Security Perimeter | Controls must be implemented to establish electronic security in depth. | |
| R 1.1 | Access Points | Are procedures in place to identify all communication access points connecting to any devices within the Electronic Security Perimeter (ESP)? | Y ___ N ___ | ITS standards should be reviewed and edited to incorporate this requirement. |
| R 1.2 | Remote Access | Are standards in place to control non-routable protocols? | Y ___ N ___ | ITS-207 Standards for Remote Access requires updating |
| R 1.3 | Communication Links | Are controls in place to adequately filter "in-band" and administrative interfaces on communication links that access the ESP? | Y ___ N ___ | ITS-207 Standards for Remote Access requires updating |
| R 1.4 | Non-Critical Cyber Assets | Are controls in place to identify and adequately protect Non-Critical Cyber Assets within a defined ESP? | Y ___ N ___ | ESM: 09.006.001 Physical Security ITS-205 Standards for Data Center Security requires updating |
| R 1.5 | Security Services | Are controls in place to ensure that all necessary security services are contained in the ESP? | Y ___ N ___ | ESM: 09.006.001 Physical Security ITS-205 Standards for Data Center Security requires updating |
| R 1.6 | Documentation | Are procedures in place to document the ESP components? | Y ___ N ___ | Documentation requirements are a facet of business management that TDF has yet to address. The policy on BCP should include these requirements. In addition a formal Change Management process must be documented and should include these requirements. |
| | | Does this documentation include all electronic access points to the ESP? | Y ___ N ___ | |

| NERC CIP-005-1 Electronic Security Perimeter(s) | | | |
|---|---|---|---|
| R 2 | Electronic Access Control | Technical and procedural mechanisms are to be implemented to control electronic access at al electronic access points to the ESP. | |
| R 2.1 | Access Control Model | Are procedures and standards in place to deny access by default? | Y | ITS-104 Standards for System Access |
| | | Are procedures in place to ensure that all Critical Cyber Assets have access restrictions in place automatically? | Y | ITS-104 Standards for System Access |
| R 2.2 | Restricted Services | Are controls in place to ensure that only necessary ports and services are implemented? | Y | ITS-214 Standards for Firewalls |
| | | Are procedures in place to monitor Cyber Assets within the ESP? | Y | ITS-212 Standards for Security Monitoring and Reporting |
| R 2.3 | Secure Remote Access | Are procedures in place to restrict remote access to the ESP? | Y | ITS-207 Standards for Remote Access ITS-217 Standards for Virtual Private Networks (VPN) |
| R 2.4 | Authenticity Controls | Are procedures and standards in place to require authentication of all parties who request access to the ESP? | Y __ N __ | ITP-02-05 IS – Physical Security Needs procedure development |
| R 2.5 | Electronic Access Controls | Are procedures in place to document access requests? | Y | ITS-104 Standards for System Access |
| R 2.5.1 | | Are procedures in place to base access on business need? | Y | ITS-104 Standards for System Access |

| | | Y / N | |
|---|---|---|---|
| R 2.5.2 | Is the authentication method documented? | Y __ N __ | Needs procedure development ITS-104 Standards for System Access |
| R 2.5.3 | Are authorization rights reviewed on a regular basis? | | |
| R 2.5.4 | Are controls defined to control remote access connections? | Y | ITS-207 Standards for Remote Access ITS-217 Standards for Virtual Private Networks (VPN) |
| R 2.6 | Are controls in place to implement an appropriate use banner at electronic access points? | Y | ITP-02-01 Information Security — Security Controls ITS-203 Standards for System Log-In Banners |

| NERC CIP-005-1 Electronic Security Perimeter(s) | | | |
|---|---|---|---|
| R 3 | Monitoring Electronic Access | Electronic or manual processes for monitoring and logging access to the ESP must be implemented. | |
| R 3.1 | Remote Access | Are controls in place to ensure that remote access to the ESP is logged and monitored? | Y | ITS-207 Standards for Remote Access ITP-02-01 Information Security — Security Controls |
| R 3.2 | Unauthorized Access Attempts | Are mechanisms in place to log and notify security personnel when unauthorized access attempts are made against Critical Cyber Assets? | Y | ITS-104 Standards for System Access |

| NERC CIP-005-1 Electronic Security Perimeter(s) | | | |
|---|---|---|---|
| R 4 | Cyber Vulnerability Assessment | Annual vulnerability assessments must be conducted on all electronic access points to the ESP. | |
| R 4.1 | Vulnerability Assessment Process | Has the vulnerability assessment methodology been documented? | Y | ITS-103 Standards for Anti-Vulnerability Protection |
| R 4.2 | Service Verification | Are procedures in place to review port and service restrictions are adequate? | Y | ITS-214 Standards for Firewalls Needs procedure development |
| R 4.3 | Access Points | Are procedures in place to identify all access points to the ESP? | Y ___ N ___ | |
| R 4.4 | Default Access | Are procedures in place to disable all default accounts, passwords, and network management community strings? | Y | ITP-02-01 Information Security — Security Controls |
| R 4.5 | Documentation | Does the vulnerability assessment documentation include an action plan to remedy any non-compliant conditions? | | ITS-103 Standards for Anti-Vulnerability Protection requires updating |

| NERC CIP-005-1 Electronic Security Perimeter(s) | | | |
|---|---|---|---|
| R 5 | Documentation Review and Maintenance | Documentation to support compliance with the requirements of Standard CIP-005 must be maintained. | |
| R 5.1 | Current Documentation | Are procedures in place to ensure that compliance documentation is current? | Y ___ N ___ | ESM: 01.001.004 Legal Compliance Internal Controls Needs procedure development |
| | | Are procedures in place to review the compliance documentation on at least an annual basis? | Y ___ N ___ | |
| R 5.2 | Update Documentation | Are procedures in place to update compliance documentation to reflect changes to the operating environment? | Y | ITP-02-02 Information Security — Applications and Data Security |
| | | Are procedures in place to ensure that all changes are entered within ninety (90) calendar days of the change? | Y | ITP-02-02 Information Security — Applications and Data Security |
| R 5.3 | Log Retention | Are procedures in place to retain electronic access logs for at least ninety (90) days? | Y ___ N ___ | Records Retention Schedule 0040 standards need to be updated |
| | | Are procedures in place to retain logs related to reportable incidents kept three calendar years? | Y | ITS-102 Standards for Security Incidents |

| NERC CIP-006-1 Physical Security of Critical Cyber Assets | | | | |
|---|---|---|---|---|
| R 1 | Electronic Security Perimeter | A physical security plan is to be documented and maintained. | | |
| R 1.1 | Physical Security Perimeter | As the Physical Security Perimeter (PSP) depicting all access points been created and maintained? | Y ___ N ___ | ITP-02-02 Information Security – Applications and Data Security needs to be documented |
| R 1.2 | Controlled Entry | Are measures in place to control entry at all PSP access control points? | Y ___ N ___ | |
| R 1.3 | Monitoring Access | Are controls in place to monitor physical access to the PSP? | Y | ITP-02-02 Information Security – Applications and Data Security |
| R 1.4 | Physical Access | Are procedures in place to grant access to the PSP based on business need? | Y | ITP-02-02 Information Security – Applications and Data Security |
| | | Are procedures in place to manage visitor access requirements? | Y | ITP-02-02 Information Security – Applications and Data Security |
| | | Are procedures in place to report loss of access credentials? | Y ___ N ___ | ITP-02-02 Information Security – Applications and Data Security Needs procedure development |
| R 1.5 | Access Requests | Are procedures in place to review and approve access authorization requests? | Y | ITP-02-02 Information Security – Applications and Data Security |
| R 1.6 | Escorted Access | Are procedures in place to escort personnel within the PSP for all appropriate visitors and unauthorized personnel? | Y | ITP-02-02 Information Security – Applications and Data Security |

| R 1.7 | Updating PSP | Are processes in place to update the physical security plan to the PSP when changes occur to the physical perimeter? | Y __ N __ | ITP-02-02 Information Security — Applications and Data Security Needs procedure development |
|---|---|---|---|---|
| | | Are the updates made at least annually or within ninety (90) days of a change? | Y __ N __ | |
| R 1.8 | Access Control Protection | Are procedures and standards in place to ensure that Cyber Assets used in access control and monitoring are properly protected? | Y __ N __ | |
| R 1.9 | Annual Review | Are procedures in place to annually review and recertify the physical security plan? | Y __ N __ | |

| NERC CIP-006-1 Physical Security of Critical Cyber Assets | | | |
|---|---|---|---|
| R 2 | Physical Access Control | The operational and procedural controls to manage physical access at al access points must be implemented and documented. | |
| R 2.1 | Card Key | Are procedures in place to ensure card access devices limit access based on least privilege criteria? | Y \_\_\_ N \_\_\_ | ESM: 09.006.001 Physical Security Needs procedure development |
| R 2.2 | Physical Locks | Are controls in place to ensure physical lock keys are restricted in their distribution? | Y \_\_\_ N \_\_\_ | |
| R 2.3 | Security Personnel | Are personnel responsible for physical security controls resident on site? | Y \_\_\_ N \_\_\_ | |
| | | Are personnel responsible for physical security controls at a monitoring station? | Y \_\_\_ N \_\_\_ | |
| R 2.4 | Other Devices | As a risk assessment been performed to determine if other access devices (biometrics, keypads, tokens, etc.) are required to provide adequate physical security? | Y | ITS-110P Security Risk Assessment Process |

| NERC CIP-006-1  Physical Security of Critical Cyber Assets | | | |
|---|---|---|---|
| R 3 | Monitoring Physical Access | Technical and procedural controls for monitoring access at all PSP access points must be documented and implemented. | |
| R 3.1 | Alarms | Are all doors, windows, and gates to the PSP fitted with alarms? | Y ___ <br> N ___ | ESM: 09.006.001 Physical Security Needs procedure development |
| | | Do the alarms sound locally and at the physical security office? | Y ___ <br> N ___ | |
| R 3.2 | Observation Points | Are controls in place to provide human monitoring of all PSP access points? | Y ___ <br> N ___ | |

| NERC CIP-006-1 Physical Security of Critical Cyber Assets | | | |
|---|---|---|---|
| R 4 | Logging Physical Access | Access logs are to be implemented to capture sufficient information to uniquely identify individual access to the PSP on a 7 X 24 criteria. | |
| R 4.1 | Computerized Logging | Have logging mechanisms been activated to capture access attempts? | Y __ <br> N __ | ESM: 09.006.001 Physical Security requires standards development |
| R 4.2 | Video Recording | Has CCTV been implemented to log all PSP access points? | Y __ <br> N __ | |
| R 4.3 | Manual Logs | Are procedures in place to require all visitors to sign in at PSP access points? | Y __ <br> N __ | |

| NERC CIP-006-1 Physical Security of Critical Cyber Assets | | | |
|---|---|---|---|
| R 5 | Access Log Retention | | |
| | Access logs must be maintained and protected. | | |
| | Are access logs retained for at least ninety (90) calendar days? | Y | ITS-104 Standards for System Access requires updating |
| | Are procedures in place to ensure that access logs cannot be tampered with or deleted? | Y | ITS-104 Standards for System Access |

| NERC CIP-006-1 Physical Security of Critical Cyber Assets | | |
|---|---|---|
| R 6 | Maintenance and Testing | All physical security systems must be properly maintained and tested. |
| R 6.1 | Testing Cycle | Are procedures in place to ensure physical security systems are tested and on a cycle no longer than three (3) years? Y ___ N ___ ESM: 09.006.001 Physical Security Needs procedure development |
| | | Are procedures in place to ensure physical security systems are maintained and on a cycle no longer than three (3) years? Y ___ N ___ |
| R 6.2 | Maintenance and Testing Logs | Are procedures in place to retain testing and maintenance logs for at least three (3) years? Y ___ N ___ ESM: 09.006.001 Physical Security ESM: 04.002.001 Records Retention requires updating |
| R 6.3 | Outage Records | Are procedures in place to record and retain outage logs for a minimum of one (1) calendar year? Y ___ N ___ ESM: 04.002.001 Records Retention requires updating |

| NERC CIP-007-1 System Security Management | | | |
|---|---|---|---|
| R 1 | Test Procedures | | TDF management will implement a program to ensure that all modifications and/or updates to the Electronic Security Perimeter (ESP) are tested to ensure the security mechanisms remain in tact. |
| R 1.1 | Limit Adverse Effects | Y | Has a testing process been implemented and documented that assures all changes to the existing environment maintain cyber security mechanisms? |
| | | | ITP-02-02 Information Security — Applications and Data Security |
| R 1.2 | Production Environment | Y | Are procedures in place to document the testing to ensure the tests reflect the production environment? |
| | | | ITP-02-02 Information Security — Applications and Data Security |
| R 1.3 | Documentation | Y | Are procedures in place to document test results? |
| | | | ITP-02-02 Information Security — Applications and Data Security |

| NERC CIP-007-1 System Security Management | | | |
|---|---|---|---|
| R 2 | Ports and Services | | Management must ensure that only those ports and services required for production processing are enabled. |
| R 2.1 | Enabled Functions | Y | Have standards been established to identify the ports and services required to support the production environment? | ITS-214 Standards for Firewalls |
| R 2.2 | Disable Unneeded Functions | Y | Have procedures been implemented to disable unneeded ports and services? | ITS-214 Standards for Firewalls |
| R 2.3 | Exception | Y ___ N ___ | Have procedures been implemented to document all unused ports and services that cannot be disabled? | ITS-214 Standards for Firewalls needs procedure development |

| NERC CIP-007-1 System Security Management | | | |
|---|---|---|---|
| R 3 | Security Patch Management | A change management process to track, evaluate, and approve all software patches must be implemented. | |
| R 3.1 | Document Patch Assessment | Are procedures in place to document the assessment of security patches and upgrades? | Y | ITS-209 Standards for Security Patch Management |
| R 3.2 | Exceptions | Are procedures in place to identify and document all security patches that have not been installed? | Y | ITS-209 Standards for Security Patch Management |

| NERC CIP-007-1 System Security Management | | | |
|---|---|---|---|
| R 4 | Malware Prevention | An active program to prevent, detect, and recover from malware attacks must be implemented. | |
| R 4.1 | Prevention Tools | Are procedures in place to ensure that Cyber Assets within the ESP are protected from outbreaks of malware? | Y | ITP-02-02 Information Security — Applications and Data Security |
| | | Do these procedures include anti-virus support and training? | Y | ITP-02-02 Information Security — Applications and Data Security |
| R 4.2 | Configuration Management | Are procedures in place to ensure that all workstations are running the most current version of the anti-malware software? | Y | ITP-02-02 Information Security — Applications and Data Security |

| NERC CIP-007-1 System Security Management | | | |
|---|---|---|---|
| R 5 | Account Management | Processes must be in place to enforce access authorization and accountability for all users. | |
| R 5.1 | Account Authorization | Are procedures in place to ensure that user access is granted based on a business need? | Y | ITS-104 Standards for System Access<br>ITP-02-01 Information Security — Security Controls<br>ITS-107 Standards for Security Administration |
| | | Are procedures in place to ensure that authorizations are granted based on the least privilege concept? | Y | ITP-02-01 Information Security — Security Controls |
| R 5.1.1 | Approval | Are procedures in place to ensure that user accounts are properly authorized? | Y | ITS-105 Standards for User Ids<br>ITS-107 Standards for Security Administration |
| R 5.1.2 | Audit Logs | Are logging mechanisms in place to record the activity generated by the user account? | Y | ITS-107 Standards for Security Administration |
| R 5.1.3 | Privilege Review | Are processes in place to ensure that user accounts and authorizations are reviewed and recertified on a regular basis? | Y | ITS-105 Standards for User IDs<br>ITS-107 Standards for Security Administration |
| R 5.2 | Acceptable Use | Are procedures in place to minimize and manage the scope of acceptable use of administrative, shared, and other generic accounts? | Y | ITS-101 Standards for Acceptable Use of Computing Systems<br>ITP-02-01 Information Security — Security Controls |

| | | | | |
|---|---|---|---|---|
| R 5.2.1 | Account Administration | Are procedures in place to ensure that the removal, disabling, or renaming of accounts is properly authorized? | Y | ITS-105 Standards for User IDs<br>ITS-107 Standards for Security Administration |
| R 5.2.2 | Shared Accounts | Are procedures in place to identify all personnel with access to shared accounts? | Y | ITS-105 Standards for User IDs<br>ITP-02-01 Information Security — Security Controls<br>ITS-107 Standards for Security Administration |
| R 5.2.3 | Shared Account Administration | Are procedures in place to ensure that shared account access is strictly restricted to those individuals with a demonstrated business need? | Y | ITS-105 Standards for User IDs<br>ITP-02-01 Information Security — Security Controls<br>ITS-107 Standards for Security Administration |
| R 5.3 | Passwords | Are procedures in place to ensure authentication passwords are properly managed? | Y | ITS-106 Standards for Passwords<br>ITP-02-01 Information Security — Security Controls |
| R 5.3.1 | Password Length | Are standards in place to require minimum password length or six (6) characters? | Y | ITS-105 Standards for User IDs<br>ITP-02-01 Information Security — Security Controls |
| R 5.3.2 | Password Composition | Are standards in place to require password consist of a combination of alpha, numeric, and "special" characters? | Y | ITS-105 Standards for User IDs<br>ITP-02-01 Information Security — Security Controls |
| R 5.3.3 | Password Change | Are procedures in place to ensure that passwords are changed on a regular basis? | Y | ITS-105 Standards for User IDs<br>ITP-02-01 Information Security — Security Controls |

| NERC CIP-007-1 System Security Management | | | |
|---|---|---|---|
| R 6 | Security Status Monitoring | The ability to monitor events impacting Cyber Assets within the Electronic Security Perimeter (ESP) is to be implemented. | |
| R 6.1 | Monitor Security Events | Are processes in place to monitor security events on all Cyber Assets within the ESP? | Y __ N __ | Needs procedure development |
| R 6.2 | Security Alerts | Are mechanisms in place to alert appropriate personnel when a Cyber Security Incident is detected? | Y | ITS-102 Standards for Security Incidents |
| R 6.3 | Log Events | Are processes in place to maintain logs of system events related to Cyber Security Incidents? | Y | ITS-102 Standards for Security Incidents ITP-02-01 Information Security — Security Controls |
| R 6.4 | Log Retention | Are controls in place to retain security incident logs for at least ninety (90) days? | Y | ITS-102 Standards for Security Incidents |
| R 6.5 | Log Review | Are procedures in place to ensure that logs are reviewed on a regular basis? | Y __ N __ | Needs procedure development |

| NERC CIP-007-1 System Security Management | | | |
|---|---|---|---|
| R 7 | Disposal or Redeployment | Formal methods, processes, and procedures must be implemented to control the disposal or redeployment of Cyber Assets within the ESP. | |
| R 7.1 | Data Storage Media | Are procedures in place to ensure that all data storage media are purged of all sensitive data prior to disposal? | Y | ITP-02-02 Information Security — Applications and Data Security ESM: 04.001.001 Information Management |
| R 7.2 | Redeployment | Are procedures in place to ensure that all data storage media are at least erased of all sensitive data prior to redeployment? | Y | ITP-02-02 Information Security — Applications and Data Security |
| R 7.3 | Log Events | Are procedures in place to record that such assets were disposed of or redeployed in accordance with documented procedures? | Y | ITP-02-02 Information Security — Applications and Data Security |

## NERC CIP-007-1 System Security Management

| | | | | |
|---|---|---|---|---|
| R 8 | Cyber Vulnerability Assessment (CVA) | An annual Cyber Vulnerability Assessment must be conducted on all Cyber Assets within the ESP. | | |
| R 8.1 | CVA Methodology | Are formal procedures in place on how to conduct a CVA? | Y | ITS-103 Standards for Anti-Vulnerability Protection |
| R 8.2 | Ports and Services | Are procedures in place to ensure that only those ports and services required to support Cyber Assets within the ESP are active? | Y | ITS-214 Standards for Firewalls |
| R 8.3 | Default Accounts | Are procedures in place to ensure that default accounts and passwords are deactivated? | Y | ITP-02-01 Information Security — Security Controls |
| R 8.4 | Documentation | Are procedures in place to ensure that an action plan to correct deficiencies found in the CVA is included in the documentation? | Y __ N __ | Needs procedure development |

| NERC CIP-007-1  System Security Management | | | |
|---|---|---|---|
| R 9 | Documentation Review and Maintenance | Documentation relating to Cyber Assets within the ESP is to be reviewed annually. | |
| | | Are procedures in place to document changes resulting from modifications to the system or controls? | Y ___ <br> N ___ | Needs procedure development |
| | | Are procedures in place to ensure these changes are documented within ninety (90) of the change? | Y ___ <br> N ___ | Needs procedure development |

| NERC CIP-008-1 Incident Reporting and Response Planning | | | |
|---|---|---|---|
| R 1 | Cyber Security Incident Response Plan | A formal Cyber Security Incident Response Plan (CSIRP) must be implemented. | |
| R 1.1 | Reporting Events | Are procedures in place to characterize and classify events related to Cyber Security Incidents? | Y | ITS-102 Standards for Security Incidents |
| R 1.2 | CSIRP Roles | Have the roles and responsibilities of the CSIRP team been documented? | Y ___ <br> N ___ | ITS-102 Standards for Security Incidents — requires updating |
| R 1.3 | Formal Reporting | Are procedures in place to ensure that all Cyber Security Incidents are reported to the Electricity Sector Information Sharing and Analysis (ES ISA) in a timely manner? | Y | ITS-102 Standards for Security Incidents |
| R 1.4 | Updating Plan | Are procedures in place to update CSIRP within ninety (90) days of any changes? | Y ___ <br> N ___ | ITS-102 Standards for Security Incidents <br> Needs procedure development to support the standards |
| R 1.5 | Plan Review | Are controls in place to ensure the CSIRP is reviewed at least annually? | Y ___ <br> N ___ | |
| R 1.6 | Plan Testing | Are procedures in place to ensure the CSIRP is tested at least annually? | Y ___ <br> N ___ | |

| NERC CIP-008-1 Incident Reporting and Response Planning | | |
|---|---|---|
| R 2 | Cyber Security Incident Documentation | Relevant documentation related to Cyber Security Incidents must be retained. |
| | Is the relevant documentation retained for at least three (3) years? | ITS-102 Standards for Security Incidents requires updating |

| NERC CIP-009-1 Recovery Plans for Critical Cyber Assets | | | |
|---|---|---|---|
| R 1 | Recovery Plans | Recovery plans for Critical Cyber Assets must be created and reviewed annually. | |
| R 1.1 | Plan Actions | Are recovery plan procedures in place to specify the required actions in response to events or conditions of varying duration and severity that would activate the recovery plan? | Y __<br>N __ | Cyber Security Policy (Status: DRAFT) — supporting procedures must be developed |
| R 1.2 | Recovery Plan Roles | Do recovery plan procedures identify specific recovery teams and responsibilities? | Y __<br>N __ | |

| NERC CIP-009-1 Recovery Plans for Critical Cyber Assets | | | |
|---|---|---|---|
| R 2 | Recovery Plan Exercises | Recovery plans for Critical Cyber Assets must be exercised at least annually. | |
| | | Are processes in place to exercise the recovery plans at least annually? | Y —<br>N — | Cyber Security Policy (Status: DRAFT) — supporting procedures must be developed |

| NERC CIP-009-1 Recovery Plans for Critical Cyber Assets | | | |
|---|---|---|---|
| Recovery plans for Critical Cyber Assets must be current. | | | |
| R 3 | Change Control | | |
| | Are procedures in place to ensure that all changes to the recovery plan are recorded within ninety (90) days of the change? | Y \_\_\_<br>N \_\_\_ | Cyber Security Policy (Status: DRAFT) – supporting procedures must be developed |

| NERC CIP-009-1 Recovery Plans for Critical Cyber Assets | | | |
|---|---|---|---|
| R 4 | Backup and Restore | Recovery plans for Critical Cyber Assets must include provisions for the backup and storage of information required to successfully restore Critical Cyber Assets. | |
| | | Are procedures in place to ensure that all necessary data, hardware, software, and documentation are backed up and stored off-site? | Y | ITP-02-02 Information Security — Applications and Data Security |

| NERC CIP-009-1 Recovery Plans for Critical Cyber Assets | | |
|---|---|---|
| R 5 | Testing Backup Media | Management must implement procedures to ensure that backup media is viable for use in the event of an emergency. |
| | Are procedures in place to test backup media to ensure it is viable in the event of an emergency? | Y | ITP-02-02 Information Security — Applications and Data Security |

## Gap Analysis Sample 3 Using Combination of Standards and Laws

| | | |
|---|---|---|
| **4 Risk Assessment and Treatment** | | |
| **4.1 Assessing Security Risks** | | |
| Risk assessments should identify, quantify, and prioritize risks against criteria for risk acceptance and objectives relevant to the organization. The results should guide and determine the appropriate management action and priorities for managing information security risks and for implementing controls selected to protect against these risks. The process of assessing risks and selecting controls may need to be performed a number of times to cover different parts of the organization or individual information systems. Risk assessment should include the systematic approach of estimating the magnitude of risks (risk analysis) and the process of comparing the estimated risks against risk criteria to determine the significance of the risks (risk evaluation). Risk assessments should also be performed periodically to address changes in the security requirements and in the risk situation, e.g., in the assets, threats, vulnerabilities, impacts, the risk evaluation, and when significant changes occur. These risk assessments should be undertaken in a methodical manner capable of producing comparable and reproducible results. The information security risk assessment should have a clearly defined scope in order to be effective and should include relationships with risk assessments in other areas, if appropriate. | | |
| *Class* | *Control Description* | |
| | | *PCI DSS* | *BIG COMPANY* |
| 4.1.1 | Risk Assessment | 12.1.2 Implement a process that annually identifies threats and vulnerabilities, and results in a formal risk assessment. | S-8.100.00 Risk Assessment |

## 4 Risk Assessment and Treatment

### 4.2 Treating Security Risks

Before considering the treatment of a risk, the organization should decide criteria for determining whether or not risks can be accepted. Risks may be accepted if, for example, it is assessed that the risk is low or that the cost of treatment is not cost effective for the organization. Such decisions should be recorded.

For each of the risks identified following the risk assessment a risk treatment decision needs to be made. Possible options for risk treatment include:

- Applying appropriate controls to reduce the risks.
- Knowingly and objectively accepting risks, providing they clearly satisfy the organization's policy and criteria for risk acceptance.
- Avoiding risks by not allowing actions that would cause the risks to occur.
- Transferring the associated risks to other parties, e.g., insurers or suppliers.

For those risks where the risk treatment decision has been to apply appropriate controls, these controls should be selected and implemented to meet the requirements identified by a risk assessment. Controls should ensure that risks are reduced to an acceptable level taking into account:

- Requirements and constraints of national and international legislation and regulations.
- Organizational objectives.
- Operational requirements and constraints.
- Cost of implementation and operation in relation to the risks being reduced and remaining proportional to the organization's requirements and constraints.
- The need to balance the investment in implementation and operation of controls against the harm likely to result from security failures.

Controls can be selected from this standard or from other control sets, or new controls can be designed to meet the specific needs of the organization. It is necessary to recognize that some controls may not be applicable to every information system or environment, and might not be practicable for all organizations. As an example, 10.1.3 describes how duties may be segregated to prevent fraud and error. It may not be possible for smaller organizations to segregate all duties and other ways of achieving the same control objective may be necessary. As another example, 10.10 describes how system use can be monitored and evidence collected. The described controls, e.g., event logging, might conflict with applicable legislation, such as privacy protection for customers or in the workplace.

| Class | Control Description | PCI DSS | | BIG COMPANY |
|---|---|---|---|---|
| 4.1.1 | Risk Assessment | 12.1.2 | Includes an annual process that identifies threats and vulnerabilities, and results in a formal risk assessment. | S-8.100.01 Evaluating the importance of assets to the organization S-8.200.01 Identifying threats, vulnerabilities, and controls S-8.300.00 Developing a risk reduction plan for the environment |

**5 Security policy**

**5.1 Information Security Policy**

To provide management direction and support for information security in accordance with business requirements and relevant laws and regulations.

Management should set a clear policy direction in line with business objectives and demonstrate support for, and commitment to, information security through the issue and maintenance of an information security policy across the organization.

| Class | Control Description | | PCI DSS | BIG COMPANY |
|---|---|---|---|---|
| 5.1.1 Information Security Policy Document | An information security policy document should be approved by management, and published and communicated to all employees and relevant external parties. | 12.1 | Establish, publish, maintain, and disseminate a security policy | UXED IT SP&S Section I IT Policy and Standards Statement |
| 5.1.2 Review of the Information Security Policy | The information security policy should be reviewed at planned intervals or if significant changes occur to ensure its continuing suitability, adequacy, and effectiveness. | 12.1.3 | Include a review at least once a year and update when the environment changes | UXED IT SP&S Section VIII Maintenance — all policies and standards will be periodically reviewed and updated by BIG IT Security |

## 6 ORGANIZATION OF INFORMATION SECURITY

### 6.1 Internal Organization

To manage information security within the organization.

A management framework should be established to initiate and control the implementation of information security within the organization.

Management should approve the information security policy, assign security roles and coordinate and review the implementation of security across the organization.

If necessary, a source of specialist information security advice should be established and made available within the organization. Contacts with external security specialists or groups, including relevant authorities, should be developed to keep up with industrial trends, monitor standards and assessment methods, and provide suitable liaison points when handling information security incidents. A multi-disciplinary approach to information security should be encouraged.

| | Class | Control Description | PCI DSS | | BIG COMPANY |
|---|---|---|---|---|---|
| 6.1.1 | Management Commitment to Information Security | Management should actively support security within the organization through clear direction, demonstrated commitment, explicit assignment, and acknowledgment of information security responsibilities. | | | S-1.100.01 UXED IT Security Council |
| 6.1.2 | Information Security Coordination | Information security activities should be coordinated by representatives from different parts of the organization with relevant roles and job functions. | 12.5 | Assign to an individual or team the information security management responsibilities. | P-1.200.00 BIG IT Security Roles and Responsibilities |

| | | | |
|---|---|---|---|
| 6.1.3 | Allocation of Information Security Responsibilities | All information security responsibilities should be clearly defined. | |
| | | 12.4 | Ensure that the security policy and procedures clearly define information security responsibilities for all employees and contractors. |
| | | | S-1.200.03 BIG IT Security Staff |
| 6.1.4 | Authorization Process for Information Processing Facilities | A management authorization process for new information processing facilities should be defined and implemented. | S-17.400.00 Information System Implementation |
| 6.1.5 | Confidentiality Agreements | Requirements for confidentiality or non-disclosure agreements reflecting the organization's needs for the protection of information should be identified and regularly reviewed. | S-6.100.04 Confidentiality Agreements |
| 6.1.6 | Contact with Authorities | Appropriate contacts with relevant authorities should be maintained. | |
| 6.1.7 | Contact with Special Interest Groups | Appropriate contacts with special interest groups or other specialist security forums and professional associations should be maintained. | |

| 6.1.8 | Independent Review of Information Security | The organization's approach to managing information security and its implementation (i.e., control objectives, controls, policies, processes, and procedures for information security) should be reviewed independently at planned intervals, or when significant changes to the security implementation occur. | 12.4 | Ensure that the security policy and procedures clearly define information security responsibilities for all employees and contractors. | S-5.400.00 Compliance |

## 6 ORGANIZATION OF INFORMATION SECURITY

### 6.2 External Parties

To maintain the security of the organization's information and information processing facilities that are accessed, processed, communicated to, or managed by external parties.

The security of the organization's information and information processing facilities should not be reduced by the introduction of external party products or services.

Any access to the organization's information processing facilities and processing and communication of information by external parties should be controlled.

Where there is a business need for working with external parties that may require access to the organization's information and information processing facilities, or in obtaining or providing a product and service from or to an external party, a risk assessment should be carried out to determine security implications and control requirements. Controls should be agreed and defined in an agreement with the external party.

| | Class | Control Description | | PCI DSS | BIG COMPANY |
|---|---|---|---|---|---|
| 6.2.1 | Identification of Risks Related to External Parties | The risks to the organization's information and information processing facilities from business processes involving external parties should be identified and appropriate controls implemented before granting access. | 12.1.2 | Implement a process that annually identtifies threats and vulnerabilities, and results in a formal risk assessment. | P-1.100.02 Chain of Trust |
| 6.2.2 | Addressing Security When Dealing with Customers | All identified security requirements should be addressed before giving customers access to the organization's information or assets. | | | S-11.300. 00 Malicious code protection required on non-BIG COMPANY systems S-14.000.00 Remote Access |

| 6.2.3 | Addressing Security in Third-Party Agreements | Agreements with third parties involving accessing, processing, communicating, or managing the organization's information or information processing facilities, or adding products or services to information processing facilities should cover all relevant security requirements | | |
| 12.4 | | | Ensure that the security policy and procedures clearly define information security responsibilities for all employees and contractors. | P-1.100.02 Chain of Trust |

# 7 ASSET MANAGEMENT

## 7.1 Responsibility for Assets

To achieve and maintain appropriate protection of organizational assets. All assets should be accounted for and have a nominated owner.

Owners should be identified for all assets and the responsibility for the maintenance of appropriate controls should be assigned. The implementation of specific controls may be delegated by the owner as appropriate but the owner remains responsible for the proper protection of the assets.

| Class | | Control Description | PCI DSS | | BIG COMPANY |
|---|---|---|---|---|---|
| 7.1.1 | Inventory of Assets | All assets should be clearly identified and an inventory of all important assets drawn up and maintained. | 9.9.1 | Properly inventory all media and make sure it is securely stored. | |
| 7.1.2 | Ownership of Assets | All information and assets associated with information processing facilities should be owned by a designated part of the organization. | | | S-9.400.01 Handling of Restricted or Confidential Information |
| 7.1.3 | Acceptable Use of Assets | Rules for the acceptable use of information and assets associated with information processing facilities should be identified, documented, and implemented | | | S-9.400.00 Classified Information |

**7 ASSET MANAGEMENT**

**7.2 Information Classification**

To ensure that information receives an appropriate level of protection.

Information should be classified to indicate the need, priorities, and expected degree of protection when handling the information.

Information has varying degrees of sensitivity and criticality. Some items may require an additional level of protection or special handling. An information classification scheme should be used to define an appropriate set of protection levels and communicate the need for special handling measures.

| | Class | Control Description | PCI DSS | BIG COMPANY |
|---|---|---|---|---|
| 7.2.1 | Classification Guidelines | Information should be classified in terms of its value, legal requirements, sensitivity, and criticality to the organization. | | S-9.300.00 Data Classification |
| 7.2.2 | Information Labeling and Handling | An appropriate set of procedures for information labeling and handling should be developed and implemented in accordance with the classification scheme adopted by the organization. | | S-9.400.00 Classified Information |

## 8 HUMAN RESOURCES SECURITY

### 8.1 Prior to Employment

To ensure that employees, contractors, and third-party users understand their responsibilities, and are suitable for the roles they are considered for, and to reduce the risk of theft, fraud, or misuse of facilities.

Security responsibilities should be addressed prior to employment in adequate job descriptions and in terms and conditions of employment.

All candidates for employment, contractors, and third-party users should be adequately screened, especially for sensitive jobs.

Employees, contractors, and third-party users of information processing facilities should sign an agreement on their security roles and responsibilities.

| | Class | Control Description | PCI DSS | BIG COMPANY |
|---|---|---|---|---|
| 8.1.1 | Roles and Responsibilities | Security roles and responsibilities of employees, contractors, and third-party users should be defined and documented in accordance with the organization's information security policy. | | P-1.100.02 Chain of Trusted Partner Agreement |
| 8.1.2 | Screening | Background verification checks on all candidates for employment, contractors, and third-party users should be carried out in accordance with relevant laws, regulations, and ethics, and proportional to the business requirements, the classification of the information to be accessed, and the perceived risks. | | S-6.100.00 Pre-Employment Screening |

## 8 HUMAN RESOURCES SECURITY

### 8.2 During Employment

To ensure that employees, contractors, and third-party users are aware of information security threats and concerns, their responsibilities and liabilities, and are equipped to support organizational security policy in the course of their normal work, and to reduce the risk of human error.

Management responsibilities should be defined to ensure that security is applied throughout an individual's employment within the organization.

An adequate level of awareness, education, and training in security procedures and the correct use of information processing facilities should be provided to all employees, contractors and third-party users to minimize possible security risks. A formal disciplinary process for handling security breaches should be established.

| Class | Control Description | PCI DSS | BIG COMPANY |
|---|---|---|---|
| 8.2.1 Management Responsibilities | Management should require employees, contractors, and third-party users to apply security in accordance with established policies and procedures of the organization. | | S-1.200.00 UXED IT Security Roles and Responsibilities |
| 8.2.2 Information Security Awareness, Education, and Training | All employees of the organization and, where relevant, contractors and third-party users should receive appropriate awareness training and regular updates in organizational policies and procedures, as relevant for their job function. | 12.6 Implement a formal security awareness program to make all employees aware of the importance of cardholder data. | S-5.200.00 Training and Awareness Elements |

| 8.2.3 | Disciplinary Process | There should be a formal disciplinary process for employees who have committed a security breach | | S-9.400.04 Disposal of Potentially Important Information<br>11-200.01 Actions to be taken when malicious code is detected<br>S-13.500.06 Special privileges and access, including "forensic" reviews |

## 8 HUMAN RESOURCES SECURITY

### 8.3 Termination or Change of Employment

To ensure that employees, contractors, and third-party users exit an organization or change employment in an orderly manner. Responsibilities should be in place to ensure an employee's, contractor's, or third-party user's exit from the organization is managed, and that the return of all equipment and the removal of all access rights are completed.
Change of responsibilities and employments within an organization should be managed as the termination of the respective responsibility or employment in line with this section, and any new employments should be managed as described in section 8.1.

| | Class | Control Description | | PCI DSS | BIG COMPANY |
|---|---|---|---|---|---|
| 8.3.1 | Termination Responsibilities | Responsibilities for performing employment termination or change of employment should be clearly defined and assigned. | 8.5.1 | Control addition, deletion, and modification of user IDs, credentials, and other identifier objects. | S-13.600.01 Notification S-13.600.07 Involuntary Termination |
| 8.3.2 | Return of Assets | All employees, contractors, and third-party users should return all of the organization's assets in their possession upon termination of their employment, contract, or agreement. | | | P-1.100.11 Exit Procedures P-1.100.02 Chain of Trusted Partner Agreement |
| 8.3.3 | Removal of Access Rights | The access rights of all employees, contractors, and third-party users to information and information processing facilities should be removed upon termination of their employment contract or agreement, or adjusted upon change. | 8.5.5 | Remove inactive user accounts at least every 90 days. | S-13.600.03 Inactive Accounts |

## 9 PHYSICAL AND ENVIRONMENTAL SECURITY

### 9.1 Secure Areas

To prevent unauthorized physical access, damage, and interference to the organization's premises and information.

Critical or sensitive information processing facilities should be housed in secure areas, protected by defined security perimeters, with appropriate security barriers and entry controls. They should be physically protected from unauthorized access, damage, and interference.

The protection provided should be commensurate with the identified risks.

| | Class | Control Description | | PCI DSS | BIG COMPANY |
|---|---|---|---|---|---|
| 9.1.1 | Physical Security Perimeter | Security perimeters (barriers such as walls, card controlled entry gates or manned reception desks) should be used to protect areas that contain information and information processing facilities. | 9.1 | Use appropriate facility entry controls to limit and monitor physical access to systems that store, process, or transmit cardholder data. | P-1.200.02 Physical Access Controls |
| 9.1.2 | Physical Entry Controls | Secure areas should be protected by appropriate entry controls to ensure that only authorized personnel are allowed access. | | | P-1.200.02 Physical Access Controls |
| 9.1.3 | Securing Offices, Rooms, and Facilities | Physical security for offices, rooms, and facilities should be designed and applied. | | | |

| 9.1.4 | Protecting against External and Environmental Threats | Physical protection against damage from fire, flood, earthquake, explosion, civil unrest, and other forms of natural or man-made disaster should be designed and applied. | | |
|---|---|---|---|---|
| 9.1.5 | Working in Secure Areas | Physical protection and guidelines for working in secure areas should be designed and applied. | | |
| 9.1.6 | Public access, Delivery, and Loading Areas | Access points such as delivery and loading areas and other points where unauthorized persons may enter the premises should be controlled and, if possible, isolated from information processing facilities to avoid unauthorized access. | | |

## 9 PHYSICAL AND ENVIRONMENTAL SECURITY

### 9.2 Equipment Security

To prevent loss, damage, theft, or compromise of assets and interruption to the organization's activities.
Equipment should be protected from physical and environmental threats.
Protection of equipment (including that used off-site, and the removal of property) is necessary to reduce the risk of unauthorized access to information and to protect against loss or damage. This should also consider equipment siting and disposal. Special controls may be required to protect against physical threats, and to safeguard supporting facilities, such as the electrical supply and cabling infrastructure.

|       | Class | Control Description | PCI DSS | BIG COMPANY |
|-------|-------|---------------------|---------|-------------|
| 9.2.1 | Equipment Siting and Protection | Equipment should be sited or protected to reduce the risks from environmental threats and hazards, and opportunities for unauthorized access | | |
| 9.2.2 | Supporting Utilities | Equipment should be protected from power failures and other disruptions caused by failures in supporting utilities. | | |
| 9.2.3 | Cabling Security | Power and telecommunications cabling carrying data or supporting information services should be protected from interception or damage. | | |
| 9.2.4 | Equipment Maintenance | Equipment should be correctly maintained to ensure its continued availability and integrity. | | |

| 9.2.5 | Security of Equipment Off-Premises | Security should be applied to off-site equipment taking into account the different risks of working outside the organization's premises. | | |
| 9.2.6 | Secure Disposal or Re-Use of Equipment | All items of equipment containing storage media should be checked to ensure that any sensitive data and licensed software has been removed or securely overwritten prior to disposal. | | |
| 9.2.7 | Removal of Property | Equipment, information, or software should not be taken off-site without prior authorization. | | |

## 10 COMMUNICATIONS AND OPERATIONS MANAGEMENT

### 10.1 Operational Procedures and Responsibilities

To ensure the correct and secure operation of information processing facilities.

Responsibilities and procedures for the management and operation of all information processing facilities should be established. This includes the development of appropriate operating procedures.

Segregation of duties should be implemented, where appropriate, to reduce the risk of negligent or deliberate system misuse.

| | Class | Control Description | | PCI DSS | BIG COMPANY |
|---|---|---|---|---|---|
| 10.1.1 | Documented Operating Procedures | Operating procedures should be documented, maintained, and made available to all users who need them. | 12.2 | Develop daily operational security procedures | |
| 10.1.2 | Change Management | Changes to information processing facilities and systems should be controlled. | 6.4 | Follow change control procedures for all system and software configuration changes. | |
| 10.1.3 | Segregation of Duties | Duties and areas of responsibility should be segregated to reduce opportunities for unauthorized or unintentional modification or misuse of the organization's assets. | 6.3.3 | Separation of duties between development, test and production environments. | |
| 10.1.4 | Separation of Development, Test, and Operational Facilities | Development, test, and operational facilities should be separated to reduce the risks of unauthorized access or changes to the operational system. | 6.3.2 | Separate development, test, and production environments. | |

## 10 COMMUNICATIONS AND OPERATIONS MANAGEMENT

### 10.2 Third-Party Service Delivery Management

To implement and maintain the appropriate level of information security and service delivery in line with third-party service delivery agreements.

The organization should check the implementation of agreements, monitor compliance with the agreements, and manage changes to ensure that the services delivered meet all requirements agreed with the third party.

|  | Class | Control Description | | PCI DSS | BIG COMPANY |
|---|---|---|---|---|---|
| 10.2.1 | Service Delivery | It should be ensured that the security controls, service definitions and delivery levels included in the third-party service delivery agreement are implemented, operated, and maintained by the third party. | 12.10 | All processors and service providers must maintain and implement policies and procedures to manage connected entities | |
| 10.2.2 | Monitoring and Review of Third-Party Services | The services, reports, and records provided by the third party should be regularly monitored and reviewed, and audits should be carried out regularly. | 10.2 | Implement automated audit trails for all system components to reconstruct events. | |
| 10.2.3 | Managing Changes to Third-Party Services | Changes to the provision of services, including maintaining and improving existing information security policies, procedures and controls, should be managed, taking account of the criticality of business systems and processes involved and re-assessment of risks. | 6.4 | Follow change control procedures for all system and software configuration changes. | |

## 10 COMMUNICATIONS AND OPERATIONS MANAGEMENT

### 10.3  System Planning and Acceptance

To minimize the risk of systems failures.

Advance planning and preparation are required to ensure the availability of adequate capacity and resources to deliver the required system performance.

Projections of future capacity requirements should be made, to reduce the risk of system overload.

The operational requirements of new systems should be established, documented, and tested prior to their acceptance and use.

| | Class | Control Description | | PCI DSS | BIG COMPANY |
|---|---|---|---|---|---|
| 10.3.1 | Capacity Management | The use of resources should be monitored, tuned, and projections made of future capacity requirements to ensure the required system performance. | | | |
| 10.3.2 | System Acceptance | Acceptance criteria for new information systems, upgrades, and new versions should be established and suitable tests of the system(s) carried out during development and prior to acceptance. | 6.1 | Ensure that all system components and software have the latest vendor-supplied patches installed. | |

**10 COMMUNICATIONS AND OPERATIONS MANAGEMENT**

**10.4 Protection against Malicious and Mobile Code**

To protect the integrity of software and information.

Precautions are required to prevent and detect the introduction of malicious code and unauthorized mobile code.

Software and information processing facilities are vulnerable to the introduction of malicious code, such as computer viruses, network worms, Trojan horses, and logic bombs. Users should be made aware of the dangers of malicious code. Managers should, where appropriate, introduce controls to prevent, detect, and remove malicious code and control mobile code.

| | Class | Control Description | | PCI DSS | BIG COMPANY |
|---|---|---|---|---|---|
| 10.4.1 | Controls against Malicious Code | Detection, prevention, and recovery controls to protect against malicious code and appropriate user awareness procedures should be implemented. | 5.1 | Deploy anti-virus software on all systems commonly affected by viruses | |
| | | | 5.2 | Ensure that all anti-virus mechanisms are current, actively running, and capable of generating audit logs. | |
| 10.4.2 | Controls against Mobile Code | Where the use of mobile code is authorized, the configuration should ensure that the authorized mobile code operates according to a clearly defined security policy, and unauthorized mobile code should be prevented from executing. | | | |

## 10 COMMUNICATIONS AND OPERATIONS MANAGEMENT

### 10.5 Backup

To maintain the integrity and availability of information and information processing facilities.
Routine procedures should be established to implement the agreed backup policy and strategy (see also 14.1) for taking backup copies of data and rehearsing their timely restoration.

| | Class | Control Description | | PCI DSS | BIG COMPANY |
|---|---|---|---|---|---|
| 10.5.1 | Information Backup | Backup copies of information and software should be taken and tested regularly in accordance with the agreed backup policy. | 9.5 | Store media backups in a secure location, preferably in an off-site facility, such as an alternate or backup site, or a commercial storage facility. | |

## 10 COMMUNICATIONS AND OPERATIONS MANAGEMENT

### 10.6 Network Security Management

To ensure the protection of information in networks and the protection of the supporting infrastructure.
The secure management of networks, which may span organizational boundaries, requires careful consideration to data flow, legal implications, monitoring, and protection.
Additional controls may also be required to protect sensitive information passing over public networks.

| Class | | Control Description | | PCI DSS | BIG COMPANY |
|---|---|---|---|---|---|
| 10.6.1 | Network Controls | Networks should be adequately managed and controlled, in order to be protected from threats, and to maintain security for the systems and applications using the network, including information in transit. | 1.1 | Establish firewall configuration standards | |
| 10.6.2 | Security of Network Services | Security features, service levels, and management requirements of all network services should be identified and included in any network services agreement, whether these services are provided in-house or outsourced. | 1.2 | Build a firewall configuration that denies all traffic from "untrusted" networks and hosts, except for protocols necessary for the cardholder data environment. | |

## 10 COMMUNICATIONS AND OPERATIONS MANAGEMENT

### 10.7 Media Handling

To prevent unauthorized disclosure, modification, removal or destruction of assets, and interruption to business activities. Media should be controlled and physically protected.

Appropriate operating procedures should be established to protect documents, computer media (e.g., tapes, disks), input/output data and system documentation from unauthorized disclosure, modification, removal, and destruction.

| | Class | Control Description | | PCI DSS | BIG COMPANY |
|---|---|---|---|---|---|
| 10.7.1 | Management of Removable Media | There should be procedures in place for the management of removable media. | 12.3.10 | When accessing cardholder data remotely, prohibit storage of cardholder data onto local hard drives, USB drives, or other external media. Prohibit use of cut-and-paste and print functions during remote access. | |
| 10.7.2 | Disposal of Media | Media should be disposed of securely and safely when no longer required, using formal procedures. | 3.1 | Develop a data retention and disposal policy. | |
| 10.7.3 | Information Handling Procedures | Procedures for the handling and storage of information should be established to protect this information from unauthorized disclosure or misuse. | 9.7 | Maintain strict control over internal or external distribution of any kind of media that contains cardholder data. | |
| 10.7.4 | Security of System Documentation | System documentation should be protected against unauthorized access. | | | |

## 10 COMMUNICATIONS AND OPERATIONS MANAGEMENT

### 10.8 Exchange of Information

To maintain the security of information and software exchanged within an organization and with any external entity.
Exchanges of information and software between organizations should be based on a formal exchange policy, carried out in line with exchange agreements, and should be compliant with any relevant legislation (see clause I S).
Procedures and standards should be established to protect information and physical media containing information in transit.

| | Class | Control Description | PCI DSS | BIG COMPANY |
|---|---|---|---|---|
| 10.8.1 | Information Exchange Policies and Procedures | Formal exchange policies, procedures, and controls should be in place to protect the exchange of information through the use of all types of communication facilities. | | |
| 10.8.2 | Exchange Agreements | Agreements should be established for the exchange of information and software between the organization and external parties. | | |
| 10.8.3 | Physical Media in Transit | Media containing information should be protected against unauthorized access, misuse, or corruption during transportation beyond an organization's physical boundaries. | | |
| 10.8.4 | Electronic Messaging | Information involved in electronic messaging should be appropriately protected. | | |

| 10.8.5 | Business Information Systems | Policies and procedures should be developed and implemented to protect information associated with the interconnection of business information systems. | | |

**10 COMMUNICATIONS AND OPERATIONS MANAGEMENT**

**10.9 Electronic Commerce Services**

To ensure the security of electronic commerce services, and their secure use.
The security implications associated with using electronic commerce services, including online transactions, and the requirements for controls, should be considered. The integrity and availability of information electronically published through publicly available systems should also be considered.

| | Class | Control Description | PCI DSS | | BIG COMPANY |
|---|---|---|---|---|---|
| 10.9.1 | Electronic Commerce | Information involved in electronic commerce passing over public networks should be protected from fraudulent activity, contract dispute, and unauthorized disclosure and modification. | 1.4 | Prohibit direct public access between external networks and any system component that stores cardholder data. | |
| 10.9.2 | Online Transactions | Information involved in online transactions should be protected to prevent incomplete transmission, misrouting, unauthorized message alteration, unauthorized disclosure, unauthorized message duplication or replay. | | | |
| 10.9.3 | Publicly Available Information | The integrity of information being made available on a publicly available system should be protected to prevent unauthorized modification. | 1.4 | Prohibit direct public access between external networks and any system component that stores cardholder data. | |

## 10 COMMUNICATIONS AND OPERATIONS MANAGEMENT

### 10.10 Monitoring

To detect unauthorized information processing activities.

Systems should be monitored and information security events should be recorded. Operator logs and fault logging should be used to ensure information system problems are identified.

An organization should comply with all relevant legal requirements applicable to its monitoring and logging activities.

System monitoring should be used to check the effectiveness of controls adopted and to verify conformity to an access policy model.

| Class | Control Description | PCI DSS | | BIG COMPANY |
|---|---|---|---|---|
| 10.10.1 Audit Logging | Audit logs recording user activities, exceptions, and information security events should be produced and kept for an agreed period to assist in future investigations and access control monitoring. | 10.2 | Implement automated audit trails for all system components to reconstruct events. | |
| 10.10.2 Monitoring System Use | Procedures for monitoring use of information processing facilities should be established and the results of the monitoring activities reviewed regularly. | 10.6 | Review logs for all system components at least daily. | |
| 10.10.3 Protection of Log Information | Logging facilities and log information should be protected against tampering and unauthorized access. | 10.5 | Secure audit trails so they cannot be altered. | |
| 10.10.4 Administrator and Operator Logs | System administrator and system operator activities should be logged. | 10.2.1 | All individual user access. | |

| | | | |
|---|---|---|---|
| 10.10.5 | Fault logging | Faults should be logged, analyzed, and appropriate action taken. | |
| 10.10.6 | Clock Synchronization | The clocks of all relevant information processing systems within an organization or security domain should be synchronized with an agreed accurate time source. | 10.4 Synchronize all critical system clocks and times. |

## 11 ACCESS CONTROL

### 11.1 Business Requirement for Access Control

To control access to information.

Access to information, information processing facilities, and business processes should be controlled on the basis of business and security requirements.

Access control rules should take account of policies for information dissemination and authorization.

| Class | Control Description | PCI DSS | | BIG COMPANY |
|---|---|---|---|---|
| 11.1.1 Access Control Policy | An access control policy should be established, documented, and reviewed based on business and security requirements for access. | 7.1 | Limit access to computing resources and cardholder information to only those individuals whose job requires such access. | |

**11 ACCESS CONTROL**

**11.2 User Access Management**

To ensure authorized user access and to prevent unauthorized access to information systems.

Formal procedures should be in place to control the allocation of access rights to information systems and services.

The procedures should cover all stages in the life cycle of user access, from the initial registration of new users to the final de-registration of users who no longer require access to information systems and services. Special attention should be given, where appropriate, to the need to control the allocation of privileged access rights, which allow users to override system controls.

| Class | | Control Description | PCI DSS | | BIG COMPANY |
|---|---|---|---|---|---|
| 11.2.1 | User Registration | There should be a formal user registration and de-registration procedure in place for granting and revoking access to all information systems and services. | 8.1 | Identify all users with a unique user name before allowing them access to systems components or cardholder data. | |
| 11.2.2 | Privilege Management | The allocation and use of privileges should be restricted and controlled. | 7.1 | Limit access to computing resources and cardholder information to only those individuals whose job requires such access. | |
| 11.2.3 | User Password Management | The allocation of passwords should be controlled through a formal management process. | 8.5 | Ensure proper user authentication and password management | |
| 11.2.4 | Review of User Access Rights | Management should review users' access rights at regular intervals using a formal process. | 12.2 | Develop daily operational security procedures that are consistent with PCI DSS requirements. | |

| 11  ACCESS CONTROL | | | | |
|---|---|---|---|---|
| **11.3  User Responsibilities** | | | | |
| To prevent unauthorized user access, and compromise or theft of information and information processing facilities.<br>The cooperation of authorized users is essential for effective security.<br>Users should be made aware of their responsibilities for maintaining effective access controls, particularly regarding the use of passwords and the security of user equipment.<br>A clear desk and clear screen policy should be implemented to reduce the risk of unauthorized access or damage to papers, media, and information processing facilities. | | | | |
| | *Class* | *Control Description* | *PCI DSS* | *BIG COMPANY* |
| 11.3.1 | Password Use | Users should be required to follow good security practices in the selection and use of passwords. | 8.5  Ensure proper user authentication and password management. | |
| 11.3.2 | Unattended User Equipment | Users should ensure that unattended equipment has appropriate protection. | 8.5.15  If a session has been idle for more than 15 minutes, require user to re-enter the password to re-activate the terminal. | |
| 11.3.3 | Clean Desk and Clear Screen Policy | A clear desk policy for papers and removable storage media and a clear screen policy for information processing facilities should be adopted. | | |

## 11 ACCESS CONTROL

### 11.4 Network Access Control

To prevent unauthorized access to networked services.

Access to both internal and external networked services should be controlled.

User access to networks and network services should not compromise the security of the network services by ensuring:

- Appropriate interfaces are in place between the organization's network and networks owned by other organizations, and public networks.
- Appropriate authentication mechanisms are applied for users and equipment.
- Control of user access to information services in enforced.

| | Class | Control Description | | PCI DSS | BIG COMPANY |
|---|---|---|---|---|---|
| 11.4.1 | Policy on Use of Network Services | Users should only be provided with access to the services that they have been specifically authorized to use. | 7.1 | Limit access to computing resources and cardholder information to only those individuals whose job requires such access. | |
| 11.4.2 | User Authentication for External Connections | Appropriate authentication methods should be used to control access by remote users. | 8.3 | Implement two-factor authentication for remote access to the network. | |
| 11.4.3 | Equipment Identification in Networks | Automatic equipment identification should be considered as a means to authenticate connections from specific locations and equipment. | | | |

| | | | |
|---|---|---|---|
| 11.4.4 | Remote Diagnostic and Configuration Port Protection | Physical and logical access to diagnostic and configuration ports should be controlled. | | |
| 11.4.5 | Segregation in Networks | Groups of information services, users, and information systems should be segregated on networks. | 1.1.4 | Description of the groups, roles, and responsibilities standards must be implemented. |
| 11.4.6 | Network Connection Control | For shared networks, especially those extending across the organization's boundaries, the capability of users to connect to the network should be restricted, in line with the access control policy and requirements of the business applications (see 11.1). | 1.1 | Establish firewall configuration standards to secure the network. |
| 11.4.7 | Network Routing Control | Routing controls should be implemented for networks to ensure that computer connections and information flows do not breach the access control policy of the business applications. | 1.1.8 | Quarterly review firewall and router rule sets. |

## 11 ACCESS CONTROL

### 11.5 Operating System Access Control

To prevent unauthorized access to operating systems.

Security facilities should be used to restrict access to operating systems to authorized users. The facilities should be capable of the following:

- Authenticating authorized users, in accordance with a defined access control policy.
- Recording successful and failed system authentication attempts.
- Recording the use of special system privileges.
- Issuing alarms when system security policies are breached.
- Providing appropriate means for authentication.
- Where appropriate, restricting the connection time of users.

| | Class | Control Description | | PCI DSS | BIG COMPANY |
|---|---|---|---|---|---|
| 11.5.1 | Secure Log-On Procedures | Access to operating systems should be controlled by a secure log-on procedure. | 8.1 | Identify all users with a unique user name before allowing them to access system components or cardholder data. | |
| 11.5.2 | User Identification and Authentication | All users should have a unique identifier (user ID) for their personal use only, and a suitable authentication technique should be chosen to substantiate the claimed identity of a user. | 8.1 | Identify all users with a unique user name before allowing them to access system components or cardholder data. | |

| | | | | | |
|---|---|---|---|---|---|
| 11.5.3 | Password Management System | Systems for managing passwords should be interactive and should ensure quality passwords. | 8.2 | In addition to assigning a unique ID, employ at least one of the following to authenticate:<br><br>∎ Password<br>∎ Token Device<br>∎ Biometrics | |
| 11.5.4 | Use of System Utilities | The use of utility programs that might be capable of overriding system and application controls should be restricted and tightly controlled. | 2.2 | Develop configuration standards for all system components. | |
| 11.5.5 | Session Time-Out | Inactive sessions should shut down after a defined period of inactivity. | 8.5.15 | If a session has been idle for more than 15 minutes, require user to re-enter the password to re-activate the terminal. | |
| 11.5.6 | Limitation of Connection Time | Restrictions on connection times should be used to provide additional security for high-risk applications. | | | |

**11 ACCESS CONTROL**

**11.6 Application and Information Access Control**

To prevent unauthorized access to information held in application systems. Security facilities should be used to restrict access to and within application systems.

Logical access to application software and information should be restricted to authorized users. Application systems should:

- Control user access to information and application system functions, in accordance with a defined access control policy.
- Provide protection from unauthorized access by any utility, operating system software, and malicious software that is capable of overriding or bypassing system or application controls.
- Not compromise other systems with which information resources are shared.

| Class | | Control Description | | PCI DSS | BIG COMPANY |
|---|---|---|---|---|---|
| 11.6.1 | Information Access Restriction | Access to information and application system functions by users and support personnel should be restricted in accordance with the defined access control policy. | 7.1 | Limit access to computing resources and cardholder information only to those individuals whose job requires such access. | |
| 11.6.2 | Sensitive System Isolation | Sensitive systems should have a dedicated (isolated) computing environment. | 1.2 | Build firewall configuration that denies all traffic from "untrusted" networks and hosts. | |

## 11 ACCESS CONTROL

### 11.7 Mobile Computing and Teleworking

To ensure information security when using mobile computing and teleworking facilities.
The protection required should be commensurate with the risks these specific ways of working cause. When using mobile computing the risks of working in an unprotected environment should be considered and appropriate protection applied. In the case of teleworking the organization should apply protection to the teleworking site and ensure that suitable arrangements are in place for this way of working.

| Class | | Control Description | PCI DSS | | BIG COMPANY |
|---|---|---|---|---|---|
| 11.7.1 | Mobile Computing and Communications | A formal policy should be in place, and appropriate security measures should be adopted to protect against the risks of using mobile computing and communication facilities. | 8.3 | Implement two-factor authentication for remote access to the network. | |
| 11.7.2 | Teleworking | A policy, operational plans and procedures should be developed and implemented for teleworking activities. | | | |

| 12 INFORMATION SYSTEMS ACQUISITION, DEVELOPMENT, AND MAINTENANCE | | | |
|---|---|---|---|
| **12.1 Security Requirements of Information Systems** | | | |
| To ensure that security is an integral part of information systems. Information systems include operating systems, infrastructure, business applications, off-the-shelf products, services, and user-developed applications. The design and implementation of the information system supporting the business process can be crucial for security. Security requirements should be identified and agreed prior to the development and/or implementation of information systems. All security requirements should be identified at the requirements phase of a project and justified, agreed, and documented as part of the overall business case for an information system. | | | |
| *Class* | *Control Description* | *PCI DSS* | *BIG COMPANY* |
| 12.1.1 Security Requirements Analysis and Specification | Statements of business requirements for new information systems, or enhancements to existing information systems should specify the requirements for security controls. | 7.1 Limit access to computing resources and cardholder information to only those individuals whose job requires such access. | |

## 12 INFORMATION SYSTEMS ACQUISITION, DEVELOPMENT, AND MAINTENANCE

### 12.2 Correct Processing in Applications

To prevent errors, loss, unauthorized modification or misuse of information in applications. Appropriate controls should be designed into applications, including user developed applications to ensure correct processing. These controls should include the validation of input data, internal processing and output data. Additional controls may be required for systems that process, or have an impact on, sensitive, valuable or critical information. Such controls should be determined on the basis of security requirements and risk assessment.

| | Class | Control Description | PCI DSS | | BIG COMPANY |
|---|---|---|---|---|---|
| 12.2.1 | Input Data Validation | Data input to applications should be validated to ensure that this data is correct and appropriate. | 6.5 | Cover prevention of common coding vulnerabilities in the software development processes | |
| 12.2.2 | Control of Internal Processing | Validation checks should be incorporated into applications to detect any corruption of information through processing errors or deliberate acts. | 6.5 6.5.1 | Cover prevention of common coding vulnerabilities in the software development processes Invalid input | |
| 12.2.3 | Message Integrity | Requirements for ensuring authenticity and protecting message integrity in applications should be identified, and appropriate controls identified and implemented. | 6.5 | Cover prevention of common coding vulnerabilities in the software development processes | |

| 12.2.4 | Output Data Validation | Data output from an application should be validated to ensure that the processing of stored information is correct and appropriate to the circumstances. | 6.5 | Cover prevention of common coding vulnerabilities in the software development processes | |

## 12 INFORMATION SYSTEMS ACQUISITION, DEVELOPMENT, AND MAINTENANCE

### 12.3 Cryptographic Controls

To protect the confidentiality, authenticity, or integrity of information by cryptographic means. A policy should be developed on the use of cryptographic controls. Key management should be in place to support the use of cryptographic techniques.

| | Class | Control Description | | PCI DSS | BIG COMPANY |
|---|---|---|---|---|---|
| 12.3.1 | Policy on the Use of Cryptographic Controls | A policy on the use of cryptographic controls for protection of information should be developed and implemented. | 3.6 | Fully document and implement all key management processes and procedures for keys used in encryption of cardholder data. | |
| 12.3.2 | Key Management | Key management should be in place to support the organization's use of cryptographic techniques. | 3.5 | Protect encryption keys used for encryption of cardholder data against both disclosure and misuse. | |

## 12 INFORMATION SYSTEMS ACQUISITION, DEVELOPMENT, AND MAINTENANCE

### 12.4 Security of System Files

To ensure the security of system files.

Access to system files and program source code should be controlled, and IT projects and support activities conducted in a secure manner. Care should be taken to avoid exposure of sensitive data in test environments.

| | Class | Control Description | | PCI DSS | BIG COMPANY |
|---|---|---|---|---|---|
| 12.4.1 | Control of Operational Software | There should be procedures in place to control the installation of software on operational systems. | 6.4 | Follow change control procedures for all system and software configuration changes. | |
| 12.4.2 | Protection of System Test Data | Test data should be selected carefully, and protected and controlled. | 6.3.2 | Separate development, test, and production environments. | |
| 12.4.3 | Access Control to Program Source Code | Access to program source code should be restricted. | 6.4 | Follow change control procedures for all system and software configuration changes. | |

## 12 INFORMATION SYSTEMS ACQUISITION, DEVELOPMENT, AND MAINTENANCE

### 12.5 Security in Development and Support Processes

To maintain the security of application system software and information. Project and support environments should be strictly controlled.

Managers responsible for application systems should also be responsible for the security of the project or support environment. They should ensure that all proposed system changes are reviewed to check that they do not compromise the security of either the system or the operating environment.

| | Class | Control Description | | PCI DSS | BIG COMPANY |
|---|---|---|---|---|---|
| 12.5.1 | Change Control Procedures | The implementation of changes should be controlled by the use of formal change control procedures. | 6.4 | Follow change control procedures for all system and software configuration changes. | |
| 12.5.2 | Technical Review of Applications after Operating System Changes | When operating systems are changed, business critical applications should be reviewed and tested to ensure there is no adverse impact on organizational operations or security. | 6.4 | Follow change control procedures for all system and software configuration changes. | |
| 12.5.3 | Restrictions on Changes to Software Packages | Modifications to software packages should be discouraged, limited to necessary changes, and all changes should be strictly controlled. | 6.3 | Develop software applications based on industry best practices and incorporate information security throughout the SDLC. | |

| 12.5.4 | Information Leakage | Opportunities for information leakage should be prevented. | 4.1 | Use strong cryptography and security protocols to safeguard sensitive cardholder data during transmission over open, public networks. |
| 12.5.5 | Outsourced Software Development | Outsourced software development should be supervised and monitored by the organization. | 6.4 | Follow change control procedures for all system and software configuration changes. |

## 12 INFORMATION SYSTEMS ACQUISITION, DEVELOPMENT, AND MAINTENANCE

### 12.6 Technical Vulnerability Management

To reduce risks resulting from exploitation of published technical vulnerabilities. Technical vulnerability management should be implemented in an effective, systematic, and repeatable way with measurements taken to confirm its effectiveness. These considerations should include operating systems, and any other applications in use.

| Class | Control Description | | PCI DSS | BIG COMPANY |
|-------|---------------------|---|---------|-------------|
| 12.6.1 Control of Technical Vulnerabilities | Timely information about technical vulnerabilities of information systems being used should be obtained, the organization's exposure to such vulnerabilities evaluated, and appropriate measures taken to address the associated risk. | 6.2 | Establish a process to identify newly discovered security vulnerabilities. | |

| 13 INFORMATION SECURITY INCIDENT MANAGEMENT | | | |
|---|---|---|---|
| **13.1 Reporting Information Security Events and Weaknesses** | | | |
| To ensure information security events and weaknesses associated with information systems are communicated in a manner allowing timely corrective action to be taken. Formal event reporting and escalation procedures should be in place. All employees, contractors, and third-party users should be made aware of the procedures for reporting the different types of event and weakness that might have an impact on the security of organizational assets. They should be required to report any information security events and weaknesses as quickly as possible to the designated point of contact. | | | |
| Class | Control Description | PCI DSS | BIG COMPANY |
| 13.1.1 Reporting Information Security Events | Information security events should be reported through appropriate management channels as quickly as possible. | 10.5 Secure audit trails so they cannot be altered. | |
| 13.1.2 Reporting Security Weaknesses | All employees, contractors, and third-party users of information systems and services should be required to note and report any observed or suspected security weaknesses in systems or services. | 12.5.3 Establish, document, and distribute security incident response and escalation procedures to ensure timely and effective handling of all situations. | |

## 13 INFORMATION SECURITY INCIDENT MANAGEMENT

### 13.2 Management of Information Security Incidents and Improvements

To ensure a consistent and effective approach is applied to the management of information security incidents. Responsibilities and procedures should be in place to handle information security events and weaknesses effectively once they have been reported. A process of continual improvement should be applied to the response to, monitoring, evaluating, and overall management of information security incidents. Where evidence is required, it should be collected to ensure compliance with legal requirements.

| Class | Control Description | | PCI DSS | BIG COMPANY |
|---|---|---|---|---|
| 13.2.1 Responsibilities and Procedures | Management responsibilities and procedures should be established to ensure a quick, effective, and orderly response to information security incidents. | 12.5.3 | Establish, document, and distribute security incident response and escalation procedures to ensure timely and effective handling of all situations. | |
| 13.2.2 Learning from Information Security Incidents | There should be mechanisms in place to enable the types, volumes, and costs of information security incidents to be quantified and monitored. | | | |
| 13.2.3 Collection of Evidence | Where a follow-up action against a person or organization after an information security incident involves legal action (either civil or criminal), evidence should be collected, retained, and presented to conform to the rules for evidence laid down in the relevant jurisdiction(s). | | | |

**14 BUSINESS CONTINUITY MANAGEMENT**

**14.1 Information Security Aspects of Business Continuity Management**

To counteract interruptions to business activities and to protect critical business processes from the effects of major failures of information systems or disasters and to ensure their timely resumption.

A business continuity management process should be implemented to minimize the impact on the organization and recover from loss of information assets (which may be the result of, for example, natural disasters, accidents, equipment failures, and deliberate actions) to an acceptable level through a combination of preventive and recovery controls. This process should identify the critical business processes and integrate the information security management requirements of business continuity with other continuity requirements relating to such aspects as operations, staffing, materials, transport, and facilities.

The consequences of disasters, security failures, loss of service, and service availability should be subject to a business impact analysis. Business continuity plans should be developed and implemented to ensure timely resumption of essential operations. Information security should be an integral part of the overall business continuity process, and other management processes within the organization.

Business continuity management should include controls to identify and reduce risks, in addition to the general risks assessment process, limit the consequences of damaging incidents, and ensure that information required for business processes is readily available.

| Class | Control Description | | PCI DSS | BIG COMPANY |
|---|---|---|---|---|
| 14.1.1 Including Information Security in the Business Continuity Management Process | A managed process should be developed and maintained for business continuity throughout the organization that addresses the information security requirements needed for the organization's business continuity. | 12.9.1 | Create the incident response plan to be implemented in the event of a system compromise. Ensure the plan addresses business recovery and continuity. | |

| | | | | | |
|---|---|---|---|---|---|
| 14.1.2 | Business Continuity and Risk Assessment | Events that can cause interruptions to business processes should be identified, along with the probability and impact of such interruptions and their consequences for information security. | 12.9.1 | Create the incident response plan to be implemented in the event of a system compromise. Ensure the plan addresses business recovery and continuity. | |
| 14.1.3 | Developing and Implementing Continuity Plans Including Information Security | Plans should be developed and implemented to maintain or restore operations and ensure availability of information at the required level and in the required time scales following interruption to, or failure of, critical business processes. | 12.9.1 | Create the incident response plan to be implemented in the event of a system compromise. Ensure the plan addresses business recovery and continuity. | |
| 14.1.4 | Business Continuity Planning Framework | A single framework of business continuity plans should be maintained to ensure all plans are consistent, to consistently address information security requirements, and to identify priorities for testing and maintenance. | 12.9.1 | Create the incident response plan to be implemented in the event of a system compromise. Ensure the plan addresses business recovery and continuity. | |
| 14.1.5 | Testing, Maintaining, and Re-Assessing Business Continuity Plans | Business continuity plans should be tested and updated regularly to ensure that they are up to date and effective. | 12.9.2 | Test the plan at least annually. | |

**15 COMPLIANCE**

**15.1 Compliance with Legal Requirements**

To avoid breaches of any law, statutory, regulatory, or contractual obligations, and of any security requirements.

The design, operation, use, and management of information systems may be subject to statutory, regulatory, and contractual security requirements.

Advice on specific legal requirements should be sought from the organization's legal advisers, or suitably qualified legal practitioners. Legislative requirements vary from country to country and may vary for information created in one country that is transmitted to another country (i.e., trans-border data flow).

| | Class | Control Description | PCI DSS | BIG COMPANY |
|---|---|---|---|---|
| 15.1.1 | Identification of Applicable Legislation | All relevant statutory, regulatory, and contractual requirements and the organization's approach to meet these requirements should be explicitly defined, documented, and kept up to date for each information system and the organization. | | |
| 15.1.2 | Intellectual Property Rights (IPR) | Appropriate procedures should be implemented to ensure compliance with legislative, regulatory, and contractual requirements on the use of material in respect of which there maybe intellectual property rights and on the use of proprietary software products. | | |

| | | | |
|---|---|---|---|
| 15.1.3 | Protection of Organizational Records | Important records should be protected from loss, destruction, and falsification, in accordance with statutory, regulatory, contractual, and business requirements. | |
| 15.1.4 | Data Protection and Privacy of Personal Information | Data protection and privacy should be ensured as required in relevant legislation, regulations, and, if applicable, contractual clauses. | |
| 15.1.5 | Prevention of Misuse of Information Processing Facilities | Users should be deterred from using information processing facilities for unauthorized purposes. | 7.1 Limit access to computing resources and cardholder information to only those individuals whose job requires such access. |
| 15.1.6 | Regulation of Cryptographic Controls | Cryptographic controls should be used in compliance with all relevant agreements, laws, and regulations. | 4.1 Use strong cryptographic and security protocols to safeguard sensitive cardholder data. |

**15 COMPLIANCE**

**15.2 Compliance with Security Policies and Standards and Technical Compliance**

To ensure compliance of systems with organizational security policies and standards.

The security of information systems should be regularly reviewed.

Such reviews should be performed against the appropriate security policies and the technical platforms and information systems should be audited for compliance with applicable security implementation standards and documented security controls.

| | Class | Control Description | | PCI DSS | BIG COMPANY |
|---|---|---|---|---|---|
| 15.2.1 | Compliance with Security Policies and Standards | Managers should ensure that all security procedures within their area of responsibility are carried out correctly to achieve compliance with security policies and standards. | 11.1 | Test security controls, limitations, network connections, and restrictions annually to assure the ability to adequately identify and stop any unauthorized access attempts. | |
| 15.2.2 | Technical Compliance Checking | Information systems should be regularly checked for compliance with security implementation standards. | 11.2 | Run internal and external vulnerability scans at least quarterly and after any significant change to the network. | |

# *Appendix M*

# Control Lists

## Overview

For years I have worked to establish a sample list of threats that could be used by risk management professionals to expedite the risk assessment process. A few years ago when I was doing a class in Brazil a student gave me a URL that has helped the threat identification process. A German organization, IT-Grundschutz, has established two important lists for the risk management professional. The first set was discussed in Appendix G; that list focused on threats. This time, IT-Grundschutz — an organization that aims to achieve a security level for IT systems that is reasonable and adequate to satisfy normal protection requirements and that can also serve as the basis for IT systems and applications requiring a high degree of protection — created a list of possible safeguards.

The safeguards catalog contains 2,056 pages of controls and safeguards in detail. The threats are divided into six categories:

| Threat Category | Number of Threats |
|---|---|
| Infrastructure | 60 |
| Organization | 306 |
| Personnel | 43 |
| Hardware/software | 232 |
| Communication | 121 |
| Contingency planning | 95 |

The URL to access this list of threats is http://www.bsi/English/gshb/index.htm

## Sample 1 — Controls by IT Group

| Control Number | IT Group | Descriptor | Definition |
|---|---|---|---|
| 1 | Operations controls | Backup | Backup requirements will be determined and communicated to Operations including a request that an electronic notification that backups were completed be sent to the application system administrator. Operations will be requested to test the backup procedures. |
| 2 | Operations controls | Recovery plan | Develop, document, and test recovery procedures designed to ensure that the application and information can be recovered, using the backups created, in the event of loss. |
| 3 | Operations controls | Risk analysis | Conduct a risk analysis to determine the level of exposure to identified threats and identify possible safeguards or controls. |
| 4 | Operations controls | Anti-virus | (1) Ensure LAN administrator installs the corporate standard anti-viral software on all computers. (2) Training and awareness of virus prevention techniques will be incorporated in the organization IP program. |
| 5 | Operations controls | Interface dependencies | Systems that feed information will be identified and communicated to Operations to stress the impact to the functionality if these feeder applications are unavailable. |
| 6 | Operations controls | Maintenance | Time requirements for technical maintenance will be tracked and a request for adjustment will be communicated to management if experience warrants. |
| 7 | Operations controls | Service-level agreement | Acquire service level agreements to establish level of customer expectations and assurances from supporting operations. |

**Sample 1 (continued) — Controls by IT Group**

| Control Number | IT Group | Descriptor | Definition |
|---|---|---|---|
| 8 | Operations controls | Maintenance | Acquire maintenance and/or supplier agreements to facilitate the continued operational status of the application. |
| 9 | Operations controls | Change management | Production migration controls such as search and remove processes to ensure data stores are clean |
| 10 | Operations controls | Business impact analysis | A formal business impact analysis will be conducted to determine the asset's relative criticality with other enterprise assets. |
| 11 | Operations controls | Backup | Training for a backup to the system administrator will be provided and duties rotated between them to ensure the adequacy of the training program. |
| 12 | Operations controls | Backup | A formal employee security awareness program has been implemented and is updated and presented to the employees at least on an annual basis. |
| 13 | Operations controls | Recovery plan | Access sourced: Implement a mechanism to limit access to confidential information to specific network paths or physical locations. |
| 14 | Operations controls | Risk analysis | Implement user authentication mechanisms (such as firewalls, dial-in controls, secure ID) to limit access to authorized personnel. |
| 15 | Application controls | Application control | Design and implement application controls (data entry edit checking, fields requiring validation, alarm indicators, password expiration capabilities, check-sums) to ensure the integrity, confidentiality, and/or availability of application information. |

*continued*

**Sample 1 (continued) — Controls by IT Group**

| Control Number | IT Group | Descriptor | Definition |
|---|---|---|---|
| 16 | Application controls | Acceptance testing | Develop testing procedures to be followed during applications development and/or during modifications to the existing application that include user participation and acceptance. |
| 17 | Application controls | Training | Implement user programs (user performance evaluations) designed to encourage compliance with policies and procedures in place to ensure the appropriate utilization of the application. |
| 18 | Application controls | Training | Application developers will provide documentation, guidance, and support to the operations staff (Operations) in implementing mechanisms to ensure that the transfer of information between applications is secure. |
| 19 | Application controls | Corrective strategies | The development team will develop corrective strategies such as reworked processes, revised application logic, etc. |
| 20 | Security controls | Policy | Develop policies and procedures to limit access and operating privileges to those with business need. |
| 21 | Security controls | Training | User training will include instruction and documentation on the proper use of the application. The importance of maintaining the confidentiality of user accts, passwords, and the confidential and competitive nature of information will be stressed. |
| 22 | Security controls | Review | Implement mechanisms to monitor, report, and audit activities identified as requiring independent reviews, including periodic reviews of user-IDs to ascertain and verify business need. |

## Sample 1 (continued) — Controls by IT Group

| Control Number | IT Group | Descriptor | Definition |
|---|---|---|---|
| 23 | Security controls | Asset classification | The asset under review will be classified using enterprise policies, standards and procedures on asset classification. |
| 24 | Security controls | Access control | Mechanisms to protect the database against unauthorized access, and modifications made from outside the application, will be determined and implemented. |
| 25 | Security controls | Management support | Request management support to ensure the cooperation and coordination of various business units. |
| 26 | Security controls | Proprietary | Processes are in place to ensure that company proprietary assets are protected and that the company is in compliance with all third-party license agreements. |
| 27 | Security controls | Security awareness | Implement an access control mechanism to prevent unauthorized access to information. This mechanism will include the capability of detecting, logging, and reporting attempts to breach the security of this information. |
| 28 | Security controls | Access control | Implement encryption mechanisms (data, end-to-end) to prevent unauthorized access to protect the integrity and confidentiality of information. |
| 29 | Security controls | Access control | Adhere to a change management process designed to facilitate a structured approach to modifications of the application, to ensure appropriate steps and precautions are followed. "Emergency" modifications should be included in this process. |

*continued*

**Sample 1 (continued) — Controls by IT Group**

| Control Number | IT Group | Descriptor | Definition |
|---|---|---|---|
| 30 | Security controls | Access control | Control procedures are in place to ensure that appropriate system logs are reviewed by independent third parties to review system update activities. |
| 31 | Security controls | Access control | In consultation with Facilities management, facilitate the implementation of physical security controls designed to protect the information, software, and hardware required of the system. |
| 32 | Systems controls | Change management | Backup requirements will be determined and communicated to Operations including a request that an electronic notification that backups were completed be sent to the application system administrator. Operations will be requested to test the backup procedures. |
| 33 | Systems controls | Monitor system logs | Develop, document, and test recovery procedures designed to ensure that the application and information can be recovered, using the backups created, in the event of loss. |
| 34 | Physical security | Physical security | Conduct a risk analysis to determine the level of exposure to identified threats and identify possible safeguards or controls. |

## Sample 2 — Controls Using ISO 17799

| Control Number | ISO 17799 Section | Class | Control Description |
|---|---|---|---|
| 1 | | Risk assessment (2) | Conduct an accurate and thorough assessment of the potential risks and vulnerabilities to the confidentiality, integrity and availability of information resources. |
| 2 | Security policy | Policy (3.1) | Develop and implement an information security policy. |
| 3 | Organizational security | Management information security forum (4.1) | Establish a corporate committee to oversee information security. Develop and implement an information security organization mission statement. |
| 4 | Organizational security | Security of third-party access (4.2) | Implement a process to analyze third-party connection risks and implement specific security standards to combat third-party connection risks. |
| 5 | Organizational security | Security requirements in outsourcing contracts (4.3) | Ensure the security requirements of the information owners have been addressed in a contract between the owners and the outsource organization. |
| 6 | Asset classification & control | Accounting of assets (5.1) | Establish an inventory of major assets associated with each information system. |
| 7 | Asset classification & control | Information classification (5.2) | Implement standards for security classification and the level of protection required for information assets. |
| 8 | Asset classification & control | Information labeling and handling (5.2) | Implement standards to ensure the proper handling of information assets. |

*continued*

**Sample 2 (continued) — Controls Using ISO 17799**

| Control Number | ISO 17799 Section | Class | Control Description |
|---|---|---|---|
| 9 | Personnel security | Security in job descriptions (6.1) | Ensure that security responsibilities are included in employee job descriptions. |
| 10 | Personnel security | User training (6.2) | Implement training standards to ensure that users are trained in information security policies and procedures, security requirements, business controls and correct use of IT facilities. |
| 11 | Personnel security | Responding to security incidents and malfunctions (6.3) | Implement procedures and standards for formal reporting and incident response action to be taken on receipt of an incident report. |
| 12 | Physical & environmental security | Secure areas (7.1) | Implement standards to ensure that physical security protections exist, based on defined perimeters through strategically located barriers throughout the organization. |
| 13 | Physical & environmental security | Equipment security (7.2) | Implement standards to ensure that equipment is located properly to reduce risks of environmental hazards and unauthorized access. |
| 14 | Physical & environmental security | General controls (7.3) | Implement a clear desk/clear screen policy for sensitive material to reduce risks of unauthorized access, loss, or damage outside normal working hours. |
| 15 | Communications and operations management | Documented operating procedures (8.1) | Implement operating procedures to clearly document that all operational computer systems are being operated in a correct, secure manner. |

**Sample 2 (continued) — Controls Using ISO 17799**

| Control Number | ISO 17799 Section | Class | Control Description |
|---|---|---|---|
| 16 | Communications and operations management | System planning and acceptance (8.2) | Implement standards to ensure that capacity requirements are monitored, and future requirements projected, to reduce the risk of system overload. |
| 17 | Communications and operations management | Protection from malicious software (8.3) | Implement standards and user training to ensure that virus detection and prevention measures are adequate. |
| 18 | Communications and operations management | Housekeeping (8.4) | Establish procedures for making regular backup copies of essential business data and software to ensure that it can be recovered following a computer disaster or media failure. |
| 19 | Communications and operations management | Network management (8.5) | Implement appropriate standards to ensure the security of data in networks and the protection of connected services from unauthorized access. |
| 20 | Communications and operations management | Media handling and security (8.6) | Implement procedures for the management of removable computer media such as tapes, disks, cassettes, and printed reports. |
| 21 | Communications and operations management | Exchanges of information and software (8.7) | Implement procedures to establish formal agreements, including software escrow agreements when appropriate, for exchanging data and software (whether electronically or manually) between organizations. |

*continued*

**Sample 2 (continued) — Controls Using ISO 17799**

| Control Number | ISO 17799 Section | Class | Control Description |
|---|---|---|---|
| 22 | Access control | Business requirement for system access (9.1) | Implement a risk analysis process to gather business requirements to document access control levels. |
| 23 | Access control | User access management (9.2) | Implement procedures for user registration and deregistration access to all multiuse IT services. |
| 24 | Access control | User responsibility (9.3) | Implement user training to ensure users been taught good security practices in the selection and use of passwords. |
| 25 | Access control | Network access control (9.4) | Implement procedures to ensure that network and computer services that can be accessed by an individual user or from a particular terminal are consistent with business access control policy. |
| 26 | Access control | Operating system access control (9.5) | Implement standards for automatic terminal identification to authenticate connections to specific locations. |
| 27 | Access control | Application access control (9.6) | Implement procedures to restrict access to applications system data and functions in accordance with defined access policy and based on individual requirements. |
| 28 | Access control | Monitoring system access and use (9.7) | Implement audit trails that record exceptions and other security-relevant events that produce and maintain to assist in future investigations and in access control. |

**Sample 2 (continued) — Controls Using ISO 17799**

| Control Number | ISO 17799 Section | Class | Control Description |
|---|---|---|---|
| 29 | Access control | Remote access and telecommuting (9.8) | Implement a formal policy and supporting standards that address the risks of working with mobile computing facilities, including requirements for physical protection, access controls, cryptographic techniques, backup, and virus protection. |
| 30 | Systems development & maintenance | Security requirements of systems (10.1) | Implement standards to ensure that analysis of security requirements is part of the requirement analysis stage of each development project. |
| 31 | Systems development & maintenance | Security in application systems (10.2) | Implement standards to ensure that data that is input into applications systems is validated to ensure that it is correct and appropriate. |
| 32 | Systems development & maintenance | Cryptography (10.3) | Implement policies and standards on the use of cryptographic controls, including management of encryption keys, and effective implementation. |
| 33 | Systems development & maintenance | Security of system files (10.4) | Implement standards to exercise strict control exercised over the implementation of software on operational systems. |
| 34 | Systems development & maintenance | Security in development and support environments (10.5) | Implement standards and procedures for formal change management process. |

*continued*

**Sample 2 (continued) — Controls Using ISO 17799**

| Control Number | ISO 17799 Section | Class | Control Description |
|---|---|---|---|
| 35 | Business continuity management | Aspects of business continuity planning (11.1) | Implement procedures for the development and maintenance of business continuity plans across the organization. |
| 36 | Compliance | Compliance with legal requirements (12.1) | Implement standards to ensure that all relevant statutory, regulatory, and contractual requirements are specifically defined and documented for each information system. |
| 37 | Compliance | Reviews of security policy and technical compliances (12.2) | Implement standards to ensure that all areas within the organization are considered for regular review to ensure compliance with security policies and standards. |

**Sample 3 — Mapping Controls to ISO 17799 — HIPAA — GLBA — SOX — FOX**

| ISO 17799 Section | Control | HIPAA | GLBA | Sarbanes–Oxley | Federal Sentencing Guidelines |
|---|---|---|---|---|---|
| | Risk assessment (2) | Risk analysis (required) | Assess risk | Assess current internal controls | |
| Security policy | Policy (3.1) | Isolate healthcare clearinghouse functions (required) Integrity (standard) | Board approves written policy and program | Policies and procedures must support effective internal control of assets | Establish policies, procedures and standards to guide the workforce |
| Organizational security | Management information security forum (4.1) | Risk management (required) Sanction policy (required) Privacy officer (required) | Involve the board of directors Assign specific responsibilities | Corporation management is responsible for assuring internal controls are adequate | Appoint high-level management to oversee compliance with program |
| Organizational security | Security of third-party access (4.2) | Business associate contracts (standard) | Contract clauses meet guidance objectives | | |
| Organizational security | Security requirements in outsourcing contracts (4.3) | Audit controls (required) | Report program effectiveness to board | Management must report on internal controls effectiveness | |

continued

**Sample 3 (continued) — Mapping Controls to ISO 17799 — HIPAA — GLBA — SOX — FOX**

| ISO 17799 Section | Control | HIPAA | GLBA | Sarbanes–Oxley | Federal Sentencing Guidelines |
|---|---|---|---|---|---|
| Asset classification & control | Accounting of assets (5.1) | Inventory all assets | Implement policies evaluate sensitivity of customer information | Identify all assets of the corporation | |
| Asset classification & control | Information classification (5.2) | Information is an asset and the property of the enterprise | Implement standards and procedures to protect customer information | Information is an asset and the property of the enterprise | |
| Asset classification & control | Information labeling and handling (5.2) | | Implement standards | | |
| Personnel security | Security in job descriptions (6.1) | | Background check on certain positions | | Enforce the policies, standards, and procedures consistently through appropriate disciplinary measures |
| Personnel security | User training (6.2) | | Train staff to implement program | | Communicate the standards and procedures to all employees and others |

| | | | |
|---|---|---|---|
| Personnel security | Responding to security incidents and malfunctions (6.3) | | Incident response program |
| Physical & environmental security | Secure areas (7.1) | Workstation security (standard) | Implement physical access restrictions |
| Physical & environmental security | Equipment security (7.2) | | |
| Physical & environmental security | General controls (7.3) | | |
| Communications and operations management | Documented operating procedures (8.1) | Response and reporting (required) Emergency mode operations plan (required) Transmission security (standard) | Implement measures to protect against information destruction or damage |
| Communications and operations management | System planning and acceptance (8.2) | | |
| Communications and operations management | Protection from malicious software (8.3) | | |

*continued*

**Sample 3 (continued) — Mapping Controls to ISO 17799 — HIPAA — GLBA — SOX — FOX**

| ISO 17799 Section | Control | HIPAA | GLBA | Sarbanes–Oxley | Federal Sentencing Guidelines |
|---|---|---|---|---|---|
| Communications and operations management | Housekeeping (8.4) | Data backup (required) | Protect information destruction or loss | | |
| Communications and operations management | Network management (8.5) | | | | |
| Communications and operations management | Media handling and security (8.6) | Device and media control (standard) Media re-use (required) | | | |
| Communications and operations management | Exchanges of information and software (8.7) | | | | |
| Access control | Business requirement for system access (9.1) | Risk analysis (required) | Risk assessment required | | Exercise due care when granting discretionary authority to employees |
| Access control | User access management (9.2) | Authentication (standard) | Authorized access only | | |
| Access control | User responsibility (9.3) | | Train users | | Communicate the standards and procedures to all employees and others |

| | | | | |
|---|---|---|---|---|
| Access control | Network access control (9.4) | | | |
| Access control | Operating system access control (9.5) | Emergency access procedure (required) | Implement incident response program | |
| Access control | Application access control (9.6) | Unique user identification (required) | | |
| Access control | Monitoring system access and use (9.7) | | Monitoring systems and intrusion detection | |
| Access control | Remote access and telecommuting (9.8) | | | |
| Systems development & maintenance | Security requirements of systems (10.1) | Risk analysis | Risk assessment | Assess effectiveness of internal control |
| Systems development & maintenance | Security in application systems (10.2) | | | |
| Systems development & maintenance | Cryptography (10.3) | | Assess encryption requirements | |

*continued*

**Sample 3 (continued) — Mapping Controls to ISO 17799 — HIPAA — GLBA — SOX — FOX**

| ISO 17799 Section | Control | HIPAA | GLBA | Sarbanes–Oxley | Federal Sentencing Guidelines |
|---|---|---|---|---|---|
| Systems development & maintenance | Security of system files (10.4) | | | | |
| Systems development & maintenance | Security in development and support environments (10.5) | | | | |
| Business continuity management | Aspects of business continuity planning (11.1) | Data backup (required) Disaster recovery plan (required) Emergency mode operations plan (required) | Implement measures to protect against loss, destruction or damage of information | | |
| Compliance | Compliance with legal requirements (12.1) | | | | |
| Compliance | Reviews of security policy and technical compliances (12.2) | Information system activity review (required) Audit controls (required) | Report findings annually to board | Management must report on internal controls effectiveness | Enforce the policies, standards and procedures consistently through appropriate disciplinary measures |

## Sample 4 — Using ISO 27002

| *ISO 27002 Section* | *Class* | *Control Description* |
|---|---|---|
| | Risk assessment (4) | Conduct an accurate and thorough assessment of the potential risks and vulnerabilities to the confidentiality, integrity, and availability of information resources. |
| Security policy | Policy (5.1) | Develop and implement an information security policy. |
| Organizing information security | Internal organization (6.1) | The organization should have a management framework for information security. Senior management should provide direction and commit their support, for example, by approving information security policies. Roles and responsibilities should be defined for the information security function. Other relevant functions should cooperate and coordinate their activities. IT facilities should be authorized. Confidentiality agreements should reflect the organization's needs. Contacts should be established with relevant authorities (e.g., law enforcement) and special interest groups. Information security should be independently reviewed. |
| Organizing information security | External parties (6.2) | Information security should not be compromised by the introduction of third-party products or services. Risks should be assessed and mitigated when dealing with customers and in third-party agreements. |
| Asset management | Accountability for assets (7.1) | All [information] assets should be accounted for and have a nominated owner. An inventory of information assets (IT hardware, software, data, system documentation, storage media and ICT services) should be maintained. The inventory should record ownership and location of the assets, and owners should identify acceptable uses. |

*continued*

**Sample 4 (continued) — Using ISO 27002**

| ISO 27002 Section | Class | Control Description |
|---|---|---|
| Asset management | Information classification (7.2) | Information should be classified according to its need for security protection and labeled accordingly. |
| Human resources | Prior to employment (8.1) | Security responsibilities should be taken into account when recruiting permanent employees, contractors and temporary staff (e.g., through adequate job descriptions, pre-employment screening) and included in contracts (e.g., terms and conditions of employment and other signed agreements on security roles and responsibilities). |
| Human resources | During employment (8.2) | Management responsibilities regarding information security should be defined. Employees and (if relevant) third-party IT users should be made aware, educated, and trained in security procedures. A formal disciplinary process is necessary to handle security breaches. |
| Human resources | Employment termination (8.3) | Security aspects of a person's exit from the organization (e.g., the return of [information] assets and removal of access rights) or change of responsibilities should be managed. |
| Physical & environmental security | Secure areas(9.1) | This section describes the need for concentric layers of physical controls to protect sensitive IT facilities from unauthorized access. |
| Physical & environmental security | Equipment security (9.2) | Critical IT equipment, cabling, etc. should be protected against physical damage, fire, flood, theft, etc., both on- and off-site. Mains power supplies and cabling should be secured. IT equipment should be maintained and disposed of securely. |

## Sample 4 (continued) — Using ISO 27002

| ISO 27002 Section | Class | Control Description |
|---|---|---|
| Communications and operations management | Operational procedures and responsibilities (10.1) | IT operating responsibilities and procedures should be documented. Changes to IT facilities and systems should be controlled. Segregation of duties should be applied where relevant (e.g., access to development and operational systems should be segregated). |
| Communications and operations management | Third-party service delivery management (10.2) | Security requirements should be taken into account in third-party service delivery (e.g., IT facilities management or outsourcing), from contractual terms to ongoing monitoring and change management. |
| Communications and operations management | System planning and acceptance (10.3) | The use of resources is to be monitored and tuned and projections made for future capacity requirements to ensure the required system performance. |
| Communications and operations management | Protection against malicious and mobile code (10.4) | Implement standards and user training to ensure that virus detection and prevention measures are adequate. |
| Communications and operations management | Backup (10.5) | Backup copies of information and software is to be taken and tested on a regular basis in accordance with SLA backup agreements. |
| Communications and operations management | Protection from malicious software (10.3) | Implement standards and user training to ensure that virus detection and prevention measures are adequate. |
| Communications and operations management | Network security management (10.6) | Implement secure network management, network security monitoring and other controls. Also covers security of commercial network services such as private networks and managed firewalls. |
| Communications and operations management | Media handling (10.7) | Implement procedures for the management of removable computer media such as tapes, disks, cassettes, and printed reports. |

*continued*

**Sample 4 (continued) — Using ISO 27002**

| ISO 27002 Section | Class | Control Description |
|---|---|---|
| Communications and operations management | Exchanges of information and software (10.8) | Implement procedures to establish formal agreements, including software escrow agreements when appropriate, for exchanging data and software (whether electronically or manually) between organizations. |
| Communications and operations management | Electronic commerce services (10.9) | The security implications of eCommerce (online transaction systems) must be evaluated and suitable controls implemented. The integrity and availability of information published online (e.g., on web sites) should also be protected. |
| Communications and operations management | Monitoring (10.10) | System monitoring should be used to check the effectiveness of controls adopted and to verify conformity to an access policy model. |
| Access control | Business requirement for system access (11.1) | Implement a risk analysis process to gather business requirements to document access control levels. |
| Access control | User access management (11.2) | Implement procedures for user registration and deregistration access to all multi-use IT services. |
| Access control | User responsibility (11.3) | Implement user training to ensure users been taught good security practices in the selection and use of passwords. |
| Access control | Network access control (11.4) | Implement procedures to ensure that network and computer services that can be accessed by an individual user or from a particular terminal are consistent with business access control policy. |
| Access control | Operating system access control (11.5) | Implement standards for automatic terminal identification to authenticate connections to specific locations. |
| Access control | Application access control (11.6) | Implement procedures to restrict access to applications system data and functions in accordance with defined access policy and based on individual requirements. |

**Sample 4 (continued) — Using ISO 27002**

| *ISO 27002 Section* | *Class* | *Control Description* |
|---|---|---|
| Access control | Mobile computing and telecommuting (11.7) | Implement a formal policy and supporting standards that address the risks of working with mobile computing facilities, including requirements for physical protection, access controls, cryptographic techniques, backup, and virus protection. |
| Information systems acquisition, development, and maintenance | Security requirements of systems (12.1) | Implement standards to ensure that analysis of security requirements is part of the requirement analysis stage of each development project. |
| Information systems acquisition, development, and maintenance | Correct processing in applications (12.2) | Data entry, processing and output validation controls, and message authentication should be provided to mitigate the associated integrity risks. |
| Information systems acquisition, development, and maintenance | Cryptography (12.3) | Implement policies and standards on the use of cryptographic controls, including management of encryption keys, and effective implementation. |
| Information systems acquisition, development, and maintenance | Security of system files (12.4) | Implement standards to exercise strict control exercised over the implementation of software on operational systems. |
| Information systems acquisition, development, and maintenance | Security in development and support environments (12.5) | Implement standards and procedures for formal change management process. |
| Information systems acquisition, development, and maintenance | Software security vulnerability management (12.6) | Technical vulnerabilities in systems and applications should be controlled by monitoring for the announcement of relevant security vulnerabilities, and risk assessing and applying relevant security patches promptly. |

*continued*

**Sample 4 (continued) — Using ISO 27002**

| *ISO 27002 Section* | *Class* | *Control Description* |
|---|---|---|
| Information security incident management | Reporting information security events and weaknesses (13.1) | An incident reporting/alarm procedure is required, plus the associated response and escalation procedures. There should be a central point of contact, and all employees, contractors, etc., should be informed of their incident reporting responsibilities. |
| Information security incident management | Management of information security incidents and improvements (13.2) | Responsibilities and procedures are required to manage incidents consistently and effectively, to implement continuous improvement (learning the lessons), and to collect forensic evidence. |
| Business continuity management | Information security aspects of business continuity management (14.1) | Implement procedures for the development and maintenance of business continuity plans across the organization. |
| Compliance | Compliance with legal requirements (15.1) | Implement standards to ensure that all relevant statutory, regulatory, and contractual requirements are specifically defined and documented for each information system. |
| Compliance | Reviews of security policy and standards (15.2) | Implement standards to ensure that all areas within the organization are considered for regular review to ensure compliance with security policies and standards. |
| Compliance | Information systems audit considerations (15.3) | Audits should be carefully planned to minimize disruption to operational systems. Powerful audit tools/facilities must also be protected against unauthorized use. |

# *Appendix N*

# Heat Charts

**Table N.1    Risk Assessment Example 1**

| Term | Definition |
|---|---|
| Probability | A measure of how likely it is that a threat may occur |
| **Threshold level** | |
| High | Very likely that the threat will occur within the next year |
| Medium | Possible that the threat will occur within the next year |
| Low | Highly unlikely that the threat will occur within the next year |
| Impact | The effect of a threat being carried out on an asset, expressed in tangible or intangible terms |
| **Threshold level** | |
| High | Entire mission or business is impacted |
| Medium | Loss limited to single business unit or business objective |
| Low | Business as usual |

**Table N.2**

| | Impact | | |
|---|---|---|---|
| Probability | Low | Medium | High |
| High | Yellow | Red | Red |
| Medium | Green | Yellow | Red |
| Low | Green | Green | Yellow |

**Table N.3**

| Color | Risk Level | Action |
|---|---|---|
| Red | High | Requires immediate action |
| Yellow | Medium | May require action, must continue to monitor |
| Green | Low | No action required at this time |

**Table N.4   Risk Assessment Example 2 Definitions**

| Probability Factor | Definition |
|---|---|
| Low | Extremely unlikely that threat will occur during the next 12 months |
| Low to medium | Unlikely that threat will occur during the next 12 months |
| Medium | Possible that threat will occur during the next 12 months |
| Medium to high | Likely that threat will occur during the next 12 months |
| High | Highly likely that threat will occur during the next 12 months |
| *Impact factor* | *Definition* |
| Low | Single work group or department affected; little or no impact to the business process |
| Low to medium | One or more departments affected; slight delay in meeting mission objectives |
| Medium | Two or more departments or a business unit affected; 4–6-hour delay in meeting mission objectives |
| Medium to high | Two or more business units affected; 1–2-day delay in meeting mission objectives |
| High | Entire mission of the enterprise affected |

**Table N.5**

| Color | Action |
|---|---|
| Red | Very high risk: immediate action required |
| Orange | High risk: action required |
| Yellow | Moderate risk: some action may be required |
| Light green | Low risk: continue to monitor |
| Dark green | Very low risk: no action required at this time |

**Table N.6    Risk Assessment Example 2 Heat Chart**

| | Impact | | | | |
|---|---|---|---|---|---|
| *High* | Moderate Low | Medium | Moderate High | High | High |
| *Medium to High* | Moderate Low | Medium | Moderate High | High | High |
| *Medium* | Low | Moderate Low | Medium | Moderate High | High |
| *Low to Medium* | Low | Moderate Low | Medium | Moderate High | Moderate High |
| *Low* | Low | Low | Low | Moderate Low | Moderate Low |
| *Probability* | Low | Low to Medium | Medium | Medium to High | High |

**Table N.7    Risk Assessment Example 3 Definitions**

| Risk Probability Rating | Definition |
|---|---|
| VHi | >99% probability of occurrence; threat occurs daily or weekly. |
| Hi | Threat is expected to occur; threat occurs monthly. |
| Med | Threat has a reasonable chance of occurring although there are no indications pointing to a greater than 50% chance; threat occurs yearly. |
| Lo | Threat has a small chance of occurring during any year. Threat is not expected to happen, but potential exists. Threat has occurred in the past, but controls have been implemented to prevent reoccurrence. |
| VLo | Threat may only occur in exceptional circumstances; a "once in a lifetime" event (<1% probability of occurrence). |

**Table N.8 Risk Impact Rating**

| Rating | Definition |
|---|---|
| VHi | Severe loss<br>Criminal penalties or material fines<br>Long-term or permanent loss of business function<br>Inability to support a significant percentage of workforce<br>Board notification required |
| Hi | Likely regulatory sanctions, criticism, actions<br>Negative media exposureLoss of significant number of assets or alliance partners<br>Key alliances threatened<br>Inability to support key workforce with extended time away from work simultaneously |
| Med | Regulatory criticism<br>Damage or impairment of a significant portion of assets<br>Injury requiring ongoing medical treatment |
| Lo | Consequences can be absorbed under normal operating conditions<br>Damage or impairment of a small portion of assets |
| VLo | Minor damage to assets with no impact to business functionality<br>Minor impact to system function not requiring outage |

**Table N.9 Risk Assessment Example 3 Heat Chart**

| | Impact | | | | |
|---|---|---|---|---|---|
| VHi<br>0.9 | .045 | .09 | .18 | .36 | .45 |
| Hi<br>0.7 | .035 | .07 | .14 | .28 | .35 |
| Med<br>0.5 | .025 | .05 | .10 | .20 | .25 |
| Lo<br>0.3 | .015 | .03 | .06 | .12 | .15 |
| VLo<br>0.1 | .005 | .01 | .02 | .04 | .05 |
| | 0.05<br>VLo | 0.1<br>Lo | 0.2<br>Med | 0.4<br>Hi | 0.5<br>VHi |

**Table N.10   Risk Assessment Example 4 Definitions**

| Impact Level | Image | Regulatory Compliance | Revenue | Productivity | Health/Safety |
|---|---|---|---|---|---|
| 5 Severe (<1% of total risks) red | Significant, sustained negative international or national media exposure Loss of strategic business partners | Criminal penalties or fines greater than $10M Major regulatory sanctions, criticism, action | Irrevocable direct loss of revenue greater than $10M | Increase in costs (i.e., maintenance, labor, supplier fees, etc.) >$10M | Loss of life or limb |
| 4 Major (orange) | Ongoing negative regional or national media exposure Key business partners threatened | Penalties or fines of $2M–$10M | Irrevocable direct loss of revenue $2M–$10M | Increase in costs (i.e., maintenance, labor, supplier fees, etc.) $2M–$10M | Severe injuries, hospitalization Major exposure to unsafe work environment |
| 3 Moderate (yellow) | Ongoing (but <2 weeks) negative local media exposure | Penalties or fines of $500K–$2M | Irrevocable direct loss of revenue $500K–$2M | Increase in costs (i.e., maintenance, labor, supplier fees, etc.) $500K–$2M | Cuts and bruises, requires first aid |
| 2 Minor (light green) | Degradation in quality, service, or products Limited negative local media exposure | Penalties or fines of $100K–$500K | Irrevocable direct loss of revenue $100K–$500K | Increase in costs (i.e., maintenance, labor, supplier fees, etc.) $100K–$500K | Minor exposure to unsafe work environment |
| 1 Insignificant | Reputation inconsistent with desired brand image No media coverage | Penalties or fines of <$100K | Irrevocable direct loss of revenue <$100K | Increase in costs (i.e., maintenance, labor, supplier fees, etc.) <$100K | Little or no impact |

**TABLE N.11    Risk Assessment Example 4 Risk Ratings**

| Category | Weight | Level | Score |
|---|---|---|---|
| Impact to health/safety | 5.0 | 0  1  2  3  4  5 | 0.0 |
| Impact to image | 4.5 | 0  1  2  3  4  5 | 0.0 |
| Legal/regulatory compliance impact | 4.0 | 0  1  2  3  4  5 | 0.0 |
| Impact to revenue | 3.5 | 0  1  2  3  4  5 | 0.0 |
| Impact to overall productivity | 3.0 | 0  1  2  3  4  5 | 0.0 |
| | | Risk rating | 0.0 |

**Table N.12    Risk Assessment Example 5 Definitions**

| Impact Term | Definition |
|---|---|
| Extreme | An event with the potential to lead to permanent or long-term damage to the organization's ability to achieve its objectives. The consequences could threaten the survival of not only the activity, but also the company, possibly causing major problems for clients/public. |
| Very high | A critical event that with proper management can be endured by the organization. |
| Medium | A significant event which can be managed under normal circumstances by the department. The consequences could mean that the activity could be subject to significant review or changed ways of operation. |
| Low | An event, the consequences of which can be absorbed but management effort is required to minimize the impact. The consequences could threaten the efficiency or effectiveness of some aspects of the operation, but would be dealt with internally. |
| Negligible | An event, the consequences of which can be absorbed through normal activity. |

**Table N.13**

| Likelihood Term | Definition |
|---|---|
| Highly likely | This event is expected to occur in most circumstances. It will occur 95% of the time. |
| Likely | This event will probably occur in most circumstance. It will occur from 60% to 94% of the time. |
| Moderate | This event should occur at some time. It will occur between 21% and 59% of the time. |
| Unlikely | This event could occur at some time. It will occur between 5% and 20% of the time. |
| Rare | This event may occur only in exceptional circumstances. It will occur less than 5% of the time. |

**Table N.14**

| Description | Color | Action |
|---|---|---|
| A subjective rating of the current residual risk related to a specific threat or risk after considering the current mitigation estimates. | Green | Low risk: no action required. |
| | Yellow | Moderate risk: monitor closely. |
| | Red | High risk: action required. |

**Table N.15   Risk Assessment Example 5 Heat Chart**

| | Impact | | | | |
|---|---|---|---|---|---|
| Highly likely | Yellow | Yellow | Red | Red | Red |
| Likely | Yellow | Yellow | Yellow | Red | Red |
| Moderate | Green | Yellow | Yellow | Yellow | Red |
| Unlikely | Green | Green | Yellow | Yellow | Yellow |
| Rare | Green | Green | Green | Yellow | Yellow |
| Likelihood | Negligible | Low | Medium | Very high | Extreme |

# Index

('f' indicates a figure; 't' indicates a table)